SOMAWISE

GET OUT OF YOUR HEAD,
GET INTO YOUR BODY

*How the body holds the answers to holistic wellbeing,
authentic change and peaceful relationships.*

DR. LUKE SNIEWSKI

Foreword by Sat Dharam Kaur

Cover Art by Timothy Brown Douglas

Edited by Tamara Kowalska

Compiled by Roland Denzel

This book does not replace the advice of a medical professional. Consult your physician or a medical professional before making any changes to your diet, regular health plan or engaging in any practices mentioned, referenced, suggested or discussed within this book.

These are my memories, from my perspective, and I have tried to represent events as faithfully as possible.

Published by NuMind Ltd. Auckland, New Zealand

www.lukesniewski.com

Contents

Per la mia regina. Sei la mia anima gemella.
Ti amo con tutto il mio cuore.

For my queen. You are my soulmate.
I love you with all my heart.

"We are dying from overthinking.
We are slowly killing ourselves
by thinking about everything.
Think. Think. Think.
You can never trust the human mind anyway.
It's a death trap."
~ Anthony Hopkins ~

And I said to my body, softly,
"I want to be your friend."
It took a long breath and replied,
"I've been waiting my whole life for this."
~ Nayyirah Waheed ~

"The deeper we live the life of our bodies,
the deeper is the upwelling of love."
~ Stanley Keleman ~

Let's Get Connected

You can learn more about Dr. Luke Sniewski, his practice, and his programs at www.LukeSniewski.com.

Take the next step in your healing journey with Dr. Luke Sniewski by scanning the QR code below, or visiting:

www.LukeSniewski.com/Somawise-Online-Program

Foreword

As co-director of the Compassionate Inquiry professional training, and a mentor to course participants learning the psychotherapy approach developed by Dr. Gabor Maté, I have the privilege to review videos from participants when they are applying for certification as a Compassionate Inquiry Practitioner after completing the rigorous year-long training.

I remember well the first time I saw Luke's work in one of these videos. I was struck by his lightning-fast perception, his confidence in interrupting the client's story to get to the underlying truth, and his ability to uncover and challenge the unconscious beliefs of the client. I immediately recognized his gifts as a therapist. That was in 2020. Since then, Luke has become a cherished member of the Compassionate Inquiry Facilitation Team and an excellent mentor to students in the program, helping them to hone their skills as practitioners. He is highly regarded by both students and colleagues.

In reading Somawise, I appreciate the combination of self-disclosure, lived experience and scientific research that entices the reader to lean into the guidelines provided. Luke's honesty, courage, vulnerability and wisdom provide a roadmap to many of us on how to approach our thoughts, our emotions, and most of all, our bodies, to optimize our lives.

I gained insight into my own traumas and addictions as I followed Luke's journey and subsequent self-examination from early childhood to adulthood. We share a few interesting similarities – having both been born premature, not breastfed, and from Polish descent. Intergenerational trauma lives in all of us, and we now know that the life histories of our parents and grandparents, and perhaps our culture, show up in our behavior. I love Luke's line, "We don't always – some would say ever – get to control the things that happen to us, but we can, with patience, determination and a sprinkle of grace and surrender, choose how we respond." Therein lies our power, when we can make that choice. Choice requires a wider perspective, the capacity to see one's options, and from a space of stillness and equilibrium, choose the option that leads to increased joy, fulfillment and individual and collective well-being.

We are all on a journey. Each journey is unique, and it is not for any person to tell another how to live. However, it is helpful to have a guide to show us possible routes to travel. I've enjoyed my travels in India, China, Europe and South America more when friends or fellow travelers suggested memorable places to visit, or have accompanied me on the journey.

Somawise is a traveler's guide to a meeting with oneself. What is required is to first acknowledge and accept what happened to us, and to our ancestors; to understand the coping mechanisms and survival strategies we used to relieve the emotional pain we held inside; to witness our thoughts and emotions, recognizing that they will pass and are not us; to befriend the body and listen to its messages, bringing attention and curiosity to any discomfort; to bring compassion to all parts of ourselves and what we discover; and to find contentment in the present moment. Luke models this for us throughout this book, and provides us with valuable tools.

May you enjoy and learn from the journey that is uniquely yours.

Sat Dharam Kaur, ND
Co-Director of Compassionate Inquiry
Author: *The Complete Natural Medicine Guide to Women's Health*
Owen Sound, ON, Canada
October 3, 2022

Preface

"Being in touch with our bodies, or more accurately, being our bodies, is how we know what is true." - Harriet Goldhor Lerner

"There is more wisdom in your body than in your deepest philosophies." - Friedrich Nietzsche

"I stand in awe of my body." - Henry David Thoreau

I found my life's passion at 15 years old. I didn't know then that my decision to play football would slowly evolve into progressively more profound dips into the deep reservoirs of wisdom found within the framework of the body. The human body – specifically my body – has been the source of never-ending insights that have transformed how I live, relate to myself and perceive the world. The rewards are worth the effort when it comes to the commitment, and regular recommitments, of doing the unavoidable 'inner work' required of such a journey. I sit and write these words with a smile on my face because I can sincerely say that I love my life and, something I never thought possible, I accept myself. My body is calm, relaxed and quiet in response. It agrees.

My exploration of the human body deepened as time passed from its superficial origins. Through football, I witnessed the body's inherent potential for physical transformation, innate resilience and incredible adaptability to its environment. I watched my body transform from its skinny and uncoordinated starting point into a body capable of playing professional sports. The body, however, is more than just a physical phenomenon, and our lifestyle impacts far more than strength, performance and aesthetics.

After my short stint of quarterbacking for the Ancona Dolphins in the Italian Football League, my obsession with the human body became more holistically oriented as I integrated yoga, mindfulness, mobility and massage practices. Our lifestyle – how we move, eat, laugh, love, sleep, think, work and rest – contributes to the interconnected and interdependent aspects of mental, physical and emotional wellbeing. In fact, caring for the body is at the very foundation of mental and emotional wellbeing. *Heal the body, the mind follows.* This understanding has been fundamental to the way I've worked with and helped others for nearly 20 years.

Eventually, attuning to the subtle language of my body provided a portal to spiritual awakening and living a life with more presence, authenticity and a sense of inner peace. This period was also the beginning of the end of no-longer-useful habits, namely pornography, workaholism and people-pleasing. I had been using these behaviors to avoid unprocessed emotions and reached for them whenever I experienced being triggered or stressed.

I thought, like many men, that sleeping with as many women as possible, watching porn, obsessing about sports, playing video games and prioritizing being busy, becoming successful and making money were a completely normal part of being a man. My body was able to unravel and integrate the subconscious conditioning and unprocessed trauma at the core of these habitual patterns once I learned how to get my mind out of the way. It's the mind, as we'll learn, that often intrudes upon and interrupts the body's natural healing and emotional integration processes.

This book emerges as a result of an unapologetic fascination with the human body and its remarkable role in healing, personal growth and thriving in all aspects of life. While my professional title – Wellbeing Coach, Somatic Therapist or Couples Counselor – changes depending on the needs of who comes to me for help, my work with clients starts and ends within the framework of the body.

The primary message of this book is that listening to the body is the key to finding answers to the biggest questions we have in our lives. *How do I experience holistic health? How do I create authentic change? How can I have more peaceful relationships?* These are the questions I've heard from clients throughout my professional career.

These three intentions sum up the *why* that brings people into my therapeutic space. While each client case may look different on the surface, the core impetus and spark for seeking help is always some iteration of these three questions. Answering any one of them requires a journey into the body, where clients learn how to listen to, reconnect with and care for their body; ultimately using it as a compass for navigating through life.

The body can be the expert, guide and barometer for improving the quality of any aspect of life. The body lets us know through internal signals and cues whether some aspect of our lifestyle (i.e., what we choose to eat or how we choose to exercise) is supporting or hindering the natural process of health. It's through learning the body's language of physical sensations that we become aware of the impulses that serve as the catalyst for permanent change. And I don't mean the kind of change that relies on the flimsy foundation of willpower, which eventually breaks when we get too stressed. What I'm referring to is a process of change that unravels and allows us to create a new path and destiny for ourselves.

When we stay connected to our body, we can practice being present with the body as it transitions from experiencing a subconscious reaction to a conscious response. In relationship with others, it's during this transition period that we learn how to differentiate between what is *our stuff* and what is someone else's. We learn how to show up and listen to others without the intrusion of our own emotional states and baggage being projected onto the other. And when we give that space for the other to be themselves, we infuse a sense of peacefulness into the relationship. I've highlighted just some of the ways that staying connected to the body impacts and influences how we experience everyday life. Many more are explored in this book.

I've written *Somawise* with a few types of readers in mind, certain sets of eyes and nervous systems that would be interested in the stories, teachings and strategies provided within these pages. Generally, this book is for people who want to create authentic change in their life but have struggled through the start-stop pattern that makes change seem impossible or unsustainable. *Somawise* can be considered uniquely appropriate for men, as I explore topics that are supremely lacking in conversations within male circles, such as emotional vulnerability and pornography. My intention is for *Somawise* to also support fellow helpers – be it coaches, counselors, therapists or psychologists – who might look at it as an educational and motivational resource for clients to use during the all-important time between sessions. It's specifically for this audience that I've included an appropriate amount of research to satisfy the mind. Finally, this book is for those who have grown tired of the materialistic success and productivity-based model for life. When blind ambition has run its course, these souls have realized that life is best enjoyed when there is a sense of ease, comfort and calmness within the body and within the relationships that make up their respective lives.

The varied types of people that will be reading this book meant that my writing style had to flow between the different audiences, catering certain sections and diction to their uniquely wired brains. You'll undoubtedly notice the academic, the helper, just a kid excitedly sharing a story or a dude trying to relate to fellow dudes. These are the many parts of myself that needed to be seen or required expression. Maybe that's what makes writing a cathartic experience, as different parts of us get to shine during the process.

You'll notice that much of the content of this book stems from direct experience. I didn't simply research these topics in order to slap some references together and write yet another book full of collated information. I took, and continue to take, repeated dives into my own somatic world because I'm passionately curious and amazed with what I continue to discover. I live and breathe the ideas, knowledge and wisdom in this book. I've been dissecting my inner experience since my teachers – Dr. Gabor Maté, Dr. Graham Mead, Rupert Spira and Dr. Phil Carter – showed me the way. It's because I've walked this path, and now embody it, that I can share from it authentically.

There's a part of me that was afraid to include some of the stories within these pages. It's the part of me that still believes I'm supposed to be the expert, doctor, clinician or academic who has it all figured out. I didn't and I don't. I'm still learning. If there truly was a perfect person out there, they'd have no one to relate to. In fact, the world doesn't need more gurus or experts. It needs fathers who role model emotional vulnerability, lovers who don't copy and paste what they see in mainstream pop culture and porn, and teachers who empower by sharing aspects of themselves that make them just as fallible, flawed and human as their students. By sharing myself through words, I've chosen the latter.

Far too many of us struggle with feeling ashamed of our own authenticity. I've witnessed how vulnerability, transparency and truthfulness have invited love and connection as regular visitors into my everyday life. It would be hypocritical if I wasn't able to display vulnerability myself. And so, within these pages,

I share the raw and naked truth of my soul. Some of my sharing is meant to teach, some to inspire and some to give you as detailed as possible an account of profound experiences that are nearly indescribable through words, though I do my best. I also share my journey through porn addiction, along with the faults and flaws I tried hiding from the world prior to knowing that it's only through radical self-acceptance that our seeming imperfections shift of their own accord. Everything I share is because we're all experiencing a slightly different rendition of the same fundamental human experience.

It's hard to take off the masks that we show the world. We think if we show our vulnerability and kinks in our armor, we won't be the invincible expert or superhero helper we think we are supposed to be. In that sense, this book is the culmination of the learning that has taught me that it's okay to take my mask off and stand as my authentic self.

As I set out long ago on my own journey of self-discovery and growth, I realized after some time that I wasn't interested in enlightenment, perfection or in reaching some pinnacle of accomplishment. *I wanted to be better at my own life*. I wanted to be more comfortable in my own skin; to show up more fully and authentically in my life and in the relationships that defined it, together with learning as much as I could about the potential of the human body. I wanted to be a better father, son, lover, partner, friend, brother and therapist. I stopped sprinting toward an illusory finish line and now enjoy a leisurely stroll with loved ones instead.

Because of this, I believe that the only thing we can *truly* be an expert in is our own life. We can know nothing more deeply and intimately than our lived experience. Indeed, one of the central tenets of *Somawise* is that everything we ever need to learn about ourselves, about the world and about life is happening *right now*. All we have to do is learn how to pay attention. The body – our understanding of it and connection with it – is the pathway to that expertise. True North always points inward.

As you are about to set out on a journey inward, know that there's nothing closer, more palpable and more accessible than your own moment-to-moment bodily experience. Yet, over and over again, we seek outside of ourselves for answers, ignorant to the fact that our greatest teacher, doctor and guide is within us. *The mind tells stories, the body speaks the truth*. Those words will be repeated throughout this book.

It may be one of life's cruelest jokes to discover that while we've been searching for the deepest yearnings of the soul externally, the answers have been quietly and subtly available within us all along. While many have sought mastery of the mind, I've dedicated my life to humbly serving the body. My hope is that this book will show you why and how tapping into the body's well of wisdom can light your own path. I thank you sincerely and graciously for reading.

Dr. Luke Sniewski
Auckland, New Zealand
September 15, 2022

Chapter 1
Introduction: The Wise Body

"This is your body, your greatest gift, pregnant with wisdom you do not hear, grief you thought was forgotten and joy you have never known." - Marion Woodman

"Within my body are all the sacred places of the world, and the most profound pilgrimage I can ever make is within my own body." – Saraha

"Only about two percent of one percent of our thoughts deserve to be taken seriously." - Mokokoma Mokhonoana

Sitting on top of a bus (yes, on top, as there are no seats left inside), I look across at a Filipino man grinning ear-to-ear. He's pointing down at a massive wild boar wrapped in cloth. "Dinner", he says, nodding his head up and down enthusiastically. The man has graciously offered to host both me and my cameraman and good friend, Daniel, in his humble, remote home in the Philippines.

The bus we're riding on top of is technically a Jeepney, an old US military vehicle repurposed for public transport. Daniel and I are sitting on massive bags of rice – the cargo of some of the passengers. Beside us, that very hairy, very dead boar. Though the smell emanating from it is anything but pleasant, I'd be lying if I said I don't feel the same enthusiasm for dinner as our host.

Our Jeepney is driving through the windy mountains of Kalinga. The destination: Buscalan, a small village where Apo Whang Od, the oldest traditional tattoo artist on Earth – 97-years-old at the time – lives and practices her craft. Her specialty, Mambabatok, is considered one of the most painful tattoos on the planet. It involves a wooden stick used as a mallet, a thorn from a lemon tree as a needle and water mixed with ash as ink. As a tattoo virgin, what better way to initiate my body to the world of tattoos than with a Mambabatok? My mind is supremely satisfied with the story it's collecting as the experience unfolds.

After a long hike into the hidden village of Buscalan, we arrive at Whang-Od's home, where she also works. I start setting up my camera equipment when I realize I haven't given the slightest thought as to what I want permanently etched onto my skin. It's an understandable oversight, given that I've been preoccupied with managing all the variables involved in finding Whang-Od.

This present adventure is intended to be the final episode of a 56-episode documentary web series, *A Million Ways to Live*. Since I don't know at this point that this episode, the series finale, will never actually be aired, I busy myself with planning the episode as if it's going to be shared with the world. Needless to say, I'm also exhausted from the bus rides and broken nights of sleep required to get here.

As I'm setting up, I watch Whang-Od work away on the back of a young woman's neck. When I ask the woman about her tattoo, she says it's a crab. A July baby myself, that immediately grabs my attention. She tells me that, in Kalinga culture, the crab is a symbol of *the wanderer* or *wandering*. Serendipity strikes again.

The Philippines is the 38th country I've visited during my global travel project. It's fitting and appropriate that a Kalinga crab be the way I memorialize my journey. My mind experiences another wave of excitement as the story that's creating itself in real-time becomes even richer with meaning and detail. Then, as if right on cue, reality deviates sharply from the expectations of my mind.

Because I'm mentally preoccupied with filming, I'm focused solely on getting enough, and the right, footage. I have to coordinate Daniel on the second camera, Whang-Od, myself and my tripod, as well as the translator. All of these parts have to be oriented in a way that allows the episode to be filmed while getting tattooed. This means no second takes unless, of course, I want a second design added to another part of my body, which isn't my preferred option.

The orientation of the filming setup is challenging because I have to make sure that the audio from my mic is recording clearly. While Whang-Od is hammering away at my back, I'm supposed to simultaneously conduct an interview with her. When I finally settle into the chair and feel the prick of the thorn enter the base of my neck, I start asking Whang-Od about the secrets of her longevity. Our dear host and boar enthusiast is the translator and is situated beside us and off-camera. I try my best to manage the many moving parts of this production while subjecting my upper back to the world's most painful tattoo. Juggling too many things at once has always been my modus operandi.

During the interview, I have to turn my head to the side to ask Whang-Od questions so that the translator can hear me clearly. To be honest, with all the mental energy required to visualize and facilitate the film shoot, I don't feel anything during my tattoo session. And with my mind intently focused on doing the interview, I fail to consider the consequences of my repeated head-turning, which become evident later that evening.

When we arrive back at our host's home after an afternoon of filming and getting inked (Daniel also got a tattoo), our host's wife busies herself with chopping and hacking away at our boar, preparing dinner for the crew. Daniel and I finally have a moment to admire each other's tattoos.

His is truly a work of art: a large, perfectly symmetrical circular design on the back of his lower leg. I can see why there was a national campaign to honor Whang-Od as a National Filipina Artist. I sit there admiring the intricate details on Daniel's lower leg. I turn around to show Daniel Whang-Od's work on my upper back. He has two words for it: "*It's crooked.*"

Those two words catalyze an intense cringe and tightening deep in my belly. I feel a wave of angst and fear seize my body. My palms begin to sweat. *This can't be real.* Nothing is more triggering to a vain perfectionist than a so-obviously imperfect tattoo. Daniel laughs out loud. I nearly cry.

All of my head turning during the interview meant that the skin on my upper back had offset slightly to one direction throughout the tattoo session. The skin moved just enough for the final product to resemble a crab *actually* wandering off my spine's center. How unfortunately appropriate.

My mind scrambles to come up with solutions, whether real or imaginary, that include waking from what I hope is a dream, laser tattoo removal and time travel. The panic eventually subsides and I'm forced, reluctantly, to accept the reality of my situation. In the end, life gave me a valuable (and permanent) lesson in vanity and perfectionism. My imperfect, wandering crab has never drawn a compliment. I'm okay with that.

The Body Speaks the Truth

I've shared my tattoo experience from the Philippines because it amusingly demonstrates how the interpretations of the mind very often differ from the reality of what is happening in the body. Thus far, I've provided a recollection of what happened from the mind's point of view, along with possible meanings and interpretations of the events. In other words, I've shared a story.

Additionally, depending on how that story is told, which details are left out or highlighted, and even my mental state or mood at the time of sharing, the story of a botched tattoo from a 97-year-old traditional tattoo artist can, and does, subtly change to meet the intention that best suits the moment. If we go into the body, however, we get a completely different story. In fact, we don't get a story at all. We get the truth. My body will spend the rest of its life removing the tattoo because the ink has triggered a permanent, low-grade inflammatory response. *The mind tells stories, the body speaks the truth.* The body – *your body* – is where you find Truth with a capital T.

Regardless of what my mind determines to be the 'lesson of the day' garnered from my tattoo experience, the body, in line with its primary function and programming for survival, will unceasingly endeavor to remove the foreign intruder from its system in order to return itself to its natural, homeostatic state. No matter how many times my mind tries to affirm that there's no harm in a bit of ink, whether I like or dislike the look of the tattoo and no matter how I reframe the story or the symbolic nature of the lessons I learned, there's no escaping the absolute *fact* that a portion of my body's immune response will be dedicated to ridding my body of the ink imprinted on its skin. The body will continue to do this every moment until it dies. Indeed, the gradual fading of a tattoo over time is evidence of the body's ongoing, yet only partial, success.

When we get out of our heads and into our bodies, we connect with what is *real* – with what is *actually happening* – rather than an interpretation of reality offered by the mind. We empower ourselves to drop the story and start observing the truth of our experience. For example, when stressed, the mind can create an endless list of things to be anxious, worried or angry about. Most of which will never happen.

However, the body's undeniable truth in this situation is that the physiological experiences of anxiety or anger are present. Both of these experiences come with specific physiological responses, including the release of the stress hormone cortisol and the activation of the sympathetic nervous system. When we attempt to soothe our body's internal discomfort by meddling with interpretations provided by the mind, we find ourselves playing a game of whack-a-mole, resolving one external variable only to find another two pop up in its place. When we instead respond to the body's need to alleviate, manage and reduce cortisol levels or soothe an activated nervous system by focusing on the body's needs in the present moment, we engage with the true source of our discomfort.

Another common example of the mind's storytelling is the firm grip on a nutritional ideology for its proclaimed health benefits. This is a story because the truth of whether food choices – and any lifestyle choice as we'll explore in the next chapter– heal or harm is better assessed by listening to the body's *actual* response to what we eat and drink. We may have been swayed by the most credible experts, studies and testimonials, but convincing the mind that a certain diet is healthy won't do much if the experience in the body reveals a contrasting reality. We can't argue or debate the objective physiological experience of the body. *The mind tells stories, the body speaks the truth.* The central crux of this book is that knowing what is real is the best starting point for navigating the oft challenging and tricky terrains of life.

***

Soma is the Latin word for 'body'. *Wise* is related to being learned, experienced and having the power of discerning and judging rightly. With the assistance of the practices provided and explored in this book, becoming *Somawise* means gaining access to the body's wisdom and then engaging that wisdom in everyday life.

I coined the term '*Somawise*' to present the case for living a body-centered life, a lifelong exploration available to anyone daring enough to journey inwards into unfamiliar and, at times, unavoidably uncomfortable experiential territory. *Somawise* is the conscious choice to live life in connection with our moment-to-moment bodily experience. The wisdom that arises from this way of being can help us cultivate holistic wellbeing, create authentic change and bring a sense of peace and harmony to our relationships. The answers we seek are in the body. *Your* body.

Researchers continue to explore and unearth findings about the importance of conscious connection with the body. For example, some studies have demonstrated that effective self-regulation involves the ability to accurately detect, assess and evaluate internal somatic cues relating to events, situations and relationships within our external environment[1]. Cultivating an awareness of the sensory information within the body, or *interoceptive awareness*, facilitates self-regulation and contributes to health and wellbeing[2]. *Somawise* provides an approach that fosters interoceptive awareness via practices (discussed in later chapters) that help us connect with our body's present moment experience.

My intention through this book is to open the reader's eyes to the awe-inspiring greatness of the human body. Specifically, *your body*. The body is a deep reservoir of wisdom that can be tapped into. The answers to the big questions, challenges and intentions that many have been seeking, maybe for years or decades, are found within the body.

Holistic wellbeing is achievable when we forge an intimate connection with our body and immerse it in an environment that supports health and healing. Our body lets us know when our lifestyle choices add or detract from our health. The body is where we can find and unravel the source of the self-destructive patterns preventing authentic change from transpiring in our lives. Connected to the body, we can experience true freedom and create new possibilities for life rather than remaining stuck on autopilot within an endless cycle of self-sabotage. Connected to the body, we can infuse more presence and peacefulness into relationships, both with ourselves and others.

It's also within the body that we unravel, process and integrate the trauma and deep emotional wounds that have been ignored, hidden, repressed, numbed or avoided for as long as we can remember. The end of our self-destructive behaviors, addictions and bad habits becomes a real possibility when we are able to go to the source and be present to what the body requires for healing. When we live life with our attention anchored in the body, we cultivate a different way of being that allows us to experience a greater sense of ease that permeates the various contexts of everyday life.

When we set aside the mind and embody our experience, we can appreciate the moment and savor it without the constant intrusions of the backseat driver living in our heads. In turn, it's through listening to and understanding the language of the body that we develop the capacity to confidently trust our ability to respond to the present moment and consciously choose where to go next. The body can be our teacher, guide and compass on the journey through life. This is the process of becoming *Somawise*; the process of connecting to the wisdom of the body.

An Ode to the Body

I love my body. Everything I write here can be considered an ode, tribute and love letter to the body... disguised as a book. These words are a long overdue acknowledgment and gesture of appreciation for the vessel that has allowed me to experience consciousness within the subjective 'I' referential point. The following passages are an acknowledgment of the intricate capacities, processes and functions that have been fine-tuned over millions of years to create a body with unimaginable physiological complexity. The body is undoubtedly worthy of worship, at least equal to the amount given to the pop culture phenomena popular at any particular time.

The body allows us to experience all the amazing things life has to offer. We require a body to savor our favorite gelato, bask in the glory of a beautiful sunset, or feel the comfort and warmth of a lover's embrace. This book explores what some might consider the radical idea that the mind – and the constant stream of thoughts we know of it – doesn't have the answers we're looking for. The answers we seek are in the body. *Your* body.

Without a body, we experience nothing at all. That's because the world isn't something that's happening *to* us. The world is happening *through* us, via the body and its senses. Absolute reality is something we'll never experience because what we experience is simply our body's interpretation of objective reality. Our body's senses come into contact with, process, filter and integrate information from our respective environments. The end product is the magnificent totality of our perceived moment-to-moment experience.

Despite this, very little inquiry, if any, is given to our inner experience. Most of us are busy focusing on what's happening 'out there' instead of seeking to understand what makes 'out there' possible to experience at all. The irony is that the more we understand our body and how it speaks through intuition and sensation, the more we understand the chaos and confusion of the external world. Life begins to flow with more ease when we direct our attention inward and return to our body's senses. We stress less and savor more when we feel comfortable in our own skin.

While many teachings and approaches proclaim that mastery of our mind is the highest achievable virtue, this book provides a different path. Mastery is for the mind. *Serving is for the body. Somawise* will show that when we respect, listen and tend to the body's needs, mastery of the mind is nothing more than a natural consequence of a body free of tension, stress and constriction. The mind's potential is realized when it isn't reacting to the constant influx of distress signals from a chronically stressed, tension-riddled and overwhelmed body. When we become humble servants to, and students of, the body, the mind bows in reverence.

The realities and demands of a mind-centered modern-day world mean that people continue doing what their mind tells them to do. Decisions are often made in response to thoughts about what is happening rather than being rooted in, or at least considering, what is objectively true within the body. This way of living comes at the expense of the body and its health. The body suffers so that a dogma or ideology can live on.

As a result, far too many are walking around with chronically accumulated tension, inflamed and protruding bellies, hunched spines, tightness and an assortment of pains, aches and discomforts. While some face these challenging realities as a byproduct of disease, genetic differences, aging, infection or other ailments, most suffer because of the detrimental consequences of their lifestyle choices, the environment they live within, and their coping behaviors. By and large, the body bears the load of our accumulated stress because its cries for help are ignored, suppressed or unheard altogether.

Of course, it doesn't have to be this way if only we listen to what our body is trying to tell us. The body does not lie. It cannot lie. It's right here, right now. Anything that originates from within the body is *true*. No blind faith is required when paying attention to the body's signals and cues. And if we're paying attention, the body is constantly providing feedback. Stress isn't allowed to accumulate to chronic levels when we listen to our body's present moment needs as they arise.

***

Before continuing, it's helpful to address two of the possible objections that may emerge within the mind of readers as they consider the uncomfortable possibility of passing the baton of decision-making to the body and thus surrendering some of its control. Losing control, any at all, is what frightens the mind most.

Firstly, as we will learn, listening to the body does not mean answering all the cravings, urges and temptations that might represent the very reason we're reading this book, such as the intention to break free from porn, alcohol, drugs or any other habit that has run its course. *Somawise* is not a license or free pass for seeking stimulation and pleasure. In many ways, it's the opposite.

Being *Somawise* means looking beneath the surface of powerful urges and impulses to get the *real* message from the body. We dive into our emotions, body sensations and triggers, and trust that our body will give us insights into ourselves that have always been just out of reach for the mind. These insights help us understand the source and root cause of our cravings, and why previous attempts to quench these insatiable cravings have fallen short.

Embracing *Somawise* as a way of life is also not a hedonistic celebration void of spirituality. On the contrary, nothing is more spiritual than embodying the fullness and richness of the present moment. Being in the here-and-now is at the core of all spiritual practice. Now is not a moment in time sandwiched between the past and future. *Now* is all that exists and where our life has been and always will be happening. A body-centered life anchors our attention in the only space where spirituality can ever exist – the present – rather than the judgmental, illusory world of thought.

Only the mind labels specific experiences or states as more 'spiritual' than others. Every moment can be revered and appreciated when we stay in our body and set aside the mind's constant and incessant judgments about what is unfolding within our present moment experience. When we connect with our body, we come back to our senses and intimately know the subtleties, nuances and uniqueness of the body. As a direct consequence, each moment is revealed as awe-inspiring and spiritual.

Living in the body is about dissolution, not solution; deprogramming, not reprogramming; being, not doing. A deeply meaningful and fulfilling life requires more than what logic, rationality and analytical reasoning alone can provide. The mind can't do it alone. What's required is a journey back into the body; a process of reconnection that is beautiful, challenging, sometimes very uncomfortable, and yet absolutely necessary. And to reconnect with the body, we must break out of the perceptual prison of the mind.

Living in the Mind

The mind is an incredible tool and an astonishingly creative power when the body is free of tension. When the body is tense and constricted, the mind's interpretations are not the most reliable assessments of any given situation. In times of stress and overwhelm, the mind incessantly ruminates on worst-case scenarios. Bouncing from thought to thought, like a ball in a pinball machine, we never end up in a calmer place. This scenario usually spirals out of control as the ruminating mind pulls us further into dysfunction and reactivity. When things start seeming chaotic, crazy or overwhelming, the body is the safest place for the mind to rest.

Modern society conditions us to prioritize, idolize and celebrate our seemingly vast intellects as if the concepts and theories that emerge from it are the holiest of grails. In reality, the miracle of our immense intellect could be the incidental byproduct of our opposable thumbs[3], which paved the way for ever-innovative tools and the simultaneous development of a brain capable of using such complex technology. Human intelligence could also result from gravity-assisted, energy-efficient bipedal movement[4]. As human movement became more energy-efficient, the brain was given free rein to feast on a larger share of calories the body consumed through food.

Other explanations for our evolved cognitive capacities could fall into the realms of silly and outrageous; assertions that our intelligence could have only emerged as a result of extraterrestrial intervention[5] or that our hunter-gatherer ancestors' consumption of psychedelic mushrooms growing on the feces of their prey led to rapid evolution and an expansion of the prefrontal cortex[6]. Whether purely accidental, intelligent design or natural selection, the mind's illusory output is relied upon as the primary authority for individual and societal decision-making.

Although they may have been complete evolutionary accidents, the experience of human consciousness and drastically improved cognitive prowess means we were bestowed with mental capabilities never before seen in the natural world. Evolutionarily speaking, it didn't take long for our great intelligence to reach the point that the mind believed itself to be all-powerful, all-knowing and exempt from the laws of nature. The mind has become the self-proclaimed master.

With the mind's sacred connection from the body broken – and thus from Nature herself – the mind has run away with its power, leaving behind it a trail of destruction equal to or greater than its creative potency, both on the micro and macro scales. The collective power of our minds has created ways of living that are presently destroying our natural environment, eroding its biodiversity and jeopardizing the entire human race in the process. It is only through reconnecting with the body – through becoming whole again – that we can begin to feel the consequences of our thoughts, words and actions. I believe that, reconnected, we can right the course of existence, both individually and collectively.

What we want out of life and what the soul yearns for most, the mind is simply ill-equipped to provide by itself. Our salvation, maybe even our sustainability as a species, depends on reconnecting with the body so that we are again connected to Nature. Ravenous, unceasing, capitalist appetites are nothing more than impulses within the body to fill a void that cannot be filled with external or material pursuits. The mind does not and cannot know when to stop because knowing when to stop is one of the messages that can only be found within the body. It's the body that teaches the all-important lesson of *enough*.

These words, however, are not intended to be a demonization of the mind. There are brilliant thinkers throughout human history who have manifested countless inventions, creations, discoveries and insights that have contributed to the beautiful and diverse entirety of the human experience. I am thankful for the technology that allows my son and his grandmother to converse face-to-face and in real-time despite being on polar opposite points of the planet. My nephew would not be alive today had it not been for medical advancements that first emerged as an idea within some genius' mind. And not a meal goes by that I don't experience a deep sense of gratitude for the technological advancements and creativity that were requisite for my taste buds' indulgence.

Even within the context of becoming *Somawise*, the mind will play a key role. As we reconnect with the body, it will be the mind's attention that rests within the body so that we can listen to what the body has to say. The mind will also initiate reflective self-inquiry processes critical for cultivating self-awareness. Living in the mind only becomes a problem when we live *solely* in the mind.

Living *exclusively* in the mind is another way of saying we're stuck in our heads. We believe everything we think, confusing the imaginary for the real. But the mind cannot penetrate reality, as it is imprisoned in the fantastical and imaginative world of thought and story. The mind can only *guess* at experience. And if there is one thing that is certain, it is that the story-telling of our mind is often far scarier than the real-world counterparts.

Most of the stories we tell ourselves are fear-based, anxiety-provoking and 'worst-case-scenario' scripts that paint the world as a scary, dangerous place. The mind doesn't understand that the bleak image projected across its landscape is often nothing more than a reflection of the accumulated tension and stress within the body.

Living solely in the mind and cut off from the body's innate intelligence is like a teenager left home alone for the weekend while the parents go out of town. You don't know exactly what's going to happen, but you know it will not be good.

The mind left to its own devices is a wildly irresponsible source of power. The mind cannot *feel* the interconnected and widespread consequences of its decisions. Without the body to let the mind know when things are immoral, unethical and have gone too far, the mind just keeps going and going; consuming and destroying everything in its path in the name of business, power, stimulation or pleasure. The mind, untethered from the body, is a problem. It is easily distracted, entranced and hijacked without the grounded presence of the body. An untethered mind is an unhappy, agitated and insane mind.

Mark Twain beautifully articulated it when he said, "I've had a lot of worries in my life, most of which never happened." People go through life as prisoners of their minds. Indeed, the only prison anyone lives in is their limited point of view. When we face our fears, no matter how big or small, we are often surprised that the mind made such a big deal about them in the first place.

Living in the mind means that instead of *being* in reality, the world, we're engaged with endlessly repeating mental stories *about* the world. The mind is great at coming up with stories that quickly hook us, take our attention away from the present moment and pull us toward reactivity.

Common stories of the mind include judgments, time traveling (ruminating thoughts of the past or the future), excuse-giving, justification and rules about how we should or shouldn't speak and behave in the world. These stories shape how we perceive and engage with ourselves and the world. However, our mind's automatic and reactive thoughts represent only *one* referential viewpoint of the world and our experience.

When we buy into our thoughts, we fuse with them and believe *we are our thoughts*. Fused, we believe our thoughts are accurate, factual and represent reality. They are not. A thought is only one possibility and often an inaccurate one. But when we continuously react to our thoughts as if they are real, *we make them real*. We make our worst fears come true because we react to them as if they have already happened. And then, we unintentionally manifest our mind's reality through our reactions. We don't realize that we keep getting stuck in a cycle of reactivity because we are watching and reacting to fear-based thoughts of the mind playing on repeat.

At the very core of our suffering are not the things that happen to us but rather the *interpretations and meanings* we give to the things that happen to us. I didn't suffer when I got a bad grade in school, when a client ended their therapeutic relationship with me or when a girl said "no" to being asked on a date. These are objective experiences that happen to everyone. Sure, they may not be pleasant, but the suffering that ensued at the time was optional and based solely on the meaning my mind gave these situations.

There is a difference between pain and suffering. Pain, a topic that will be explored in immense detail throughout this book, is inevitable in life. Suffering, however, is holding on to our interpretations of the events leading to our pain and wishing they were otherwise. I *suffered* because I interpreted my bad grade as me being stupid, the client leaving meant I was useless, and the rejection confirmed I was unworthy of love. We suffer because of the meaning that our mind attaches to the things that happen to us.

Believing that our thoughts are inherently true is like believing that our dreams are true. Sometimes dreams can seem real. We wake up with a racing heart, sweating and eyes wide open. It can take some time to recalibrate as we slowly realize we were just dreaming. Eventually, we let go of the nightmares we *thought* we had experienced as we come back to our senses. Similarly, when we believe every thought and live a life predominantly in our head, we are essentially living in a dream. We are asleep in a waking state.

Who's in Control?

The mind, aka conscious thought, likes to believe it's in control of its fate, destiny and everyday decision-making. The mind *thinks* it can create change simply by having *thoughts* of change (more on that in a later chapter, *Radical Self-Acceptance*). But the truth is that the vast majority (upwards of 95%[7]) of human behaviors, thoughts and actions stem from the activity of the subconscious mind. The subconscious mind thus dictates how we experience, interpret and respond to the world.

The subconscious mind exercises its influence over cognitive decision-making because it can gather, filter and process information at an exponentially higher rate than the conscious mind can react with a conscious thought. While these processes occur automatically and help prevent the conscious mind from being overloaded or burdened by simple or mundane routine tasks, we underplay and under-appreciate the extent to which the subconscious mind impacts the choices and decisions we've mistakenly assumed are made by the conscious mind[8].

But where is the subconscious mind? I agree with neuroscientist and author Dr. Candace Pert when she says that the body *is* the subconscious mind. Where else would it be? Dr. Pert's research provided an inside look at the molecular activity within every cell of the human body to back up her assertion.

One of the ways that the body subconsciously exerts influence over thoughts, words and actions is via the nervous system. If we are sympathetically aroused or triggered, our body's fight-flight-freeze mechanism becomes activated or ready for action. When this system is oversensitive, any external stimulus, no matter how big or small, will initiate this self-preserving way of relating to the external world. Everything and everyone could be perceived as a threat.

When we begin reconnecting with our body, however, we start sensing, feeling and understanding the state of our nervous system. Through this process, we learn to listen to what the body is saying. We can then determine how to bring ourselves back into balance and effectively cope with what is happening within us.

The Somatic Marker Hypothesis (SMH) provides another conceptual framework for understanding how the body calls the shots even though the mind likes to think it does. The SMH, developed by António Damásio, asserts that a *physical sensation* occurs on the body, at the experiential level, before cognition kicks in as *a reaction* to physical sensation[9]. In other words, the body *feels* before the mind *thinks*[10]. *The mind tells a story about the truth of the body's experience.* This is why awareness of the body's physical sensations is the foundation of becoming *Somawise*. We'll detail how to cultivate this capacity for feeling physical sensations in later chapters.

Somatic markers, aka the physical sensations experienced within the body, influence the mind's decision-making because they can immediately lead us to dismiss or consider one option over another based on how they make us *feel*. The body's senses collect, process, filter and send information to the brain *before* a conscious thought emerges as a consequence of this *bodily* process. The real-world implication of this phenomenon is that our conscious decisions end up being significantly determined by what we feel or don't feel in the body.

Brands and clever marketers continue to leverage this feedback loop between the body and mind by seeking to elicit specific emotional states via their ads[11].

The mind's rational reasoning, hypothetical scenario modeling and verbal narratives are invariably impacted by various sensory inputs experienced within the body. What the conscious mind decides in any moment is influenced by anything from unpleasant physical sensations, physiological states like hunger, and external stimuli like environmental temperature, to our partner's mood, how much we slept, stress levels, loud noises, or even lunar positioning[12, 13].

I've already demonstrated how this process might play out when I shared the many different stories and narratives that emerged from my tattoo experience. Indeed, this process is why sometimes the stories of our greatest difficulties and traumas radically shift to stories of triumph, acceptance and resilience when we find ourselves on the other side of our challenges. When the experience of the body shifts, so, too, does the story of the mind.

The so-called 'free-thinking' mind is – as one of my teachers, Dr. Phil Carter, would say – *always* a step behind the action, one step behind the body, even though the mind likes to puff its chest as the supreme autonomous power and decision maker. In reality, the whole universe contributes to the single output labeled as a conscious thought.

It's truly a humbling experience when we recognize and appreciate the influence of the body over the mind. The mind's conscious intentions for change and responsiveness to the present moment are often bulldozed by the sheer power of subconscious bodily drivers, because we are unaware and disconnected from the sensations at the core of subconscious reactivity. The mind stands no chance against an activated nervous system and a body full of tension and stress. Freedom and free will may very well be inaccurate illusions of the mind.

Disengaging from the Mind

It takes time to stop believing every thought that crosses the mind. It takes even longer to realize those thoughts aren't even *you*. Most of the content automatically popping up in our mental landscape is old conditioning. These are the reactions, behaviors and habits shaped by our genetics at conception and programmed into our body's nervous systems due to life experiences, mostly during early childhood[14]. These programs have been embedded in our bodies ever since.

As living in the mind is modern society's status quo, we don't realize there's an alternative to experiencing the mind's incessant clutching, interpreting, measuring, judging, labeling and story-telling. As we gradually immerse ourselves in our sensory experience by reconnecting with the body and its felt sense, the mind begins to loosen its firm grip over decision making and the enticing nature of thought begins to lose its seductiveness.

Of course, this process of settling back into our somatic experience requires committed, intentional and consistent practice. It requires more than simply reading the pages of this, or any, book. But the process of becoming *Somawise* starts with understanding why living in the mind became our default way of being. We cannot move away from an old way of being and authentically change without first understanding, and then accepting and thanking, the origin and function of that which we intend to move away from. This is discussed in extensive detail in a later chapter, Radical Self-Acceptance. In short, if we want to reconnect with the body, we have to appreciate why it was necessary to retreat from the body's experience to begin with.

Dr. Gabor Maté taught me not to criticize the mind, and certainly oneself, for our way of mentally engaging, or disengaging, with the world. Maté showed me that living in the mind was, first and foremost, a survival mechanism from, and an adaptation to, our early childhood environment. Maté emphasizes via his teachings that we distance ourselves from our unpleasant, uncomfortable and oft-painful bodily experiences because we *learned* to do so as children[15].

Instead of someone teaching us to articulate, be present with, validate our emotions as normal, and be present with us as they are processed, we got some iteration of *don't be sad, stop your whining* or *I'll give you something to cry about if you don't shut up*. The body's experience of the present moment thus became something to be ignored, suppressed or rejected, lest the environment we were dependent upon should reject us. It was safer to disconnect from ourselves. At the time, no other option was possible or available to us, as we depended on our immediate environment for survival.

While it may have been necessary to do that then, the disconnection from the body set us down a path that would prevent us from engaging authentically with the world moving forward. As a result, anything and everything could be a threatening, unfamiliar, scary or painful experience. The chasm between mind and body has grown so vast that bringing our attention to the body can seem like being a stranger visiting a foreign land, like a backpacker being dropped in the middle of a foreign country with no understanding of the local language or culture.

Disconnected from the body, we try to figure out the source of our perceived discomfort by jumping from thought to thought. We cannot find more than momentary relief because we don't speak or understand the language of the body, where the distress signal is actually coming from.

No matter what someone's mind thinks, and whether that particular mind believes its challenges are related to parents, genetics, chemical imbalance, early childhood environment, intergenerational trauma, or even past life trauma, *all reactions* arise firstly within the body as a sensation. When we engage with our thoughts to quell our pain and discomfort, we are trying to extinguish a fire by fanning our hands through the ethereal smoke in front of our faces, unaware that the fire causing our pain is within us, not *out there*. The Great Disconnect we learned through our experiences in childhood ensures we no longer have access to the source of our pain and discomfort.

The Great Disconnect

We don't experience objective reality. We experience the world through our body's senses. The senses of our body are filters through which we receive, analyze, process and interpret the world. If our filters are full of tension, constriction and pain, then the mind will follow with similarly-themed perceptions. If the body is riddled with tension and constriction, this will be the lens through which we view, interpret and understand the world, along with everything and everyone within it. If we are unaware of or disconnected from, the tension that has chronically accumulated in the body, then the world becomes the outward expression of an internal state. As tension dissolves from our bodies, so, too, do many of the negative perceptions and interpretations we have of the world around us.

Disconnected, we don't feel the emotional states and sensations that trigger the impulse toward addictions and habitual self-soothing. When we blindly reach for the pantry, a glass of wine or a porn site, we don't sense there was a spark that ignited, firstly, within the body. We fail to see that when we are engaged in a heated argument with a loved one, we are actually in relationship with the discomfort arising within our own bodies. The body is experiencing anger and the physiological sensations associated with it, yet we are reacting to the thoughts in our head as if they are real. As a result, we don't truly see the person in front of us because we are reacting to the mental story, narrative and projection playing in our minds.

Disconnected, we find it impossible to create and sustain authentic change because we aren't aware that the origin of our reactivity is within, not external to us. Rather than attending to the somatic trigger driving the reaction, we try to manipulate the external world. *It's not me; it's them.* We all know what happens when we try to change and control the people around us.

Disconnected, we don't see that the habits that continue to repeat themselves are an expression of our body's commitment to healing old patterns. *Why does this keep happening to me* is more accurately reframed as *this situation is creating yet another opportunity to explore what needs healing within me.* The subconscious mind, aka the body, is constantly setting up conditions of cyclic reliving and re-enactment so that it can process, integrate and heal old relational wounds. Though the same things seem to keep happening repeatedly, this can be reframed as a gift and opportunity to face old problems with new potential, possibilities and awareness. In other words, life keeps giving us the same lessons until we learn them, until the lesson is *embodied.*

Disconnected, we require an external authority for morality, such as precepts, commandments or rules. Yet it's the body that lets us know it's wrong to hurt, manipulate, exploit, steal, kill, lie or intentionally cause any other kind of harm to another. When we're disconnected, our mind justifies immoral actions with its insanity: *they deserved it, she made me do it,* or *it's just business.* We don't have to wait until we die or the next life to know if what we're doing is just or right. The body is the moral and ethical compass giving us feedback if an intention or act is misaligned with morality. Tension and agitation let us know immediately if something is right or wrong. The body is giving us this feedback from moment to moment.

To be disconnected from the body means we are disconnected from the most natural way of navigating life with morality. We are subject to the interpretations and words of what others have judged as right or wrong. Jesus, Buddha, and teachers from various traditions have all pointed in the same direction: *Know thyself. The kingdom of heaven is within. You have to find your own path. That path is inward.* The meanings of these teachings are strengthened and made more profound when we reconnect with the body.

Disconnected, we forget that we are intimately linked with the world and everything within it. The separation we perceive is nothing more than an illusion of the mind. The mind dissects, labels and separates everything in its awareness to bring a sense of control and understanding to its experience of reality. This separation is not real. For example, the mind dissects a tree into its constituent parts – the roots, trunk, branches and leaves – but all of these seemingly separate parts make up *one whole* tree. Even the mind's separating of the tree's surrounding ground, air and water is misleading as the tree cannot exist without these surrounding contexts. They are as much a part of the tree as what the mind labels as a tree. If that is hard to grasp or believe, then consider that only after the mere passage of time the tree's surrounding water and air become part of the tree as they are absorbed and integrated into it. The same illusion of separation applies to our respective bodies and experience of ourselves. Our body is intimately connected to, dependent upon, and *one with* our external environment.

Disconnected, we disregard our body and fail to give it what it needs to thrive. We rely on smartphones to tell us if we've moved enough during the day, slept enough during the night, and eaten correctly in between. Third-party apps have replaced the ancient wisdom of the body. We don't listen to, or rather cannot understand, the body's pleas for nurture, rest and care. Despite the tireless, endless and unceasing efforts the body has given, it has been forgotten, ignored, taken for granted and misused. We reach for myriad quick fixes instead of providing the body with what it needs to heal and thrive. We treat our body like it's just another commodified good that can be replaced when the next model or upgrade releases and don't truly appreciate that we get only one body.

One. If we truly grasped and appreciated this reality, we wouldn't treat the body in the loveless ways that many of us do.

Disconnected, we do not appreciate the body's vast inherent healing capacity. There are an estimated thirty-two trillion cells in the human body. Every single one contains the fundamental program, instincts and compulsive drive toward healing. These survival programs are as old as life and could be considered biological life's original coding and programming. Instead of acknowledging the body's inherent healing capacities, many opt to take a pill for every ill.

Disconnected, we don't understand or appreciate the different ways the body heals itself. The process of healing isn't always comfortable and the mind prefers to avoid such states of discomfort. We even take pills to intentionally *avoid* therapeutic physiological states, such as fever, diarrhea or vomiting. Yet the fever, diarrhea and vomiting, regardless of how uncomfortable or frightening the mind perceives them to be, are three of the body's natural healing mechanisms. The mind doesn't like experiencing discomfort, so it impedes the process of healing and reacts with the thought that *some ibuprofen or Panadol will make me feel better.* It will not. It will only temporarily numb. *Feeling is healing.* There is often more to gain when we acknowledge and sit with our pain than getting dragged into the mind's story and narrative about it. I'll dive into the many benefits of consciously facing discomfort later in this book.

Most importantly, disconnected, we don't trust our bodies. Our complete and utter lack of trust in the body means that even a single sensation of discomfort can induce a state of fear and panic. Google has replaced an intuitive sense that has taken Mother Nature countless millennia to evolve, refine and perfect. We've forgotten how to live, relying on external sources and authority figures to tell us how to eat, move, laugh, love, sleep, work and think. Despite this seemingly infinite amount of information the mind has access to, we *still* aren't any closer to living a fulfilled life. Disconnected, we are truly lost.

***

Arguably the most significant and evident consequence of The Great Disconnect is the present state of our health and wellbeing, both individually and collectively. The average body struggles to get through everyday life as it's riddled with unending inflows of stress. Without energy in the morning, we reach for coffee only to flood the body with caffeine, an anxiety-promoting stressor, throughout the day. When in pain, we reach for pain relievers, though our body's expression of chronic pain is its way of saying something requires investigation and attention. We consume a near-perpetual amount of fear-mongering and anxiety-inducing content while our bodies feel the detrimental effects of circulating cortisol and inflammation that come as a consequence. The body, shell-shocked from the daily war games we play with it, refuses to fall asleep naturally because it's *too stressed* to sleep. So, we reach for sleeping pills instead. We wake the next morning tired and fatigued. In comes the coffee to start the cycle again.

A stressed body does not change. It gets stuck in repetitive patterns of self-sabotage. A stressed body doesn't want to have sex because it's solely focused on its survival. Reproducing is very far down on the list of necessities when the body is carrying loads of stress. A stressed body is tired, moody, distracted and easily triggered. A stressed body gets sick and stays sick more often. A stressed body won't allow the mind to explore the realms of creativity because the mind is engaged in a near-constant external search for the source of its perceived discomfort.

The mind and its thoughts are only reacting to messages from the body. When the body is sending signals that something is not working (like not being able to sleep, a lack of energy or a bad mood that doesn't seem to shake), we ignore the calls for help with quick fixes so that we can continue living following our mind's meticulously designed routines, work demands and life expectations. The body bears the brunt of this cumulative stress burden.

The body is stressed, but because we don't understand the language of the body, we have no idea that it is sending us distress signals. We've either never learned or forgotten how to care for the body when it lets us know it needs nurturing and care. To cope with chronic stress, we've become masters at numbing, sedating, ignoring, repressing and drowning out the body's messages to keep pace with the mind's demands. This is where the mind's insanity starts to make sense, as it's trying its best to solve a problem the only way it knows how: *doing, doing and more doing*. But when the root cause of our discomfort and the path toward healing both point to the body, that severed connection leads to the perpetual hunt for something *out there* that cannot be found outside ourselves.

***

We can escape the world of thought and come back to reality by coming back to our senses. And where do our senses reside? In the body, of course. In a world where most people live solely focused on exploring the outside world in an attempt to understand its many complexities, people rarely turn their attention in the other direction. The mind has been given plenty of time and opportunities to prove its power. Countless books, teachers and quotes have shown that they provide only temporary relief. Why are we so drawn to the ethereal world of thought, to *what is out there*, rather than what is palpable, real and *now* within the body? It's time to trust the body.

Why not flip the referential point around? Why not turn the microscope in the opposite direction and focus on the body instead of being enamored with the world of thought? We can learn about the universe by observing that which is made out of the same substance and governed by the same principles: the body.

The mysteries of life reveal themselves when we begin to understand the frames, lenses and filters through which we interpret the world. The naked truth emerges from the ashes of our burnt beliefs when we choose to follow our direct experience rather than our imagination.

Our body knows the most important things it needs, what feels uniquely right when it comes to whom and how to love, the nourishment it needs for healthy functioning, and how to rest, restore and heal so that it can flow with the demands of everyday life. Our body carries the mysteries of our lineage, history, conditioning, and all of our potential selves. The challenge faced by all of us is learning to trust our respective bodies as teachers and guides. It's time to learn *how*.

Somawise: A New Way of Being

Chances are that, if you're reading this, then you're starting this journey because you want to change something in your life. You might relate to some of the challenges and problems presented thus far. Maybe you're someone who needs to consistently perform at a high level. Perhaps you've been trying to quit a habit that doesn't serve you anymore. Or you just want to enjoy the simpler things in life without your mind being elsewhere. More than likely, you've reached the end of the path that leads to answers *out there* and suspect that the answers have been *here* all along. You've been on a long journey of exploring and experimenting, only to return to where you started. Your body is your home, regardless of how uncomfortable being in it may seem right now.

Change is hard. But health, habits, choices, addictions and behavioral patterns don't have to be life sentences. The answers we seek require us to travel a path that points inward, where we'll get to know our body, come back to our senses and learn how to understand the many messages the body is trying to tell us.

The body is worthy of worship for being the incredible gift that it is, its innate wisdom and its tremendous healing potential. Most importantly, in a world dominated by thoughts, ideas and head-based living, anchoring to the body may be the only way to settle the mind's chaotic state. This book is the beginning of a journey that takes us toward a calm, peaceful and still place within ourselves, that has always been there and is available to us at any given moment.

The chapters within *Somawise* are organized to support cultivating awareness of the body from the inside out. It's challenging to stay present with our bodily experience in relationship with others. Before we can bring an embodied sense of self into relationship with others and the external world, it's essential to learn how to stay connected with the body within contexts that are more focused on individual practice and thus contextually less complex.

To start the process of reconnecting to the body, the introduction being read now is intended to assist the mind in understanding why living *solely* in the mind is like being trapped in a perceptual prison, and why reconnecting with the body is a vital step toward holistic wellbeing, authentic change and peaceful relationships. Disarming and softening the automatic defenses of the mind is a necessary step for receiving the teachings of this book. When the mind understands and accepts the role the body plays in relation to the mind's intentions and goals, it makes it easier to engage with, and commit to, the practices explored in the following five chapters.

The five chapters following this introduction – *The Environment of Health and Healing, Stillness, Change through Stillness, Conscious Discomfort,* and *Radical Self-Acceptance* – explore the tools, techniques and practices that support the initial process of reconnecting to the body. Each practice teaches nuances and subtleties as we learn to trust the body's intuitive sense and refine our understanding of its present moment experience and needs. After the connection with the body becomes easier, we can begin utilizing the body's wisdom as a guide and teacher in relationship with others and the world. Indeed, the gifts we cultivate through individual practice become helpful when we share them in relationship with others.

Essentially, the final three chapters are intended to connect the dots of *Somawise.* The first of these concluding chapters, *Relationship,* can be considered a mini conclusion, as being in relationship with others brings all the lessons of personal practice into a context where they can be applied and utilized. What makes the context of relationships particularly unique is that being in relationship also provides another way of practicing being *Somawise.* When we embody our experience in relationship with others, we can access wisdom and teachings that are otherwise inaccessible through personal practice alone. For example, if we have trouble meeting, connecting with and being present with people, we cannot meditate in a cave and expect our interpersonal problems to disappear. In relationship, we can heal old relational wounds and discover new ways of being in and navigating the relationships that make up our life.

The last two chapters are the true conclusions of the book. First, *The Miracle of Healing Trauma* connects the dots of *Somawise* further, by incorporating the practice of being in relationship into the holistic equation of health, healing and wellbeing. Lastly, the second conclusion, *A New Way of Being,* is intended to set the path for acquiring new learnings, which will be different for every reader. We will have different lessons and insights from our respective lived experience.

We all live within contexts specific to us. Thus, the wisdom that emerges from being connected to our body will be unique for us and our respective lives.

Each chapter of *Somawise* is summarized in the following paragraphs:

The Environment for Health & Healing

What happens when we live a body-centered life and embody our life experience? Wellbeing becomes more than just a mental construct that requires tracking with an app. Our body lets us know what is or isn't supporting its health. When connected to the body, we can't avoid the truth that we've been overworking, over-stressing and overwhelming ourselves in the name of productivity and keeping up with the rat race. We also realize the importance of slowing down and caring for the body. *Self-care is about giving the best of you, not what's left of you.*

This chapter also explores how to put the body in an environment that supports its innate healing processes. We don't need fad diets or intricately designed workout plans when a lifestyle is designed in such a way that cultivates health as a direct consequence. Health is the natural byproduct of a healthy lifestyle and an automatic process. We don't have to stress about it or overthink it. The body will naturally and effortlessly move toward optimal health and wellbeing when nourished and cared for in alignment with the Healthy Lifestyle Principles discussed in this chapter.

Stillness

The world has become loud and chaotic from the near-constant stream of notifications and pings. To hear the body's subtle language, however, we must get quiet. Intuition speaks with a soft tone. It's hard to hear the body over the screaming of the mind and the external noise aimed at grabbing the mind's attention. More than meditation, it's through practicing and embodying the quality of stillness that the mind settles and the body heals.

Stillness also represents the bridge and portal through which we'll begin the journey back into the body, where we'll be able to learn to differentiate between the thoughts of the mind and messages emerging from the body. Reconnecting to the body through stillness requires becoming aware of and learning the language through which the body speaks: sensations. Detecting subtle physical sensations before they reach the level of intense emotional states or impulsive behavioral triggers is the key to breaking the cycle of reactivity and moving toward authentic change.

Change through Stillness

Stillness is the birthplace of self-awareness. When we truly understand ourselves, we are empowered to make more conscious and responsive decisions rather than falling into the same old habitual, subconscious reactions. To become aware of ourselves, we must practice being still.

Self-awareness is also the key driver of authentic and permanent change. When we are still, we become aware of the specific thoughts, emotions and body sensations that fuel automatic reactions that keep us stuck in the cycle of reactivity. Through stillness, we allow these impulses deep within the body to settle, thus cultivating the capacity to choose something new, fresh and different. Connected to the body, we discover the possibility of choice that is inherently available in every moment if we remain attentively present.

Conscious Discomfort

We've learned to avoid discomfort rather than face it. This reactive and habitual way of being manifests in our lives in many ways. We take an elevator instead of the stairs. We avoid the potential pain of failing to reach our goals by not taking a single step away from our present circumstances. We pop pills to numb the discomfort of pain. These are just a few examples. *Everyone* is doing their own rendition of the dance of avoidance.

If we want to create authentic change in life, however, we must lean toward discomfort instead of turning away from it. We remain stuck until we befriend the pain we've been avoiding because change is an uncomfortable process regardless of context. It's not a pleasant experience to oppose the conditioned reactions embedded within the body. Consciously pivoting toward pain and discomfort is a pivot toward meaning, purpose and authentic change.

This chapter explores how we can practice a different way of relating to the uncomfortable experiences of everyday life by embracing the sensations they involve. When we get more comfortable being uncomfortable, it doesn't mean life's stresses and problems go away; it just makes passing through stressful situations easier because we've practiced sitting with and passing through the experience of discomfort.

Radical Self-Acceptance

We wouldn't use the labels and criticisms we unconsciously project at ourselves toward a friend, child and sometimes even an enemy. And yet, we don't think twice about the words we use to describe ourselves and our perceived limitations. Reacting with harsh self-judgment, shame and self-criticism perpetuates the very habits and patterns we wish to end. It's like being in a fight with ourselves. No matter the outcome, we're always the loser at the end of this fight. With each fight, we add more stress and tension to the body's already overwhelmed system. As we infuse more self-acceptance into our respective lives, however, the body reveals how differently it responds to compassionate and kind self-talk.

On the journey of change, self-discovery and personal growth, we inevitably hit roadblocks, get stuck for some time, and even take steps that seem to go backward sometimes. It's self-judgment, and the stressful physiological reactions that come with it, that perpetuates old ways of being because it sparks the next cycle of habitual reactivity. Learning how to be radically accepting of ourselves helps us break free of the habits that no longer serve us.

Relationship

Our hard-earned gifts of insight, reflection and self-awareness become useful within relationship. When healthy lifestyles cultivate a greater sense of energy and vitality, we have more to give others. The self-awareness garnered through stillness helps us understand who we are and how we behave when relating to others. When we've developed the capacity to be present with discomfort through conscious discomfort practices, it's easier to be present and less reactive with another person when we invariably get triggered. Through relationships with others, we can share our hard work and insights.

When we enter into any relationship with another person with our attention anchored in the body, we can better differentiate between 'our stuff' and the experience of the other. When triggers do arise in our body, we can stay present with them without reacting to the thoughts about the other person that might automatically arise. We are thus empowered to take responsibility for what is our reaction and choose, instead, to respond. In turn, relationships become a mirror that provide us with unique learning and healing opportunities that are only possible within relational contexts.

The Miracle of Healing Trauma

This chapter is a nod to Dr. Gabor Maté's life work in the field of trauma, as well as the impacts that those teachings have had on me, both personally and professionally. The main concepts in this chapter stem directly from or have been heavily influenced by Maté and Compassionate Inquiry, the psychotherapeutic approach developed jointly by Maté and Sat Dharam Kaur. While the detailed exploration of trauma is outside the scope of this book, when we seek to understand the source and origins of our automatic thoughts, conditioned reactions and habitual behaviors that keep us stuck in the cycle of reactivity, we invariably travel back in time to explore the environments of our past that would have led to such adaptations.

The conditioning that emerges as a result of the things that happen to us is not a purely psychological response. Trauma is the conditioning and reactivity programmed *into our bodies* as an adaptation to life experiences, primarily, according to Maté, our early life environment. Our conditioned reactivity is *embedded in our body*, often like a tightly wound ball. And because it is within the framework of our body, it invariably impacts and influences our present moment experience. This means that managing, processing and integrating can *only* happen in the present moment, because that is where our body is *experiencing the effects of trauma*, no matter how far back its origin may go.

Trauma leaves its signature in the present moment experience of our respective bodies as *tensio*n. Indeed, I far prefer the term *tension* to *trauma*, as it's more neutral, carries less connotation, and has less potential for identification with a victim-based narrative. *Tension is an indifferent, impersonal and natural phenomenon.* The topic of trauma has also become commercialized, watered-down and laden with socio-political ramifications, making it an ambiguous term that means something different to every nervous system.

Replacing the word 'trauma' with 'tension' assists us in focusing objectively on the present moment, direct experience and reality of the body, rather than a story. We can only deal with trauma – the accumulated tension in the body – *in the present moment*. We can only heal *now*. Within the context of Somawise, thus, trauma is primarily related to that box of programming, reactivity and conditioning presently embedded within the body.

The culmination of the inner work proposed by *Somawise* is reconnecting to the body so that we gain the capacity to heal trauma and unravel that ball of conditioned reactivity. Processing, integrating and healing our deepest wounds is work only the body can do. And this is no small task. While healing trauma is supported by all of the practices outlined throughout this book, it still requires a sprinkle of the magical ingredients of surrender, trust and faith. In other words, the mind has to get out of the way for this healing process to occur, and it may never understand or be able to explain how it happened. When the mind doesn't have an explanation for something, that experience is sometimes called a miracle. That is why healing trauma is a miracle.

A New Way of Being

Life looks very different when we embody our present moment experience. Living a life anchored in the body is a new way of being in the world. Books, teachers and experts become sources of helpful information and provide guidance, but only when necessary, rather than being the singular source of answers to our woes. This shift occurs because the body becomes our compass and roadmap for navigating everyday life.

Everything we ever need to learn about life, ourselves and the world is happening *right now*. When we stay attentive to how our body responds to our lived experience, we find lessons, insights and nuggets of wisdom particularly relevant to our own life. In the final chapter of *Somawise*, I share some of the lessons, insights and gems that my own body has taught me on my own journey. I hope these short anecdotes are helpful to read, but I also recognize that our respective bodies will have their own lessons to teach.

***

As this book offers many stories and experiences from my journey of healing beyond my conditioned reactivity, it's fitting and appropriate that I have saved those stories and experiences for the book's final chapters. The reader might arrive at the concluding chapters, only to think that the stories shared in the last chapters would have been helpful to know right from the start. However, this book's organization reflects the process of discovering new insights about ourselves while on the path of healing and personal growth. Sharing the stories that provide insight into the potential origins of my trauma and conditioned reactivity mirrors that process.

The long journey of healing starts on the surface level and moves progressively deeper, just as the chapters within this book do. We might feel the call to change because we are experiencing stress, dis-ease or some challenge in our life. We might start creating change with diet and exercise strategies, focusing primarily on superficial means and goals. We may find that, as we continue to grow and curiously look inward, new practices and insights begin to reveal more profound aspects of ourselves previously hidden from conscious awareness. We are then called to dig deeper and embark on excavations of the soul, where we unearth new understandings of ourselves. Eventually, we illuminate the deepest and darkest parts of our shadow self, paving the way for an awareness that transforms how we perceive ourselves, the people closest to us, and the world.

Of course, it would have been helpful to know something deep and meaningful about ourselves at the start of the journey. But that is not how the process of self-inquiry, self-awareness and inner work tends to go. We learn our biggest truths and most significant insights only after investments of consistent practice and patience. This is also why our most precious insights are held with immense gratitude when they are finally discovered.

Finally, while this may not immediately appeal to some readers who are accustomed to being given step-by-step instructions for how to live or do something, becoming *Somawise* is an inside job. We attune with, and tune into, our internal compass and learn how to listen to our intuitive senses. *The body is the real teacher.* The words in this book are here to point and guide us as we pave our own path. The support we're looking for comes from within. Little by little, as we settle into the body and learn to trust its wisdom, the external supports gradually drop away, and we consciously embrace the responsibility of navigating the incredible inner journey of life.

Consider these chapters and the teachings within them as training wheels. This book is not intended to be a mere transmission of information. The words in this book might serve to help or inspire, but real change only happens when these words are applied in practice. Reading this book is not enough. Agreeing with the passages of this book does not result in spontaneous health, harmony or enlightenment. *Direct experience is what turns knowledge into wisdom.* Becoming *Somawise* requires intentional practice. No one is exempt from the work that is necessary for personal growth.

The teachings in this book may ignite the fires of curiosity, prompting an exploration of many more modalities than those offered within these pages. That's a good thing because the path to reconnecting with the body is uniquely our own. While each chapter includes several questions that can be used for reflective self-inquiry, my words, stories and approach provide only the starting point. After that, it's up to the reader to explore their life experience with a childlike naivety. We can, if we want to, become the masters and experts of our own respective lives.

I can think of no worthier challenge in this lifetime than reconnecting to and understanding the body. The greatest call to adventure we can answer is to explore the potential, possibilities, nuances, subtleties, complexities and paradoxical simplicity of the body. This has been my meaning of life and the only way of living that makes any sense to me. I explore, investigate and observe my body with curiosity and wonder, because freedom has been the ultimate experience of such a wildly exhilarating journey.

We see the world with new eyes as we reconnect with the body. Everything will be different even though things look the same on the outside. We may even seem the same to those around us. Internally, however, we'll humbly smile because the truth is that the inner transformation that has taken place has changed our entire world. Nothing will be the same when the body is free of the tension, constriction and trauma that has been stored since early childhood (and likely long before that). We'll have wiped clean the lens through which we experience the world, and witness with clarity how rich and full every moment truly is. This is what becoming Somawise is all about. Enjoy the dive!

Chapter 2
The Environment of Health & Healing

"The greatest miracle on Earth is the human body. It is stronger and wiser than you realize, and improving its ability to heal is within your control." - Dr. Fabrizio Mancini

"The more we see health as a practice rather than as a problem to fix, the more we encourage the body's natural potential to be healthy." - Aarti Patel

"Complete health and awakening are really the same thing."
- Tarthang Tulka

The whistle blows. Again. I don't know how many more whistles I'll hear on this hot summer day, nor can I accurately recall how many I've already heard. All I know is that when I hear its sound vibrating through the air, I will sprint to the cone 53 yards away with as much effort as my body can muster. If I don't cross the marker before a specific time, there will be a price. During these infamous midday summer workouts, my coaches always ensure that crossing the finish line in time is the preferable option.

During the short breaks between sprints, the volume of my inner experience is turned up so high that it drowns out the voices screaming, cheering and jeering in the background. I can feel the sweat pouring off my face and dripping onto the knuckles of my hands resting on my knees as I slouch over trying to catch my breath. My heart beats with the intensity of a bass drum, each racing beat sending waves through my body that make my eyeballs quiver. My body vibrates with pain as it struggles to recover between the blows of the whistle. The physiological intensity of my experience makes my body vomit. This is what happens when the body is pushed to levels well beyond where the mind would have allowed it to go without the collective presence and pressure of coaches and teammates. Even as a young student-athlete, I can appreciate the incredible strength and adaptability of the human body as I walk back to the starting line for the next sprint.

The mind's protesting thoughts to stop have given up. My mind knows I won't listen. I only respond to the whistle. I trust my body – and my coaches – more than my mind. Even as my body struggles to get enough air and oxygen into itself, I feel *safe*.

I am fully and completely in my body, so I feel every explosive stride required to reach the marker, only looking forward to relishing and savoring a few brief moments of rest. From time to time, I allow myself to look around and see an increasing number of teammates with their hands and knees or flat on their backs. I smile internally.

With each successive sprint, I find myself closer and closer to the front of the pack. I may be one of the slowest players on the field, but I know I've gotten this far, both during this workout and as a collegiate athlete, because I outwork everyone around me. I keep going until the whistle stops. I always do. I don't give credence to the mind's stories trying to convince me otherwise. I've already learned that I can trust my body as it passes through such challenging experiences. Even though it's not comfortable – indeed, it can be pretty painful – moments like these have shown me that the body is much stronger, more capable and far more resilient than the mind can fathom.

***

I'm lucky to have found my life's passion at age 15. I didn't know then, but playing high school football would serve as my introduction to the incredible potential of the human body. As a result of my efforts and the environment my body was exposed to, my skinny and uncoordinated body transformed into a body capable of playing professional sports.

I had never played sports before trying out for football because the body I was born with was anything but athletic. I was tall, but I was also *really* skinny. During tryouts, teammates laughed as I ran because my running resembled a baby giraffe learning to walk. I was so unathletic that the coaches hesitated to put me in a game out of fear that my frail body would get snapped in half the first time I got tackled. If it weren't for my ability to throw a football, which was surprising given the underwhelming nature of my body's athletic abilities, my time as a football player would have ended after tryouts.

Despite my evident athletic shortcomings, I turned down academic scholarships to pursue football at a local junior college. I knew I could lean on a solid academic resumé if things didn't work out with athletics. And I wanted to prove wrong all the coaches and players who said I'd never play college football. There was a chip on my shoulder.

Football became my single-pointed focus. What I lacked in athleticism, I made up for in unrelenting drive and stubborn determination. I placed my body in an environment centered solely on football and activities that developed athleticism. My body had no choice but to transform in response to my consistent and sustained efforts.

Throughout the following six years of rigorous training, I put on 30 kilograms (nearly 70 pounds) of muscle, with proportionate increases in strength, power and athletic ability. An athletic scholarship to a Division IA University served as the supporting evidence that I had made the right choice for myself.

After college football, I fulfilled my teenage dream of playing professional football when I signed a contract with the Italian Football League as the Quarterback for the Ancona Dolphins. Unfortunately, the IFL doesn't pay nearly as much as the NFL, so after my first season, I retired from the sport that had given me so much. It was an easy decision to hang up my cleats. I had the closure I was looking for.

***

My dedication to becoming a professional football player revealed the transformative potential of the human body. The body adapts to the environment that it regularly and consistently lives within. When I put my body in an environment that supported the development of athletic capabilities, that's precisely how it responded.

That same adaptive process happens no matter the goal or intention. If we seek improved holistic wellbeing and subsequently immerse the body in an environment that supports those goals, that's exactly what we'll get. The body has no choice as it responds to the consistent stimuli that its environment provides.

No additional ingredients or extras are necessary as the environment dictates the body's physiological adaptations. I witnessed this slow and steady transformation firsthand, step-by-step and year-by-year, as my lanky, clumsy and unathletic frame slowly morphed into that of a professional athlete. I've never forgotten this important lesson. Whenever a client sits down in front of me, I see more potential in them than they see themselves because I know what the body is capable of doing and being. I've lived the challenging experience of physical transformation.

Of course, the body doesn't adapt to its environment in beneficial ways alone. The body adapts to its surrounding environment whether or not our mind wants the specific adaptations. If, for example, our body lives in an environment that involves predominantly desk work, then it will adapt to be efficient and effective at sitting. But that's not an adaptation that's healthy for the body.

I learned this the hard way during my brief career as a Certified Public Accountant. My time as an accountant was short because it was while working in a cubicle that the paradoxical irony of desk work revealed itself. After getting tossed around and tackled as a football player, I was left scratching my head in confusion when nursing aches and pains that had accumulated during my short stint of long hours of office work. Why was my body experiencing *more* pain sitting at a desk than playing the violent sport of football?

I was also faced with the humbling insight that after years of committing myself to working out and eating in ways that transformed my body, I hadn't learned *how* and *why* my physical transformation had occurred. Blindly following instructions (and whistles), I hadn't yet learned how the interconnected parts of my body's surrounding environment contributed to my transformation. I didn't know how to take care of my own body.

Health, however, is a personal responsibility because every respective body is unique and different. Everyone must find the formula that works for them, their goals, values and unique physiological needs. If I wanted health to be the foundation of my life, I had to learn how to attend to my body's needs.

While listening to coaches had proven helpful, I hadn't prepared myself for the inevitable transition from taking direction to being *personally responsible* for my body's wellbeing. When starting down the path toward improved health, the process can be made easier by starting with an established professional or evidence-based approach. Once momentum and consistency start turning conscious choices into habitual behaviors, it's important to start shifting the focus to the body to see how it responds to our lifestyle choices.

When strictly adhering to a nutrition, exercise or lifestyle dogma as if it is universally true, we put all our eggs in the mind basket, trusting that our thoughts, beliefs (or, more accurately, someone else's thoughts and beliefs) know what's best for our unique body. Unfortunately, every modality, philosophy and approach of the wellness industry trumpets its own set of studies, testimonials, products, documentaries and celebrities endorsing its effectiveness and superiority. Each, however, also has plenty of criticisms attached to it. It's easy to get overwhelmed or confused.

Despite the good intentions of the mind, the body needs to be involved in the process of determining what it needs to thrive. *Should I go Vegan or Paleo? Keto or low-fat? Should I skip breakfast and avoid snacks, or eat six small meals daily?* We can get as many answers as external sources we seek answers from.

My body and its health were and will always be my responsibility. It was this realization that ignited my passion for health and wellbeing. Whatever processes contributed to my athletic transformation, I was determined to learn them so that I could reclaim my health. That my career path involved empowering others to do the same was the icing on the cake.

As I began learning about how our body's environment supports its capacities for health and healing, I started with movement and exercise. My first job in the health and wellness industry was as a personal trainer, but it didn't take long to see that exercise alone wasn't enough to create the transformation I knew my clients were seeking. Exercise represents only one aspect of a health-promoting environment.

I continued my learning by exploring the various aspects of health that connected the interdependent dots of holistic wellbeing. I learned to care for the body's soft tissue through Neuromuscular Therapy and an immersive body-work curriculum called Functional Soft Tissue Transformation, taught by one of my first teachers and mentors, Lenny Parracino, now one of the NBA's leading Soft Tissue Therapists.

While exercise is one of the best long-term strategies for developing and maintaining physical health, massage and soft-tissue care represent immediate and compassionate gifts we can give our bodies *today*. It's true that our muscles need a challenge, but they also need rest. We hold tension in our muscles and connective tissue for various reasons, rigorous exercise being one of them. Left unattended, tension can lead to pain because tense muscle tissue doesn't receive the necessary blood and oxygen circulation.

It wasn't long before I devoured nutrition and healthy eating certifications, went to cooking school and earned a Master's degree in Sustainable Food Systems. I sought to deepen my understanding of the most intimate connection we have with the external world: food. At this point, I had become fully immersed as a student of the human body.

I eventually leveraged my knowledge and experience as I opened a holistic wellness studio in Santa Monica, California. My wellness studio was the blank canvas onto which I could paint with the modalities and approaches I had learned over years of study and practice. I held the intention for each of my clients to be a work of art.

When running the studio, my clients brought into focus the emerging revelation that wellbeing is dictated by the environment within which the body lives. When someone works with a health professional, the time they spend with them pales in comparison to the time in-between sessions. No matter how good, one to three hours per week with a health and wellness professional doesn't offset the remaining 166 hours of a week. This is especially true if those remaining hours are spent within an environment of highly processed food, sedentariness, poor sleep, endless work and tension-laden relationships. Regarding health, our lifestyle choices – how we move, eat, sleep, talk, laugh, love, think, work and rest – collectively contribute to the interconnected aspects of mental, physical and emotional wellbeing.

Aside from rare genetic diseases and disorders[16], it's lifestyle, aka the body's surrounding environment, that dictates the overall state of our health. The body is our ally with this intention as our cell's sole drive is to survive and thrive, something I've already mentioned and described in the previous chapter.

Our daily lifestyle choices are either supporting or resisting the body's inherent collective cellular strive toward health. Every lifestyle choice either moves us toward or away from holistic wellbeing. Every moment counts because health is a *process*, not some static state or destination. And the whole environment matters. But once the environment is in place, the body naturally takes care of the rest because that is what it has evolved to do. When the body lives within an environment that supports health and healing, we can focus on being present in our life while our body takes care of the rest.

Healthy Lifestyle Principles

An environment focused on health and healing supports the interconnected physical, mental and emotional aspects of holistic wellbeing. What determines a health-promoting environment can be distilled down to simple and straightforward principles. When we remove the scientific jargon, ethically questionable marketing and media hype from healthy lifestyle choices, what remains are fundamental principles that are universally applicable across people and cultures. I feel confident that this assertion is true because I checked myself.

Several years before writing this book, I traveled the world filming a documentary series, A Million Ways to Live, which showed how people were finding health and happiness in accordance with healthy lifestyle principles. The six fundamental Healthy Lifestyle Principles, aka the environment that supports health and healing, that I previously wrote a book about and showcased in my documentary are:

- Real Food
- Movement
- Rest & Recovery
- Lifelong Learning
- Community
- Love

This is what my body, my studies and my clients taught me. While the Healthy Lifestyle Principles' simplicity may not immediately appeal to a mind seeking fancy complex solutions, these principles are the foundation of what the body needs to thrive.

Real Food

The first Healthy Lifestyle Principle is Real Food. Real Food doesn't need mascots, slogans or health claims to prove its suitability for consumption. It's the primary food groups that every child learns about in elementary school: fruits, vegetables, meat, nuts, dairy, whole grains and legumes. Various options within these food groups carry healthful qualities that play complementary roles in building a solid foundation of health.

Real Food has more essential vitamins and minerals, nutrient density, fiber and water than its processed counterparts, meaning we eat less and feel more satiated from the meal[17]. Real Food is free of the chemicals and additives that leave us unsatisfied, unsatiated and craving for more. That craving is not a real physiological need. It is often a trick the additives in our food play on us. Once digested, the body metabolizes real food more efficiently and effectively, making it the ideal choice over processed foods for metabolic health and weight management[18].

Real Food is also the best diet for health because the body has evolved to eat real food. When we eat a diversity of whole foods, variables like cholesterol, sodium and sugar become largely redundant since whole food doesn't contain the unhealthy amounts and ratios of these substances that their processed alternatives do.

Real Food means less stress because the need to log, weigh and track food choices disappears, especially as we learn to connect to the body and its response to the food we eat. There are other questions to ask and nuances to consider when choosing particular foods, such as: *How was it grown? Where did it come from? How was it prepared? Is it best consumed raw, fresh, soaked, cooked or fermented? Is this food choice healthy and appropriate for my specific bodily needs, goals and intentions?* Generally speaking, however, whole and unprocessed foods, as close to their natural state as possible, represent the starting point for *every* healthy diet.

Movement

The second healthy Lifestyle Principle is Movement. Daily movement isn't just about exercise and its associated health benefits. We *need* movement. Everyday.

Movement supports many physiological functions required for wellbeing because it supports the body's circulatory processes. The circulation initiated by movement is the principal mechanism through which all the health benefits associated with movement are derived. Movement makes the muscles and connective tissue of the body act as a biological pump that assists the heart in pumping water, oxygen and nutrients throughout the body, as well as metabolic waste out of the body. Indeed, the body's lymphatic system depends almost entirely on movement to support its detoxification processes because our body's lymphatic system doesn't have its own contractile properties[19].

Digestively, movement supports the natural motion of our internal organs that keep bowel movements regular by increasing blood flow throughout the digestive system[20]. Moving the body after meals triggers a process called *peristalsis*, a series of wave-like muscle contractions that help food move through the body's digestive tract. By moving the body, the digestive system gets a push of encouragement from our muscles and connective tissue.

When we move, we keep our body younger, stronger and more capable because the body adapts to working against the force of gravity by maintaining and improving bone density and lean muscle tissue[21]. When we are sedentary and our body doesn't receive the environmental cues that accompany weight-bearing activities, the body responds by shifting its metabolic resources from muscle and bone maintenance to other physiological functions. In other words, when we don't move, the body's bones weaken and its muscles and connective tissue atrophy. Movement and exercise are thus the closest things to a fountain of youth our body will experience and represent a potent anti-aging therapy[22].

Rest & Relaxation

The third Healthy Lifestyle Principle is Rest & Relaxation. To understand its importance, it's helpful first to explain how the body experiences and processes stress. Hans Selye, considered one of the early pioneers of modern stress theory, defined stress as the nonspecific response of the body to *any* demand, whether it is caused by, or results in, pleasant or unpleasant conditions. This means that with every lifestyle choice we make or behavior we engage in, we are, to some degree, stressing the body.

As I've already discussed, the body is incredibly adept at managing and coping with stress. The body takes stresses, in all forms and from all sources, directed toward any specific system in the body and then distributes that stress throughout the whole body so that it can lower the direct effect of stress on any single part of the body[23]. One example is when we stub our toe while walking. While we may feel the pain and see the consequences of the injury at a particular location, the entire body shares the inflammatory burden as the body begins to heal. This is a remarkable survival strategy of the body.

Regardless of the source – whether a stubbed toe, intense workout, long workday, argument with a loved one, or unhealthy meal – the body has to expend energy as it copes with the stresses placed on it. That means our body treats junk food, traffic, toxic relationships and intense workouts similarly: it's all physiological stress that the body must manage. While the human body is an incredible adapter to stress, putting the body under too much stress for too long will lead to breakdowns. The body *needs* rest and relaxation. The body needs time to recover.

Stress is countered by relaxation practices, which release muscle tension, lower blood pressure, and slow the heart and breath rates[24]. During recovery, all the benefits of healthy lifestyle choices – like healing, fat loss and muscle gain – actually happen. When we exercise intensely, it's during the recovery period that we burn fat and build muscle, not during the workout. This is because the workout breaks down our muscles and connective tissue. In other words, working out *injures* the body. During recovery, our body expends energy to heal the damaged connective tissue and build it back stronger.

When we work long hours, days or weeks on end, stepping away from our work environment to rejuvenate is the most productive thing we can do for ourselves and our productivity[25]. Even small investments in restorative strategies can significantly improve the body's physiological wellbeing.

Of course, the king of recovery strategies is sleep. Unfortunately, sleep is also the lifestyle choice many struggle with. The body needs high-quality sleep to function. A sleep routine can include a preparatory ritual that lets the body know it's time to get ready to sleep. Like Pavlov's dogs responding to bells by salivating in anticipation of being fed, a series of consistent behaviors and actions before bed every night can trigger the physiological and biochemical processes that make it easier for the body to fall asleep. While the body is an incredible adapter to stress, an environment that includes Rest & Relaxation strategies will support the body's metabolic processes of managing stress.

The Big Rocks of Healthy Living

There's an anecdote about a professor who puts large rocks in a glass until they reach the top of the glass. When he asks the class if there is any space in the glass for more, they reply *no*. He then adds small pebbles to the glass to fill the space between the big rocks. The professor again asks the same question and receives the same answer, only to pour sand into the glass until it is filled to the top again.

The lesson the professor was teaching his students related to the choices that fill our daily lives. He told his class that the glass was analogous to our life and that we should first fill each day with big rocks, the most meaningful and important things to us. Only then do we fill the remainder of our glass of life with less important things, the pebbles and, lastly, the sand. If, however, the glass is first filled with the sand and pebbles – the things in life that aren't as important or don't hold significant meaning for us – there won't be any space for our big rocks.

With that analogy in mind, the food we eat, how we move, and how we balance our stress equation with rest and recovery make up the first three Healthy Lifestyle Principles. These Healthy Lifestyle Principles are the big rocks of healthy living. Revisiting the remaining three Healthy Lifestyle Principles (Lifelong Learning, Community and Love) is outside the scope and context of *Somawise*. That is why Real Food, Movement and Rest & Relaxation have been, and will remain, the primary focus of this chapter. When the big rocks of healthy living guide our daily lifestyle choices, the body responds to this environment by cultivating energy, strength and vitality. As we'll soon learn, these qualities permeate and positively impact every aspect of life.

Heal the Body. The Mind Follows.

Throughout my career, my passion for learning about the human body has never waned. I may have stopped prescribing exercise for weight loss and body fat reduction, but I continue to empower clients to move and exercise because I know movement supports their mental wellbeing and emotional healing. I'm situated as a mental health professional at this point in my career, but I know that psychological healing and emotional processing start and end with the body. The answers we seek for healing are found within.

The intellectual understanding of *what happened to us* is only a tiny piece of the puzzle, maybe the first piece, and only an invitation for the journey of healing that begins thereafter. The mind may *understand*, but understanding alone is not enough to heal. Healing is work only the body can do. Just because the mind *thinks* it knows the source of its suffering, it is the body that processes the physiological residue remaining in the body. That process of integration and metabolization takes time.

A healthy body created by an environment of health and healing simultaneously supports us as we process the painful stories and acquired understandings of our past. The stronger the body, the more capable it is of passing through the invariably uncomfortable processes of emotional integration. That's why no matter the external presentation, narrative or story, my therapeutic priority is getting the body within an environment that supports its natural healing processes. Indeed, as we *feel* better in our body, many of the mind's worries diminish or disappear altogether because how we think and feel is largely impacted by the overall health of our body.

Healing starts and ends in the body. As the body heals, the mind follows. What good is *talking about* anxiety if someone drinks 8 cups of coffee daily? With that much caffeine coursing through the body, the mind will conjure up thousands of reasons to be anxious. Someone experiencing a depressed mood unknowingly contributes to their state by drinking alcohol. Alcohol is a depressant, drowns out emotions, and only pushes uncomfortable feelings down for a short while before the discomfort bubbles back up again more intensely than before.

As a result of this intimate connection between the body and mind, we can begin to make some pretty good guesses at someone's mental and emotional state by examining the environment the body is surrounded by. How would we expect someone to think and feel after a series of 60-hour work weeks at a desk, a diet predominantly made up of takeaways and little to no movement and exercise?

Taking care of the body first can help us see if the perceived challenges dominating the mental landscape are cries for help from a body riddled with physiological stress. On many occasions, the chaotic thoughts of the mind are merely symptoms of a distressed body crying out for help. When we listen to our body when it whispers, we won't have to hear the screaming of the mind.

***

There's no shortage of psychological approaches to help us better analyze what is going on within our respective minds. It makes sense that we gravitate toward strategies that focus on the mind to resolve the battles happening within our mental landscape. But with a sole focus on cognitive interventions, we forget that the mind, and our mental health state, are inexorably linked to the health of the body.

It seems too simple, and maybe far too obvious, to examine physical lifestyles and their contributing role in how we show up mentally and feel emotionally. And yet, most of the debilitating symptoms we experience, as well as the benefits we want to feel, are the result of the physiological factors stemming from the environment the body lives within.

Jim Carrey isn't a doctor, researcher or scientist. Still, the actor and comedian offered some poignant words on depression that demonstrate the wisdom of having lived through mental health challenges: *I believe depression is legitimate. But I also believe that if you don't exercise, eat nutritious food, get sunlight, get enough sleep, consume positive material or surround yourself with support, then you aren't giving yourself a fighting chance.* Carrey was essentially summing up the Healthy Lifestyle Principles and their role in supporting mental wellbeing. *Heal the body, the mind follows.*

Real Food

Aside from breathing, we primarily interact with our external environment through the food we eat and drink. The impact of food on the body cannot be overstated. From gestation into adulthood, dietary habits influence the body's energy balance, mental attention, emotional state, behavior, as well as susceptibility to illness and mental health disorders[26]. Hippocrates said to *let food be thy medicine and medicine be thy food.*

Academics and scientists have explored the 'shouldn't-it-be-common-sense' notion that what we eat and drink greatly influences our health and how we experience the world. Research on these topics has emerged from a myriad of different angles, shaping our understanding of how, and the extent to which, our mental and emotional wellbeing is linked to the food we eat.

Nutritional deficiencies and mental health challenges are inescapably linked. The food choices we make influence the development, severity and duration of depressive episodes[27]. And while this is a chicken and egg debate (*which came first, the dietary habits or the symptoms of depression?*), the clinically-relevant dietary patterns linked to depression tend to be established and present *before* depressive symptoms emerge. This means that nutrition-related behaviors or qualities, such as poor appetite, skipping meals and a dominant craving for sweet food, could represent some of the contributing factors to the development of depression, not the symptoms and signs of it. This subtle difference is significant because it can help determine how a person navigates their healing process.

A closer look at our digestive system shows connections between gut health and mental wellbeing. Looking at our digestive system under a microscope, we see that it's not just our body and its cells that we nourish with the food we eat. Most cells that make up the body are bacterial cells[28]. The body's microbiota, the bacteria that call our digestive system its home, plays a critical role in how we feel and behave[29]. Dysbiosis, a microbial imbalance heavily influenced by diet[30], is one of the contributing variables to mental health challenges, linked to both anxiety and depression[31]. Probiotic-rich fermented foods provide a protective, low-risk food choice for improving mental health and emotional mood[32] because they support a healthy microbiome[33].

The relationship between mental wellbeing and nutritional interventions like probiotic-rich diets works in both directions. Food choices impact the onset and development of mental health concerns, but food is also an effective strategy for treating and managing mental health symptoms when they do arise. What we eat, or don't eat, helps manage the symptoms of anxiety[34], depression[35,36] and supports overall mood and mental wellbeing[37]. And what food choices represent the best strategy for managing mental health challenges? Real food[38], of course.

Movement

The next big rock of healthy living is movement. Movement is one of the magic bullets for mental health challenges. Emotionally, movement helps us feel better and provides nearly immediate relief from the symptoms of anxiety and depression[39,40]. When the body moves, it releases powerful endorphins that improve our mood. Mentally, movement helps us think more clearly because it boosts cognitive function and learning capabilities[41]. This is because movement and exercise create new neurons and increase blood flow throughout the body. Psychologically, movement provides an efficient and effective way of processing and metabolizing stress[42] because it helps regulate cortisol, the key hormone involved in stress. With challenging emotions out of the way, it's easier to improve our decision-making and organizing abilities.

Despite marketers pushing the trends that pay their bills, the kind of exercise matters little as *all* forms of exercise lower our mental health burden[43]. It's moving the body that counts. How we do that is up to us. Whether it's yoga, rock climbing, powerlifting, Pilates, hiking, rowing or tai chi, choose the type of movement that best supports our respective wellbeing goals and intentions. Becoming *Somawise* means choosing what feels right and good for our individual and unique bodies. If we listen, the body will tell us which forms of movement and exercise it needs most. More on that later in this chapter.

Rest & Relaxation

Finally, Rest & Relaxation represents the third big rock of a healthy lifestyle. It's not surprising that sleep difficulties are one of the root causes of many mental health concerns[44], as low-quality sleep impacts our mood, as well as our ability to process information and recall memories. Our ability to consciously and openly engage with life deteriorates due to poor sleeping habits. If we don't get a good night's rest, even a quick afternoon nap can boost cognitive function and offset sleep loss[45]. This is why getting good, high-quality and regular sleep is consistently at the top of the list for treating and managing mental health challenges[46].

***

The three big rocks of healthy living build the foundation of a healthy body, allowing us to experience a clear, focused and healthy mind. But how and why does this happen? What's the connection other than experts telling us so? While it's easy to talk about the mind and body being linked, it doesn't help us understand *how* and *why* this connection expresses itself. If we want this information to stick around, the mind will need an anchor of understanding. As such, exploring the physiological ramifications shared by all healthy lifestyle choices and how these commonalities influence our mental and emotional landscape can be helpful. This exploration requires an understanding of inflammation.

Inflammation: Connecting the Dots

Inflammation is a natural defense mechanism of the human body. Acute inflammation is beneficial and part of the body's immune response[47]. Stress to the body, and the resulting inflammation, is a necessary and unavoidable part of growth, whether physical, mental or emotional.

Short-term periods of stress enhance human function and, in many ways, are vital for survival. Short-term stress boosts mental capabilities to cope with the demands and pressures of a task or challenge. We can consciously face stress and, as a result, reap many benefits.

Acute stresses like these are beneficial in small doses. We experience them, adapt to them, recover from them and, consequently, the body becomes stronger and more resilient. The kind of stress that is not beneficial is the unabated, free flow of stress circulating through the body for long periods. This is when we enter the world of chronic stress.

Chronic stress is the body's physiological and psychological response to its stress system staying activated over a long period of time. Carrying the constant and cumulative burdens of being unhappy at a job, working long hours, eating an unhealthy diet, remaining sedentary and many other lifestyle stresses lead to a constant rush of stress hormones that put a lot of wear and tear on the body, causing it to age more quickly and making it more prone to illness. Chronic stress hinders immune function, making it more likely to get sick[48]. Stressed people also have more heart attacks, more depressive symptoms, more colds and less sex[49].

Chronic stress, and the chronic state of inflammation that follows, is like driving a car with the gas pedal pressed all the way down. The engine is pumping on all cylinders and RPMs are red-lining. Fuel is getting burned quickly and the tires are screeching and leaving skid marks on the ground. For a while, a car may function fine at that level of demanding performance. But a car can only handle this for a short period before it starts breaking down. Cars are not designed to be pushed to their limits for long periods because they require maintenance when pushed to these performance thresholds. Even cars need time to rest and recover.

Today's non-stop, fast-paced world has us living under constant and continuous stress. We are driving on all cylinders without the understanding that our bodies cannot perform at these peak conditions for sustained periods of time. The effects of this kind of living are ever present and evident: being easily agitated, unable to focus, low energy, low-quality sleep, or the presence of aches and pains throughout the body. Chronically stressed people exercise less, mainly because they are time-stressed and feel they have no time for exercise. They are constantly tired yet can't relax enough to get a good night of sleep.

Chronic inflammation, the physiological experience of the body when exposed to chronic stress, is characterized by slow, long-term exposure to inflammation lasting for several months to years. Chronic inflammation is the root cause of most chronic diseases of modern-day life[50]. Though inflammation is a physiological phenomenon that occurs at the physical level, it influences the expression and state of the mind because of the impacts of chronic inflammation on mental health diagnoses[51,52,53]. Put simply: *harm the body, the mind follows.*

Lifestyle choices significantly influence the inflammatory state and processes of the body[54]. This is why reducing bodily inflammation and decreasing the activation of inflammatory pathways both support mental health and wellbeing[55]. For example, food can either add to or subtract from our body's inflammatory load. Foods like olive oil, garlic, blueberries, bone broth and cocoa powder can be anti-inflammatory and contribute to health and wellbeing. These foods have anti-inflammatory effects that help reduce the inflammatory burden on the body[56,57]. Or food can be pro-inflammatory and cause chronic, low-grade inflammation[58], thus moving the body and mind toward discomfort and disease. Examples of inflammation-promoting foods and drinks are the ones that most of us already know aren't healthy options: sugar-laden foods, highly-processed fast food and alcohol.

The other big rocks of healthy living – Movement and Rest & Relaxation – have equally profound influences on inflammation[59,60]. Belonging to a connected community[61], exposure to nature, outdoors and sunshine[62,63] and meditation[64,65] are a few more examples of healthy lifestyle choices that have demonstrated a wide range of positive mental health benefits. Indeed, every healthy lifestyle choice, not just those associated with the big three, directly impacts the body's inflammatory pathways.

This means that how we live directly impacts *how we think and feel*[66]. The body's environment influences how the mind perceives the world. This is why Jim Carrey's words so brilliantly bring it home. The actor, who himself publicly battled with depression, didn't identify *one* healthy lifestyle choice. His formula for health and healing didn't even stop with the big rocks. Carrey listed many other lifestyle decisions – social support, sunshine and consuming positive content – that are strikingly aligned with the remaining Healthy Lifestyle Principles.

Every lifestyle choice is either pro-inflammatory or anti-inflammatory, either adding or reducing stress, and either helpful or detrimental to our mental and emotional wellbeing. Our lifestyle is the antidote to chronic stress and inflammation. Every lifestyle choice, day-to-day, and moment-to-moment, matters. How we eat, move, sleep, laugh, love, think, connect, talk and rest all come into play in the cumulative equation of stress and inflammation, and thus in our health and healing. *Every decision, breath and choice either adds to or detracts from the body's health.* Let the gravity of that statement genuinely sink in.

If we want to know how healthy we are, we can examine our life from the moment we wake up until we fall asleep and note how well we sleep that night through to the following morning. Our health directly results from how our body interacts with its environment 24 hours a day. The whole lifestyle matters.

The keyword from the previous sentence is *whole*. The collective whole of daily lifestyle choices is greater than the sum of its individual parts. For example, food choices are made exponentially healthier when we focus on *how* we eat rather than solely on *what* we eat. Food is an experience that's better shared in the company of others. Healthy eating can be slow rather than fast, social rather than solitary, and fun rather than monotonous. We learn new things, foster and grow relationships and enjoy the health benefits of being socially connected when we share meals with others. Combining a mindful and calm state with eating through the practice of gratitude also improves wellbeing[67]. This is because our mindset before, during and after eating impacts our digestive, biochemical and hormonal systems. Indeed, when we infuse the meal in front of us with thankfulness and gratitude[68], we shift our physiology and improve our digestion function[69].

Healthy lifestyle choices are interconnected and interdependent. They support each other, compounding their health-promoting benefits. For example, exercise and meditation improve sleep quality[70,71]. As does the food we eat[72]. The complementary relationship works in the other direction as well.

How we sleep contributes to how much we move and how we eat. Quality sleep not only influences daytime activity levels[73], it also encourages healthy eating behaviors[74]. *No single choice exists in isolation* as that choice reverberates and ripples outward, impacting other contexts of our physiological and psychological experience. The point here is that the collective whole that comprises our lifestyle is greater than any individual or single lifestyle choice.

The body, and its health, is often overlooked, undervalued or considered secondary when attempting to improve how we think and feel. We are solely engaged with the mental stories of our pain and suffering. What would happen if we first started with the body's health to see how many of our perceived difficulties and challenges were resolved naturally as a consequence of improving our body's physiological function?

If the foundation of an individual's mental and emotional challenge is related to the body's physiological factors, it doesn't matter how much talk therapy is involved, it might be a long and possibly never-ending road to recovery as the root cause will remain unaddressed. Or, we can try a different way: *heal the body, and the mind will follow.*

***

Becoming *Somawise* is more than just about getting healthy. While being healthy is a worthy intention in and of itself, this is not a book about healthy living. What makes healthy lifestyle choices particularly relevant within the context of *Somawise* is that the very same lifestyle choices that make life easier can be used to teach us how to listen to the body and its needs. When we focus on the body and its responses to our daily lifestyle choices, we can begin to decipher the body's subtle messages.

When we start paying attention to lifestyle choices, the body tells us when a choice is either promoting or detracting from health and wellbeing. Every meal, every chosen form of exercise and every recovery strategy results in an experience within the body that we can tune into as we begin intuitively discerning whether the choice is healing or harming. The body is constantly giving us information about its present moment experience, whether it's gas or indigestion after a meal, or an ache or pain after a workout. By staying connected to the body, we learn how to use it as a compass that points toward holistic wellbeing. Over time, we develop the capacity to identify and respond to our body's needs as they change and evolve.

Daily lifestyle choices are the quickest and easiest way to start learning and understanding the body's language because we don't have to do or add anything new to our life. We're already living our lives and making choices throughout the day. The only difference is that now we can start paying attention to our bodies as we make those choices.

Each lifestyle choice is an opportunity to listen to how the body responds and the different ways the body speaks. When we create an environment of health and healing, we get two birds with one stone: holistic health and a reconnection with the body. This is the starting point for becoming *Somawise*.

Listening to the Body

While it may seem daunting to overhaul our whole lifestyle, the longest journey starts with a single step; a single lifestyle choice. Over time, as each additional choice is added or subtracted, a completely new lifestyle and way of being emerges. The journey might start with the decision to be kinder to ourselves (a worthwhile starting point, as we'll see in a later chapter, *Radical Self-Acceptance*). Then daily walking and stretching may be added in. Soon, the inspiration to experiment with cold showers and fasting may arise.

When it comes to real food, the journey to a cleaner way of eating may begin with small and gradual shifts, such as cutting calories and reducing sugar, but eventually end up with dietary choices that might have seemed difficult, impractical or strange at the start, such as fermenting vegetables or eating organ meats. The point is to start somewhere – anywhere – and gradually build our unique healthy lifestyle as we listen to and refine our understanding of what the body needs. What we'll notice is that our healthy lifestyle practices will constantly evolve when we are connected to the body because the body – and its physiological needs – is continuously changing.

Reconnecting with the body isn't a process that happens automatically when the mind decides it wants to do so. It's hard to reconnect, especially when someone's nervous system has been engrained with programming and conditioning that directly opposes reconnection. Self-protective defense mechanisms (i.e., self-judgment, defensiveness and self-soothing behaviors) that have been active for decades often stand firmly in the way of such intentions. These defenses are always activated because the triggers of everyday life are constantly turning them on.

When the body gets physiologically overwhelmed, reactivity kickstarts the subconscious, conditioned reactions that grab the steering wheel of decision-making. We might get stressed out at work due to long hours or an impending project deadline. Or we might be activated from an argument with our partner. Before consciously aware of it, we might find ourselves eating chocolate, drinking a glass of wine or watching porn. This is how quickly and subtly our programmed reactions can initiate reactive behavior. It's so fast that we don't even know when or how it happened.

When we are reactive, we say things we didn't mean to say and do things we apologize for later. It may be an engrained form of protection, but the reality is that this reactive form of protection may not be as helpful as it once was. Rather than solving the problem, reaching for food, alcohol or porn makes things worse. These defenses originated as necessary survival and self-protection adaptations, but they have outlived their utility as the sole strategy of responding to the people and situations that activate certain emotions and experiences in the body.

Building a lifestyle that cultivates health and supports healing paves a calmer pathway for reconnecting with the body and becoming *Somawise*. Indeed, it's easier to pay attention to how our body responds to a meal than to stay connected and attentive to our body when we get emotionally triggered and physiologically overwhelmed. Daily lifestyle choices are happening throughout the day no matter what. By checking in with the body, we can use daily events, such as eating, walking, sitting, exercising or resting, to teach us how to listen to the body.

***

The rituals, routines and practices of a daily lifestyle provide several opportunities throughout the day to check in with the body to see what's happening. Over time, these consistent check-ins cultivate *interoceptive awareness*, a concept discussed in the previous chapter, *Introduction: The Wise Body*) as our sense of the body's internal state is brought into the light of conscious awareness[75]. *The body always has something to tell us.* All we need to do is pause, rest our attention on the body and wait for it to respond in its subtle language.

The body speaks through the felt sense, with physical sensations (this will be expanded upon in the next chapter, *Stillness*). Our body, specifically the physical sensations through which it speaks, becomes our guiding light and a key contributor to making decisions in daily life.

The hardest step of pausing and becoming more aware is the first one, especially if this is new and uncharted territory. As such, it's natural to start with some approach or philosophy that we have previous experience with or knowledge of.

Maybe we start with Paleo (or keto, vegan or vegetarian) because that's what worked in the past or for a close friend or family member. We might have experience with yoga, so we know we can start with that as a movement strategy. Regardless of choice, it's helpful during this initial phase to lean on books, articles, experts and professionals to make the transition to a health and wellbeing-oriented lifestyle smoother.

Finally, what's important to note is that our chosen professionals should empower us to move toward self-sufficiency rather than depend on them and their knowledge. After that, a healthy dose of curiosity fuels the lifestyle exploration as we experiment and experience firsthand how our body responds to new ways of eating, exercising, resting and living. Some helpful reflective self-inquiry questions we can ask ourselves as we reconnect to the body through lifestyle choices are: *how does my present choice impact my energy levels, concentration, sleep, sense of calm and peace, strength and even body weight? What is happening in my body before, during and after this choice? Are these choices supporting my holistic wellbeing intentions?* These questions can guide our experimentation with lifestyle choices.

Real Food

Real Food is the starting point. While Paleo advocates face-off against devout Vegans and Keto-converts proclaim their superiority over low-fat proponents, what they don't mention is that their respective dogmas are more alike than not. The differences between the diets tend to be trivial, while their effectiveness for promoting holistic wellbeing is generally comparable[76]. This is because regardless of which healthy eating strategy people choose, the decision to be healthier almost always comes with a simultaneous consequence of subtracting unhealthy eating habits, such as ditching junk foods and sugary-laden snacks and beverages, or drinking less (or abstaining from) alcohol.

The subtractions that come with choosing a healthy eating approach, arguably more than the additions, are what support and enhance the body's natural processes that move it toward health. Many of the benefits people experience at the start of their wellbeing journey result from what is *taken out* of their diets rather than what is added in. For example, the transition from low-quality processed foods to high-quality, nutrient-rich and minimally-processed Real Food is what begins building the foundation of health[77,78]. When the body isn't struggling to manage and metabolize toxins from unhealthy food choices, it can devote more resources to healing, health and thriving.

We begin to look, feel and think better because highly inflammatory choices are replaced with health-promoting ones. As Real Food replaces less healthy options, we can also pay attention to how the body responds to removing the things stressing and inflaming it.

The body lets us know our diet is working when we don't experience the signs that clearly show our body may not agree with the foods we are eating, symptoms such as bloating, indigestion, lethargy, energy crashes or excessive gas. When we begin to feel how our dietary choices impact things like energy levels, concentration and mood, it is the motivation and evidence to keep going. Once we experience health, it's easier to stay on track, especially when old patterns quickly remind us of how we feel when the body is flooded with stress and inflammation.

We continue refining our somatic connection via dietary choices as we explore the impact of specific foods, macronutrient ratios and meal frequency on the body. We can experiment with different combinations to determine which best suits our body and its needs. The depth and degree we do this is a personal decision and journey. To assess and monitor this process, we can use one of the many variables that require us to pay attention to the body.

We can use subjective measures like mood, energy levels, sleep quality, sex drive or our ability to stay focused and concentrate. We can also pay attention to how our body functions after meals, such as the presence of joint aches and pain or digestive symptoms like bowel irregularity, indigestion or bloating. The body's responses thus serve as barometers for whether we're on the right track. For example, if the body is sensitive to certain foods, they will impact one or more of these functions. We can test our hunches by removing certain foods for some time and then adding them back to see what impact they might have on the body.

Movement

Move daily because it's a gift for the body, not because a program says so. The body speaks to us before, during and after we move and exercise. Intense muscle soreness may tell us to lighten the load of an upcoming workout or to rest altogether. Sharp pains or discomfort while we move could be letting us know we're doing something with incorrect form. Relief and relaxation after a workout are sure signs that the body got precisely what it needed.

Listening to the body lets us know when it's safe to push the body or whether it's appropriate to relax and focus on recovery instead. When we blindly adhere to a practice without checking in with the body first, the body might let us know we missed an important cue when we experience aches, pains or injuries. Indeed, injuries from exercise often manifest because of the repetitive strain placed on the body from the unconscious implementation of a single form of movement.

I've heard many yoga and CrossFit loyalists speak of their injuries as badges of honor instead of cries from the body that something might not be working. Our movement strategies are intended to improve our capacity for kinesthetic freedom, not hinder it. Yoga and CrossFit are both beneficial modalities when applied appropriately, while connected to the body rather than followed blindly.

Whether a movement or exercise is helpful or harmful depends on what movement qualities our body needs at any given time. The body tells us if it needs more strength, flexibility or cardiovascular conditioning. Sometimes the workout of the day or sequence of the week isn't aligned with our body's present moment needs. By listening to the body, we are empowered to choose what's right for us, whether in the moment or within the context of a long-term development need.

Balancing the capacities and functionality of the body is critical. Flexibility and mobility are essential for a healthy joint range of motion, but hyper-mobility and hyper-flexibility increase the risk of injury[79]. Running has cardiovascular health benefits, but relying on it as the sole movement strategy dramatically increases injury risk[80]. Physiotherapists around the world love runners because they keep them in business. Strength training sustains the long-term health of the body's muscles and bones, but too much could lead to tightness, decreased range of motion and connective tissue strains and tears.

To know where to start, we can quickly assess ourselves to determine an appropriate starting place. *Can't touch your toes?* Maybe flexibility is lacking and would be an excellent place to start. *Are you feeling puffed after taking a flight of stairs?* Maybe cardiovascular fitness and conditioning should take priority for some time. *Do you experience difficulty doing a pushup?* Strength training could be the right choice for you.

When we pay attention to the body, we can utilize awareness of our movement strengths and limitations to creatively mix up our exercise strategies to keep our body's functional capacities balanced. This kind of diversified movement variety helps to keep the body pain-free and brain fit as our cognitive processes are simultaneously challenged to learn something new[81]. As a bonus, the body burns more energy while adjusting and adapting to the new form of exercise[82].

Every form of exercise is healthy for the body, which makes it easier to follow the heart and choose the ones that feel the best and most fulfilling. This is one of the reasons why I incorporate so many different forms of exercise as part of my regular movement practice. Any week will include swimming, weight training, yoga or salsa dancing. Not only am I more entertained and motivated by the variety of movements, but my body's risk of overuse injury is reduced because the diversity of activities keeps my joints moving through various ranges. My body lets me know I'm getting the equation right because it's open and pain-free. Indeed, one quick variable and barometer of movement wellbeing anyone can use is checking in with their body's ability to move, stretch, reach and jump through its natural range of motion without pain.

The invitation on offer is to try it all. Anything and everything. Diversifying movement and exercise strategies balances and enhances our movement qualities, helps prevent injuries, trains the brain, and allows us to experience more fun and enjoyment during movement and exercise.

Rest & Recovery

Finally, the body tells us when it's time for the all-important period of rest and recovery. We cannot heal if we don't turn off the physiological tap that floods the system with inflammation and stress. Aches, pains, soreness and fatigue are often the body's way of telling us to slow down or that something isn't working.

Rather than ignoring the body's signals or numbing them out with ointments or pills, we can get curious about what our body is trying to tell us and investigate which aspect of our lifestyle might be a contributing factor or cause. Muscle soreness, low energy or aches and pains might signal the body to slow down. Whether our body feels refreshed, rejuvenated or recovered are some ways we can determine whether our rest and recovery strategies are fulfilling their intended purpose.

***

We can use objective body-based data to assess our overall lifestyle. Whether it's body weight, body fat percentage, lean mass, circumference measurements, clothing size or blood tests, these objective measures can be used over time to see how the body responds to the food we eat and our lifestyle as a whole. Even sex drive can be useful to track, as a healthy body wants to have sex. When the body is stressed and struggling to survive, reproduction doesn't register as one of the body's immediate needs.

Regardless of what we choose, the body and our direct experience can serve as the ultimate judge and jury of whether our chosen strategies are actually working for us. The body always speaks the truth. It cannot lie.

A final way to check in with the body to see if we are choosing a healthy lifestyle is if we are enjoying that choice. If a lifestyle choice doesn't feel good or isn't fun, then the chances of sticking with it are low. If living healthy is experienced as a punishment, it's only a matter of time before old habits creep back in.

Eating should be an enjoyable experience, so if we don't like the taste of the foods we're eating, we probably won't eat them for too long. The same goes for our movement and exercise choices. If we don't like a particular form of exercise, we can find one that's more fun. Enjoyment is what makes lifestyles sustainable.

The body is not static. It is undergoing a constant process of change in relation to the environment that it lives within. With every passing moment, cells of the body are dying away while new, healthy cells are being created. The rate of these processes, called *apoptosis* for cell death and *cell division* for the creation of new cells, is determined by variables such as age, genetics and, not surprisingly, our lifestyle. With every decision, moment, lifestyle choice and breath, the body is in a constant state of flux and change. Every seven to ten years we essentially embody a new body because, in that time, every cell within us has been replaced by a new one. Nothing in the body is static, so why should our dietary, movement and lifestyle choices be set in stone?

This means we can invite openness, curiosity and exploration to our lifestyle choices as they change according to how our body changes over time. Be open to the body's inevitable shifts and changing needs. What our body needed *then* may not be what it needs *now*. If we are ruthlessly honest with what we see, feel and experience in our bodies, we can find the unique formula for what we need to thrive.

Finally, one of the biggest complaints about healthy living is that it takes too much time to maintain. But it doesn't have to be this way. Despite what many think, healthy living doesn't have to be all-consuming and overwhelming. Health doesn't have to require monotonous and time-consuming tracking, monitoring and measuring, though, admittedly, these processes can be helpful at the beginning of the journey as we learn about our own bodies.

What's important to remember is that health is the natural byproduct of a healthy lifestyle. It's far less stressful to live a healthy life when that lifestyle doesn't require a full-time job's worth of hours to maintain.

Designing and building a life on top of the foundation of Healthy Lifestyle Principles reveals that holistic wellbeing doesn't have to be complex or confusing. If our lifestyle supports and promotes health, health will naturally and effortlessly follow.

The process of creating, sustaining and fine-tuning our lifestyle connects us to our body as we learn to understand its needs, when those needs shift and how to adjust our choices accordingly. This is how we become students of our respective bodies. It's a practice. It takes time. But what we can be absolutely sure of is that the body will respond to the environment we place it in. We make the lifestyle choices. The body takes care of the rest.

Lean on a Regular Practice

Getting into my body is my answer when I need to hit the reset button or de-stress. When I gift my body with healthy lifestyle choices, it reciprocates by giving my mind a sense of peace. This is especially true when I need that sense of calm amid external chaos and overwhelm. When the external world seems out of control or things get stressful, my lifestyle is what I lean on to help me get through. I listen to my body, and it tells me whether cooking a healthy meal, going for a swim, sitting in a sauna, dunking in an ice bath or some meditative stillness is what the present moment requires.

The initial bodily impulse might be to reach for sugar, alcohol, porn or some other short-term fix. I've learned from experience that following that path triggers the downward spiral toward mental catastrophizing and increases the stress load on my body. Leaning on my healthy lifestyle practices, even when my mind's default responses tell me otherwise, helps to slow, stop or reverse the downward spiral before it has a chance to gain momentum. The first few moments of my proactive lifestyle choice may be challenging, but my body and mind always feel relief thereafter. The quick fixes, on the other hand, invariably make things worse.

When the body is stressed, it's hard to see past our shoes. While our practices aren't intended to make problems go away, we can see our stresses and challenges more clearly when the body is settled. As we lean on our practices in this way, we begin to see that most of the time we are stressed out because we are reacting to distressing perceptions. The mind is telling stories.

These perceptions are likely related to or initiated by a distressed body. At the very least, our perceptions are exaggerated and made more prominent by a stressed body. When I drink too much coffee (which is *any* amount of coffee for me), my mind can create a long list of things to be anxious and worried about. When the body is relaxed, however, the worst-case scenarios of the mind don't seem as certain or even possible.

As we commit to leaning on our healthy lifestyle practices, we develop a foundation of physical, mental and emotional resilience. This baseline level of resilience created by healthy living buffers us from the stresses of everyday life. When the body is happy, content and at peace, it's easier to get through the invariably difficult moments of everyday life.

The physical resilience cultivated through healthy choices also supports us as we process emotions and heal trauma, a topic that will be discussed and expanded upon throughout this book. Sitting with the pain of trauma, aka opposing the conditioned reactivity of our nervous system, isn't easy, which is why we spend much of our lives avoiding it one way or another.

When answering the body's natural inclination toward processing, integrating and healing emotional wounds, a healthy body will help us move through that process with more ease. It doesn't mean that we get to avoid the pain and discomfort of healing and integrating (more on that later as well), just that we can lean on the qualities and capacities cultivated through healthy living practices. These are the beginning stages of learning to trust the body's capacity to pass through challenging experiences.

A resilient body has more freedom to direct attention toward serving others and being creative. As health and wellbeing emerge as a natural consequence of lifestyle choices, our time, space and energy are freed to focus on other things. When the body is healthy, thriving and not sprinting toward a collision with chronic disease, we are free to give attention to the things that matter most in our life. Living with meaning and purpose is easier when we have the strength, energy and vitality that emerge from a healthy lifestyle. Without a healthy body, it's only a matter of time before there isn't enough fuel left in the tank to follow through on our intentions.

In neglecting the body along our journey back to health, we arrive at the mind's perceived destination with a sinking ship, if we get there at all. A healthy body is a strong and sturdy vessel that allows us to savor the fruits of our labor when we periodically reach our goals and intentions. What's the point of reaching a destination if we cannot enjoy it?

***

The body is the temple of God, according to the Bible. This declaration, however, seems to be often overlooked as fundamental Christian teaching. I've already mentioned that the body is worthy of worship. When we treat our body as sacred, holy and something of great value, our daily lifestyle choices are transformed from menial tasks into offerings of reverence and respect. When our body is a temple, we don't desecrate it or allow it to be desecrated by others. Regardless of our religious beliefs, our body houses the spirit.

Treating healthy lifestyles as gifts to the body – as offerings of worship – changes the intention, meaning and purpose of each choice. Healthy food is a gift to the body because it's what our body needs to thrive. When we gift our bodies with movement, we do so because we know that the circulation provided by movement is essential for health. The body will respond not only to our lifestyle choices but also to the intention behind those choices. It's a worthwhile experiment for us to pay attention to how the body experiences our lifestyle choices when we frame them as gifts.

I treat my lifestyle choices as offerings of worship placed at the altar of my body. I know and trust in the body's incredible healing capacity and offer it daily doses of healthy food, rigorous movement, meditative stillness and restorative sleep. The more I tend to and care for it, the easier it is to be present for, attune with and attend to the needs of those around me.

In closing this chapter, let me offer a few words to those who might think it selfish to focus on their health and wellbeing, as I've worked with many who hold this limiting self-belief. I can sum up my thoughts on this with a single quote: *self-care is about giving the best of you, not what's left of you.*

It's easier to listen, be productive, be creative and be of service to others when the body is strong, resilient, healthy and calm. It is then that we are best prepared to focus on attending to the needs of those situations, projects and relationships that require our attention. When we choose to be compassionate to our bodies, we set the groundwork for health and healing. The body, in return, quietly serves us so that we can, in turn, be of service to the world. The lesson is clear: *take care of your body and it will take care of you.*

Chapter Summary Points and Key Takeaways

- The body's surrounding environment can support its innate and inherent health and healing processes. Look at the *whole* lifestyle when assessing the body's environment.

- The 'big rocks' of the Healthy Lifestyle Principles are Real Food, Movement and Rest & Relaxation.

- Healthy lifestyles reduce overall stress load and lower the inflammatory burden on the body.

- Healthy lifestyles cultivate the strength, vitality and resilience that make everyday life easier.

- More than a health strategy, healthy lifestyles help you start learning how to listen to the body, understand how it speaks, and provide it with what it needs.

Three Ways to Get Started with Practice

1. **Use your daily lifestyle choices to start connecting to your body.** Before meals, workouts or recovery strategies, check in with your body before, during and after to see how your body responds. How are your energy levels? How does your stomach and digestive system respond? Try new things. The more you experiment, the more you learn about your own body. The body can help you determine which choices are helping or harming.

2. **Keep a food, movement and rest journal.** It's helpful to track your choices at the beginning of the journey. It makes it easier to remember choices that work and investigate possibilities if something doesn't feel right in your body. Remember to note how your body responds.

3. **Take out one food or drink you know or have a hunch is unhealthy for your body.** Remember, taking *out* lifestyle choices is essential and helpful as you learn to listen to your body. Over two weeks, pay attention to how your body responds to removing the food or drink.

Chapter 3
Stillness

"Within yourself is a stillness and sanctuary to which you can retreat at any time and be yourself." - *Herman Hesse*

"There is nothing as certain as silence, stillness and solitude to introduce you to the secrets of yourself." - *Guy Finley*

"The thing about meditation is: You become more and more you." - *David Lynch*

I'm now reaching the 10th hour of the day that I'm quietly maintaining a single-pointed focus on my inner world. This is the 6th sitting of the day, lasting between 1-2 hours each, cumulatively comprising the 10 hours. Curious, I watch my unfolding experience without preference or expectation of what my conscious mind will come into contact with next. It may look like nothing in particular is happening to the casual observer. They may see nothing more than a bald man with closed eyes, sitting cross-legged and statue-like on a meditation cushion. My perspective, however, tells a very different story. What the steady and consistent application of stillness provides a portal to is nothing short of remarkable.

Within deep states of meditation, I feel every cell and molecule of my body vibrating and pulsing with a distinctive buzz. I experience massive currents of electric energy, stretching far wider than the perceived width of my body, originating from below my seat and surging up through and out of the top of my head. I watch as my breath reaches rates and depths so few and subtle that I doubt they would register as breathing to someone watching.

Starkly contrasting my body's seemingly imperceptible breath is the immense current of energy flowing within the framework of my body. The slightest shift of attention sends waves of energy flowing through my body in that same direction. During these deep explorations, I've learned that my body may dissolve into nothingness or expand into everything-ness; both equally astonishing states to experience.

The Newtonian Laws of the physical world seem to become null and void when my present moment experience is put under the microscope of meditative stillness. I suddenly appreciate and understand how Stan Lee could have dreamt up superheroes like Thor and The Invisible Man. In these deep states of concentration, superpowers like channeling electric energy and making the body invisible seem possible.

These consciousness-altering experiences are held together by the delicate and fragile container of stillness. The slightest movement, or a breath too deep, and the entire structure collapses, flooding the system and overwhelming the senses with intense sensations. The mind often doesn't have a label for the sensations buzzing through my body. They are equal parts pain and bliss.

When the set and setting allow for such experiences, I don't want to miss the opportunity to observe and learn. This depth of meditation is not easy to access. Arriving at this moment requires patience, surrender and trust. When I encounter these experiences, I want to give my body the time and space it needs to process, integrate and heal.

Tension in my body releases as I feel more unraveling and dissolving within the inner landscape of my body. My mind has learned how to step aside and trust the body, no matter how uncomfortable the mind perceives the present moment to be. Opposing mental reactivity, I soften, surrender and watch the process unfold. I do nothing. My body feels freer after each sitting.

In these moments, my intention is to stay objective, surrendered and, most importantly, *still* because there always seems to be something new to learn within these states. Not the traditional kind of learning that involves cognitive processes. This is a very different type of learning. Wisdom like this is only accessible when we allow our awareness to penetrate the deepest layers of our somatic experience. What is discovered there isn't an idea, image or words, which require perpetual debate or defense. The wisdom being described here is embodied *knowing*.

My experience has shown me that the critical difference between the two is that the learnings of my mind are temporary, fleeting and flimsy. The wisdom excavated from the depths of the body, however, creates permanent shifts in my understanding of myself and my way of being in the world. When we *know* something to be true, we don't feel an urge or impulse to defend ourselves from the opinions of others. Truth doesn't require a defense. We know we've arrived at this level of intuitive knowing when the body is correspondingly calm and relaxed in response to our declaration, intention or decision.

***

Experiencing meditative states like those described above made me change my opinion of meditation from something fluffy and pointless to a transformative modality. Meditation turns words and intellectual teachings into direct experience. When teachers told me there is no "I" or that "I" is merely a thought or an illusion, it sounded like some riddle I'd never solve. And yet, in deep meditative states, I've searched for the 'I' within my own experience of all-encompassing vibration and buzzing and found nothing. *I* was definitely not my body. Nor was *I* my thoughts, which had long stopped as my attention dropped into a highly concentrated state within the body. So where, or what, was *I*?

It took time to witness these kinds of experiences in a detached way. My virgin dives into these depths convinced my naïve ego that these states were the goals of meditation in and of themselves. I honestly thought, and it pains me to admit, that I had reached enlightenment the first time I witnessed my body dissolving. I can't help but smile and laugh at the mind's childish naivety. Indeed, consciousness-altering meditative states can entice and tempt meditators. Some chase these euphoric experiences that meditation can elicit as if the pleasant experience is the goal of meditation. Of course, like chasing any high, it's a trap, a subtle form of spiritual materialism and bypass. These states are like every other life experience: destined to pass away.

Meditation provides the container within which lessons like this – *all experiences in life are temporary, constantly changing and destined to pass away* – become the kind of embodied *wisdom* and *knowing* described above. It's one thing to intellectually accept or agree that challenging sensations and emotions are destined to pass away. It's quite another to be present and attentive as this natural phenomenon is observed, witnessed and experienced during meditation. The experiential evidence provided by meditation practice is what turns information into wisdom, knowledge into knowing.

Non-duality teacher, Rupert Spira, said that meditation is not something we do. It is the essence of who and what we are. Stillness has served as the window I've peered through to see the essence of *what* I am. I know that whatever 'I' am, it is not my mind, nor my body, because I've experienced myself as the blank canvas of awareness through which all experience perpetually flows. In this experience, the solidity of the physical world reveals itself to be an elaborate and convincing illusion of the mind. Beneath the experience of the physical body, thoughts, emotions and sensations, there is only the observer. Pure Awareness. Stillness. The Self. Only direct experience could have made these words Truth.

The profound insights that emerged through meditation found their way into my everyday life experience. When it became clear that I was not the self-defeating thoughts, judgments and limiting beliefs that painted my picture of the world, I could start choosing something new. My destiny was no longer predestined.

It was easy to choose a different path when provided with clear evidence that I wasn't my thoughts. I was merely having an experience of them. I didn't have to believe the inner critic because he revealed himself as nothing more than an illusion of the mind. Previously, I hadn't known what freedom felt like in my body. I can only guess (and often I do) how meditative experiences like these create real change in my everyday life. What I know for sure, however, is that every time I emerge from such experiences, profound and permanent shifts soon follow.

I've been called selfish for disconnecting from life responsibilities for 10-days at a time, that it's unacceptable to leave behind my life's responsibilities –such as work or being a father – for such long periods. I know the contrary to be true. Knowing what I know now, the time and space taken for intentional inner work is one of the most selfless acts we can engage in. It would be selfish and irresponsible *not* to go.

Vipassana is where I learned how to face, sit and be with my pain. Vipassana served as the cauldron that brewed my capacity to have empathy for others. Each course has proven to be an opportunity to grow as a person, develop as a therapist and be a better partner upon emerging from my yearly cocoon. Vipassana made me a convert and believer in what is possible through meditative stillness.

Vipassana: New Understandings

I had leisurely dabbled in meditation for a couple of years before arriving at my first Vipassana Meditation Course in Prachinburi, Thailand. For those unfamiliar with these 10-day silent meditation retreats, here is what to expect: between 6 and 11 hours of meditation each day. No cell phones, books, electronics or entertainment of any kind. The kicker is the unintentionally enforced intermittent fasting, as the only two meals of the day are at 6:30 am and 11:00 am. During the ten days of complete silence, meditators have just their thoughts to keep them company, and there's no shortage of those (at least at the beginning).

When it comes to meditation, Vipassana isn't an experience intended for beginners. I was genuinely shocked when I met people that had never meditated before attending the course with me. I thought I was ready for what awaited. No one ever is.

The circumstances in my life had certainly set the stage for making Vipassana a pivotal moment in my life. I had reached the end of *A Million Ways to Live*, my 13-month documentary project. I was tired. And after traveling, filming and editing 56 episodes, I was also bankrupt. Not just financially, but physically, mentally and emotionally. I had stubbornly persevered through a project while attempting to maintain an amicable relationship (side note: I failed miserably) with my co-host and co-creator of the project, who happened to be my ex-girlfriend and mother of the 8-month child we had in tow, my son, Jack. Yes, you read all of that correctly.

With the benefit of hindsight, no one would attempt to persevere through such an idiotic set of circumstances. Still, I have routinely been comically stubborn and doggedly persistent. This was another one of those shining moments.

While I ticked the box for completing the massive project, it cost me almost everything.

I was lost, depressed and confused. I had no idea in which direction to take my next step. If there was ever a time to attend a Vipassana course, this was it. What seemed to be the shared commonality of those arriving for their inaugural Vipassana was a life event of a similar texture or flavor.

Vipassana ensures an environment where there is nothing to do except meditate. Everything is meticulously planned, arranged and scheduled. From 4:00 am until 9:00 pm, gongs let meditators know where to go next. The daily schedule is structured to support introspection and maintain a near-continuous awareness of the body's moment-to-moment experience. I've found no better environment for excavations into the innermost parts of the mind and body than at Vipassana, which is why I return routinely for sittings.

My understanding of meditation has matured over the years like a fine wine. The motivations that sparked my initial dives into the practice have long been discarded, replaced with more profound yearnings of the soul. My meditation practice isn't like consuming a multivitamin or nutritional supplement, which is often nothing more than taking a daily pill without ever really feeling whether it's helping, hindering or doing anything at all. The changes I consistently experience and discover through meditation are palpable, tangible and real. Benefits from my practice have permeated into everyday life.

My practice started with the 'this-for-that' mentality at the core of many short-term fixes to problems with deeper sources. I didn't like how stress felt in my body, so I meditated to feel better. It wasn't porn, work or sports content. However, I was still using meditation as an antidote for stress reduction, as if the experience of stress was something to be unequivocally avoided. Eventually, I understood that wanting to get something from meditation – thus using meditation in response to a specific experience – had become another iteration of reactivity. Whenever I experienced something uncomfortable, I could quickly avoid the experience by meditating. In other words, I was using meditation as an avoidance strategy.

I've grown to appreciate that stress is an inherent and vital part of our growth as fulfilled human beings. Stress is at the heart of building a healthy and strong body, as the stress of exercise leads to the adaptation of strength and muscle development. The body adapts to the stresses placed upon it in ways that make it more resilient against the stress it experiences in the future. Indeed, hormetic stress practices (covered in greater detail in a later chapter, *Conscious Discomfort*) create health for the body precisely because they stress the body at levels that aren't physiologically harmful or dangerous.

Rather than avoiding stress, we can learn to face it without reacting to it. Meditation has empowered me to face life's stresses without being controlled by them or swayed too far off my center. I learned that it's possible to remain calm and responsive despite the presence of stress. I witnessed as relationships in my life experienced more ease, my mental and emotional wellbeing stabilized, and my everyday life experience transformed.

I stopped viewing meditation in the usual 'this-for-that' way that so many practices are initially used for. Sure, improved sleep and stress management are excellent starting points and motivators for practice, but I realized there was much more to the practice. Meditation helps me show up more authentically and be more present in my life.

Patience is critical as it often takes a long time to notice how meditation slowly, subtly and gently transforms the world – *your* world – from the inside out. We often can't see how meditation impacts our life until we put down the practice for a bit. In this sense, meditation is kind of like brushing our teeth. The first time we skip a brushing, it's not too noticeable. But the longer we go without brushing, the worse and more obvious our oral hygiene becomes, both to ourselves and others.

Similarly, when we maintain mental hygiene with meditation, we may not be aware of the subtle shifts that alter our way of being. When we stop meditating for a few days, we notice old habits and triggers sneaking back into life, tension creeping back into the body and friction in our relationships. We might feel moody, irritable, or triggered more easily. Those are certainly the signals that let me know my practice has slipped. This happens to everyone and has served as a humbling periodic reminder to stay consistent.

I've often become aware of how meditation has changed my life when I see old habits alive and expressing themselves in others. I remember driving one day and watching someone ahead of me throw a tantrum and yell through their car window when cut off by another driver. *That was me once.* I smiled when I realized getting cut off didn't bother me much anymore. I hadn't even noticed when or how the reaction had unraveled until I witnessed my 'old' way of reacting alive in another. This is the subtle way meditation creates authentic and permanent change.

Reactive behaviors shed themselves naturally and effortlessly over time. Nothing necessarily changes externally. And that's because meditation transforms the internal, specifically how we relate to the body, how we relate to our moment-to-moment experience, and how we relate to the world. This, however, changes everything.

It was easy to empathize with the angry driver because I knew, quite intimately, that particular flavor of anger and rage coursing through his veins in that precise moment of perceived sleight. *How fucking dare he cut ME off!* Reading that last sentence may hit the reader hard, but let's be honest about the content that pops up in our respective minds. Those potentially triggering words are likely a downplay of the labels, thoughts and images that actually arise in moments of intense anger. The physiological impulse in the body that triggers these kinds of words and reactions is immensely powerful when we first start paying attention to it.

When first becoming aware of anger as it arises within the body, it can seem impossible to prevent the reaction that instantly follows. Even with the precious blessing of time that might allow for the acknowledgment that *any* variation of an outwardly projected tantrum *always* leads down the same self-destructive path, the anger-laden reaction follows through to its conclusion.

Our internal programming and conditioning are much stronger than our conscious thoughts and intentions. When we anchor our attention in the body, we feel the flooding waves of sensations and emotions that drive and dictate our thoughts, words and behaviors. Despite the mind's best intentions to oppose, pause or stop our programmed conditioning, our subconscious reactions often bulldoze conscious intentions as they express themselves until they are fully completed. Self-judgment tends to follow soon after.

It was a humbling experience when I realized I didn't have as much freedom and free will over my decisions as my mind had assumed. This is why, in the end, willpower always fails. The mind doesn't comprehend and has great difficulty accepting the power of the subconscious forces at play in the body.

For a long time, anger controlled me. It took a long time to break free of that ball-and-chain and to relate to this powerful emotion in a different, more productive and healthier way. I had to practice consciously sitting with anger without letting it drive my decision-making. This process required time and patience. I quietly hoped for the gift of awareness to find this stranger ignorant to the fact that he was being held captive by a conditioned reaction. A reaction, ironically, that cannot be overpowered with willpower. Instead, the conditioned reaction can be softened and extinguished through the quiet surrender of meditative stillness.

The Body Meditates. The Mind Follows.

As my meditation practice seasoned over time, so did my understanding of what was happening while I sat in states of stillness and silence. I was initially taught that meditation is an activity of the mind. Indeed, meditation is often described as something the mind *does*. And the many benefits of meditation are explained by their impact... *on the mind*. For example, meditation has been called a *mind gym*, where we go to strengthen concentration muscles and train our ability to focus, recall and remember. Summary: *meditation is for the mind, not the body*.

My understanding and explorations of the body catalyzed appreciating meditation as a somatic experience. I asked myself: *what would happen if we viewed meditation from the referential point of the body? Would this shift my understanding of the practice and its associated benefits? Is meditation yet another phenomenon that could be better understood and appreciated more nuancedly if we stayed anchored to and reverent of the body's experience during meditation?*

The more I sat with the possibility that meditation was more somatic than cognitive, the more it seemed that what the mind experienced because of meditation, as well as the many associated benefits that go hand in hand with meditation, was the result of what was happening in the body. I reached my own conclusion about the practice: *meditation is for the body, not the mind*.

***

Let's examine meditation from the referential viewpoint of the body to appreciate this stance fully. Firstly, is the act of meditating. The *body* prepares for meditation by finding a comfortable position and posture on a cushion, chair or bed. Then the body closes its eyes to avoid distractions caused by visual stimulation. The body knows it must give the mind something to busy itself with so it can rest, process and integrate without being distracted by the mind's near-perpetual stream of thoughts. Without some kind of mental stimulation to appease it, the mind will attempt in earnest to interrupt the body's intention for silence and stillness. The body understands the mind, aka the stimulation junkie in denial, needs this distraction because it will otherwise react to every shiny object that shows up in its periphery.

The lack of stimulation during meditation also happens to be why the mind often hates the states of stillness and silence. When nothing is happening, uncomfortable withdrawal symptoms quickly kick in. *What should I eat for lunch? What do I have to do today? This is so boring. I have better things to do. Where is my phone?* Is it surprising that we require mental stimulation via smartphones when we go to the bathroom? Like a stressed parent giving their child a device when they desperately need a break from the full-on demands of parenting, the body provides the mind with something to watch for an extended period: its own breathing.

By paying attention to the breath, the mind can pause its endless state of seeking and consuming. As a result, the body can sigh in relief as it initiates its innate healing processes. With the mind occupied by the breath, the body finally has space to process and integrate, rest and digest, heal and restore. As the body settles into the state of stillness required for this work, it invariably experiences myriad sensations as it gently, naturally and intrinsically moves toward a more balanced state. The mind often becomes aware of these new, odd, uncomfortable sensations as they arise in the body. This is because releasing tension isn't a comfortable process. But before the mind can interrupt the body's natural healing process by suggesting a reactive thought, the mind is gently instructed to turn its attention back to the breath. The body is thus left to continue processing deeper and deeper layers of tension, constriction and trauma.

The mind sits and plays with the breath as the body runs its intrinsic restorative processes. One of the hardest things for the mind to comprehend, and accept, is that it literally must stop its endless *doing* for the body to do the actual work of healing itself. Every cell, all 30 or so trillion of them, of the human body is ceaselessly moving toward healing and thriving because that's Nature's original programming. Programming that has been intricately fine-tuned through the millennia by evolution. All the mind has to do is step aside so the body can do what it's been programmed to do. Anyone who has tried meditating, knows this is easier said than done.

Nothing is scarier and more necessary for the mind than recognizing its futility in this process. As the body continues to rest in this uniquely rare and sacred space of stillness and silence, it can relax and release its accumulated tension. The body slowly begins to soften and relax as these constrictions dissolve. Not surprisingly, many measurable, palpable and objective changes associated with meditation occur within the body: increased metabolism, lowered blood pressure and an improved heart and breath rate[83]. The mind can only intrude, stop and prevent these processes if it tries to barge in with its destined-to-fail help.

With the body free of tension, the mind naturally calms and settles as a direct consequence. This meditation-induced, tension-free body allows the mind to sustain attention for more extended periods without distraction[84], to remember things[85] and to make more conscious decisions in the present moment without being drawn into thoughts of the past or future[86].

A similar phenomenon happens when we get a massage. The body's tension is massaged away by the hands of a masseuse or therapist. At the end of the massage, we open our eyes and experience a distinct sense of peace and calm in the mind. The mind didn't create this state, yet it's acutely easier to think clearly after gifting the body with a massage. In the case of meditation, however, the mind quickly takes credit for the benefits. The body, however, is happy to humbly enjoy its peaceful state and let the mind take whatever credit it needs in an attempt to quench its insatiable egotistical desires. Both body and mind benefit as both get to savor a sense of relaxation and peace.

The plethora of physiological and psychological benefits associated with meditation can be explained by changes within the body. This is because meditation reduces inflammation[87], a concept already discussed in detail in the previous chapter. As such, any condition caused or worsened by inflammation can thus be improved through meditation because of the practice's anti-inflammatory effects on the body[88]. Not only does this include chronic diseases like cancer, heart disease, diabetes, digestive disorders or Alzheimer's[89], it also includes psychological disorders like anxiety and depression, which are associated with inflammatory biomarkers and states[90,91]. Maybe meditators are loving, kind[92] and exude a positive mood[93] because it's easier to be more loving, kind and positive when the body is free of tension, constriction and inflammation.

***

Meditation allows us to practice a different way of being in the world. We learn and practice observing thoughts, emotions and body sensations without reacting to or identifying with them. We, quite literally, *do* nothing. And by doing nothing, we slowly begin to realize we *are* nothing. Meditation showed me that I could *be* without meddling or reacting. I don't have to react. I can observe. This understanding has profound implications for everyday life.

We all like the sound of mindfulness and, given a choice, most would *acknowledge, observe and accept* their internal experience rather than try to change, suppress or react to it. The former invites responsiveness and enables responsibility. The latter leads to saying things we regret and reactions ultimately requiring an apology.

Choosing to *behave* mindfully is more than merely accepting mindfulness concepts on an intellectual level. If we don't *practice* relating to the world in this way, we will, without fail, fall back into reactive behavioral patterns repeatedly. No matter how convinced the mind is that living mindfully is beneficial, practice is necessary. *The real work is in the body, not the mind.*

Meditation is often called a practice because we are practicing a different way of relating to our present moment experience. By meditating, we *practice* acknowledging, observing and accepting our internal experience. We *practice* response-ability. We are developing an ability to respond to our everyday life experience by responding with stillness to our present moment experience within meditation. Mindfulness teachings become more than buzz words when we embody them through consistent practice. When the body practices mindfulness, the mind follows.

Let's revisit the driver who threw a tantrum on the road. Response-ability is what is needed to empower the angry driver to respond differently. Responding, in this case, might be the driver being able to experience being cut off, to notice the anger and its related sensations arising in his body, to momentarily reflect on whether his perception of ill-will is correct, and to consider what response, if any, is warranted. If we don't practice this slower way of relating, it won't magically happen in real life.

We don't know what it means to observe and accept something – like an uncomfortable emotion, unwanted outcome or a tragic loss – until we've actually practiced observing and accepting an experience as we pass through it. Meditation facilitates this process by showing us what acceptance *feels* like in the body. When we have an experiential reference point for acceptance, we are empowered to carry this way of being into relationship with the world. The mind can *think* it's accepting something, but only the body can tell us if we're embodying the quality of acceptance.

All of this leads to the conclusion that *how* we meditate matters. The external posture, attire and location are not as important as what's happening on the inside. Specifically, how we relate within practice to our internal moment-to-moment experience. Three people, sitting eyes-closed and cross-legged next to each other, might look identical to an observer. One could be planning their upcoming workday and fidgeting every few moments. The second might be mentally considering lunch options. The third might be intently focusing the mind and embodying an internal posture of surrender and stillness. Only the third meditator is meditating.

All three might experience a refreshing and enjoyable sense of relaxation and calmness after taking some time to rest, but only one is paving the way for the transformational benefits possible with meditation. With meditation, what's happening on the inside is what matters. *How you meditate matters.* There's a quality that must be practiced and embodied within meditation that unearths the treasure troves of self-awareness, personal growth and transformation. That quality is *stillness*.

The Quality of Stillness

In a world that places perpetual busyness and never-ending *doing* on a pedestal, the virtue of stillness, and the gifts that it bears, has nearly become a lost art. Rarely do people brag about being able to spend the weekend sitting quietly by a lake watching the wind ruffle the water, lying in a park and watching the clouds slowly pass overhead, or spend time with eyes closed observing the unconscious muscle twitches, beating of the heart and rhythms of the inner workings that give the amazing human body its life. Instead, we are riding on the edge of over-stimulation with sensationalized media headlines, sugar-laden processed foods, work deadlines, the endless swiping of online dating and the perpetual buzzing of smartphone notifications. Stillness is needed now more than ever.

In the broadest sense, stillness represents a solution to the global crises of sustainability humans are currently facing. In the face of rampant capitalistic consumption and environmental degradation, stillness represents a way of being that can quell the destructive flames of modern-day consumerism. When we stop reacting, individually, organizationally and collectively, to the internal impulse for *more-more-more*, we see that our ravenous, unceasing, capitalist appetites are nothing more than an effort to fill a void that material pursuits cannot fill.

When we consider that most of the food we eat and products we buy are born out of an inability to manage our most primal bodily urges, temptations and emotions, then we can see that learning how to respond to our internal cues can stop us from consuming the world and destroying ourselves in hopes of soothing an agitated internal state. Late comedian George Carlin said, quite accurately, that trying to be happy by accumulating possessions is like trying to satiate hunger by taping sandwiches all over your body. He's right. The peace, joy and happiness we seek is an inside job, not an external purchase.

Moving from the broadest sense to the most subtle, stillness is the quality that reveals the true Self. Through stillness, I *experienced* Rupert Spira's non-dual teachings of Aware Presence, the essence of our beingness. There is always something still within us, but it is not absent of movement. Our beingness remains unaffected by any movement, action or *doing* even though it moves, acts and does. It is naturally present at the heart of all experience for everyone. It is called the witness, the observer and the ever-present 'I' of all experience, which remains unchanged regardless of external circumstances.

Of course, these words are understandably difficult for the mind to conceptualize and comprehend if they haven't been made real with direct experience. I, like many readers, didn't know what to make of these descriptions when first exposed to them. It wasn't until the steady application of meditative stillness, serving as the microscope through which I observed the subtlest aspects of my beingness, that these words were brought into perfect clarity.

***

As we saw in the previous chapter, we can improve our health and wellbeing by listening to the body's reactions to our lifestyle choices and the environment that our body lives within. Through stillness, we can start fostering a deeper connection with the body. When our eyes are closed and our attention is focused inward, we begin learning the language of the human body and attune to its many subtle learnings and messages. Stillness is slowing down to hear what the body is trying to tell us.

Stillness heals the body because *all healing* – physical, emotional and psychological – starts and ends within the body's framework. Our body's natural and inherent healing superpowers are activated in stillness, just as they are when we sleep. Stillness heals emotional trauma by removing the straitjacket of a traumatic past as it gently summons to the surface unresolved and unprocessed emotional energy. Stillness enables the unavoidable confrontation with the deeply rooted experiences that drive reactive behaviors that have been subconsciously or consciously avoided.

Stillness is the gift we bring into relationships that allows us to see the person in front of us more clearly. We develop the capacity to stop reacting to internal states and learn how to be present for the other. Interpersonal harmony naturally flows as our way of being becomes a calming gift for those we encounter. Relationships become more connected when reactivity is replaced by stillness.

The pinnacle of practical utility related to stillness becomes apparent when it permeates into and transforms various contexts of everyday life. Stillness is the teacher that shows us a different way of relating to ourselves and being in the world. Stillness deconditions reactive behavioral patterns, as we will learn in the next chapter.

Through practice, stillness softens reactivity, with the capacity to extinguish it entirely. When we first start paying attention to the reactive impulse within the body, it can seem like the external stimulus and the corresponding physiological response are a single, overlapping event. This is what we label as a *reaction* because the mind doesn't perceive there is a space between stimulus and response.

The underlying energetic impulse in the body that catalyzes the cycle of reactive self-soothing behaviors loses its charge when the quality of stillness wedges a gap between the stimulus and response. Reactions transform into responses and automatic and conditioned habits run their course, fizzle out and lose their power because we learn how to *do nothing* and *simply observe*. Through stillness, the experiences of authentic freedom and free will reveal themselves.

When we can feel the arising physiological experience of our triggers and impulses without reacting to them in our programmed and conditioned way, we experience momentary freedom. We can respond rather than react, thus deviating from a predestined path and toward a consciously created future. And life, as we all know, gives us plenty of opportunities to practice being with triggers as we move toward such noble and virtuous intentions.

Practicing Stillness

We don't control the things that happen to us. We don't control how our body reacts, either. We can't control when uncomfortable body sensations or intense emotions arise within us, nor can we make them go away simply because we don't want them there. There's no switch in the body to turn our triggers on and off.

As much as we'd like to sometimes, we also can't stop the frequency or nature of our thoughts. The mind's primary function is to think; we can't turn that off either. Automatic thoughts pop up of their own accord. While sometimes we try numbing, sedating or avoiding our internal experience when it gets overwhelming, that only works for so long. Ultimately, we realize that attempts to run from our uncomfortable inner world are temporary at best. A day, and a life, can quickly slip by when stuck in the constant state of avoidance. Avoidance is exhausting.

We can plan and prepare for the best, but despite our best efforts to control the chaos of everyday life, meditation is a gentle reminder that we don't have as much control over what happens to us as we think we do. But while we can't control the things that happen to us, we can, with practice, choose how we respond. This is where practicing stillness comes in.

Meditation gives us a practical way of learning how to face and be with the certainty of uncertainty that comes with life. When we can be with our internal experience without reacting to it, our habitual reactions slowly unravel and lose their power to dictate and determine our actions and choices. This is the essence of freedom and free will. Stillness, thus, is the golden nugget we dig toward in meditation.

We begin cultivating non-reaction in everyday life by practicing stillness during meditation. Practicing stillness within meditation involves three aspects: physical, mental and internal posture. The first aspect of stillness is *physical stillness*.

While meditating, it's important to remain physically still. Settling into a sense of physical stillness makes it easier to begin connecting to the body. The absence of external movement and visual stimulation makes it possible to perceive the subtle ways the body speaks and communicates. This is the language of physical sensations.

Sensations exist everywhere throughout the body. Whatever we can distinctly feel, however intense or subtle, is a sensation. Our capacity to notice, locate, feel and, most importantly, stay present with sensations is directly related to cultivating fluency with the language of the body. We know we are improving our somatic vocabulary as we get more comfortable clearly articulating the details of what we notice emerging within our somatic world.

Sensation is at the very core of our bodily experience. All experience begins firstly as sensation. Powerful emotions like anxiety, sadness and anger all have corresponding sensations within the body. It's helpful to know how our body experiences these states – sensations such as tension, constriction, heat or pain – because they are easier to regulate and manage at the level of sensation; before the strong emotion floods the nervous system. It's much harder to manage and respond to intense emotions in their full expression.

Sensations also trigger subconscious habits and reactive behaviors. Detecting subtle physical sensations before they reach intense emotional states or impulsive behavioral triggers is the key to breaking through reactivity and creating authentic change.

If you're new to the concept of physical sensations or uncertain of what I'm trying to describe, you can do an exercise as you read this paragraph. Direct your attention and awareness to your fingertips. You don't have to look at your hands. In fact, for this exercise, it's best to either close your eyes or keep them fixed on these words or an object in the distance. In other words, don't look at your hands.

Now, rest your attention, not your eyes or gaze, at your fingertips. What you'll undoubtedly notice is that you can distinctly *feel* something. Whether your mind labels the experience as tingling, prickling, pulsing, vibrating or pressure is secondary. If you're following along, then what you've just become aware of is sensation. The mind may be looking for something significant or special, but sensation is nothing more than that distinct feeling that you're now paying attention to even though your eyes are not presently looking at your hands. Sensations like these exist throughout the body and are perceivable at any moment. Just like your fingertips, all that is required is directing your awareness and paying close attention.

Using the chart on the next page as a starting point and reference guide, you can practice feeling sensations. Direct and rest your attention on different body parts and see if you can notice what sensations are present at any given time.

When it comes to meditation, we never know what sensations we will experience. Sensations come and go, sometimes flickering in and out of awareness and other times sticking around for what seems like forever. Some sensations may be pleasant. Others are uncomfortable, nagging or even painful. At times, we may be focusing our attention on one part of the body, only to feel sensations somewhere else. Sometimes we feel nothing at all. Experiencing any, all or none of these sensations during meditation is precisely *as it's supposed to be*.

Meditation is not about expecting to experience something or to feel a certain way. It's about being present and feeling *what actually is*. We don't know what we're going to get. Stillness is a universal 'yes' to everything.

Sensations: The Language of the Body

Examples of Sensations				Body Location	
Achy	Expansive	Numb	Stabbing	Head	Stomach
Bloated	Flowy	Painful	Spinning	Face	Arms
Bubbly	Fluttery	Paralyzed	Stiff	Eyes	Hands
Buzzy	Frozen	Pounding	Still	Nose	Fingers
Clammy	Full	Pressure	Sweaty	Cheeks	Thighs
Cold	Fuzzy	Prickly	Tense	Chin	Buttocks
Constricted	Heavy	Pulsing	Tight	Mouth	Genitals
Contracted	Hot	Queasy	Tingly	Neck	Knees
Dry	Itchy	Quivery	Trembly	Teeth	Ankles
Dull	Jittery	Restricted	Twitchy	Throat	Calves
Dizzy	Jumpy	Shaky	Throbbing	Shoulders	Feet
Empty	Light	Spacious	Warm	Chest	Toes

Instead of reacting to impulses to scratch, fidget, adjust or move in any way, notice these sensations as they arise and observe what happens when we allow our internal experience to unfold without intrusion. Simply noticing, observing and feeling is enough. Indeed, doing nothing and remaining physically still in relation to these sensations is precisely what's required. Stillness is achieved when we are merely observing in a non-reactive way.

The second aspect of stillness, *mental stillness*, is related to the capacity to notice the mind's mental chatter – the thoughts, judgments and labels that invariably pop up – without getting on the roller coaster and going for the ride. This requires patience. If you've tried meditating before, you already know how difficult it can be to sustain a focused and concentrated state of mind for prolonged periods. You bring your attention to your breath only to find that the mind is elsewhere a moment later. In the first few days of meditating, many people become disheartened or quit because of this common meditative experience.

When we feel frustrated or think we're doing it wrong, remember that we're developing a new skill. Understand that developing the ability to focus takes time, like any new skill. And it really doesn't matter how often the mind wanders when we meditate, because refocusing and *coming back to the breath* is at the core of meditative practice.

The breath is the perfect object of focus for meditation. Firstly, if we're breathing then we're alive. And knowing we're alive is an excellent place to start when trying to create positive change in life. Secondly, realize we're breathing *now*. When we're not attentive to what's happening here and now, it's easier to get overwhelmed by life's many stresses or overreact to unwanted thoughts or negative emotions. The breath, thus, is an anchor to the present moment. We can't breathe in the past or the future, so when we shift our attention to our breath, we're really shifting our attention to the here and now.

Finally, the breath invariably keeps our attention on the body, which means that we're already practicing attuning with and listening to our body as soon as we close our eyes to meditate. When our eyes are closed and we're focusing on the body breathing, it's easier to pay attention to our inner world and what we're experiencing within the body's framework.

I call the third and final aspect of stillness an *internal posture of stillness*. This describes the way we relate to our experience from moment to moment. Just because someone looks like they are sitting still on the outside, their internal way of relating to their arisen experience could be fraught with tension: an internal resistance against some sensation or experience.

When our internal posture is one of tension, our inner experience is akin to fighting tension with more tension. This is like an internal struggle with our bodies. This kind of forced, tense and rigid stillness isn't what is being asked for with stillness practice.

Resisting an uncomfortable thought, emotion or body sensation invariably creates more tension. Embodying stillness as an internal posture requires surrendering to, rather than resisting or fighting, an experience. Welcome any experiences that arise. Any thinking, labeling, analyzing or understanding is unnecessary, even when we want to run. Even though we're not quite sure of the way through, we can practice softening and surrendering into stillness. Trust that the body knows what it's doing. Relax into what comes up within the framework of the body.

A final consideration to include in this section is to acknowledge that trusting one's body isn't always easy or doesn't always seem possible. Some experience only pain, discomfort and dysregulation due to their life experience or unique genetics when they attempt to connect to their somatic experience in this way. For those readers and clients, the final section of *Conscious Discomfort* (Encountering Resurfacing Trauma) addresses and explores both my philosophical alignment with this topic, as well as considerations for such individuals.

I'll close this section by stating that I naïvely hold, and will always hold, the belief that reconnection with the body is possible for everyone, regardless of how much pain, discomfort or trauma their body has experienced. I believe that healing is possible for anyone seeking to work toward it.

Stillness in Everyday Life

Outside of formal meditation practice, daily life – every moment of it – can become an informal stillness practice. Indeed, transferring the quality of stillness from our cushions and into our respective lives is the goal. Practicing stillness in everyday life means adopting a new way of being that involves staying present, attentive and responsive to what emerges in the moment rather than reacting to life's experiences like a pinball.

When we get triggered, we can STOP: Surrender To Own Presence. When we STOP, we begin to see that the impulses in the body don't have to result in habitual reactions. With practice, we can choose something different.

When we notice moments when a trigger or internal discomfort arises, we can give ourselves a bit of time and space to be with them to create the opportunity to choose a different response. Taking a few moments throughout the day to bring focus to the breath provides bite-sized experiences of stillness that allow us to feel the subtle states and shifts within the body. We can even practice articulating what we feel, thus improving our somatic comprehension and vocabulary. Most importantly, we can acknowledge and celebrate choosing a different path by telling ourselves: *you've just changed your destiny. Nice job. You deserve it.*

***

Stillness is not easy. I once held the belief that meditation is nothing but relaxation and peace. Instead of nirvana, however, I got a wild, uncontrollable mind and a fidgety body to match. I've spoken with many who have waved the white flag and dismissed the practice because they thought they 'weren't good at meditation' when initial roadblocks like these presented themselves. The backdrop of stillness and silence doesn't mean that what we will find when we close our eyes are peace and serenity. Stillness very quickly reveals to us what we've been avoiding, running from and are now consciously choosing to face.

Each time meditation practitioners close their eyes, they *practice* acknowledging, observing and accepting their internal experience rather than trying to change, suppress or react to it. That sounds easy and simple enough, but in the world of behavioral change, *acknowledging, observing and accepting* are anything but comfortable. Furthermore, modalities that make behavioral change the end goal in and of themselves inherently invalidate the capacities of *acknowledging, observing,* and *accepting.*

Sometimes, the present moment, and all the unwanted thoughts, negative emotions and unpleasant body sensations that come with it, are too uncomfortable to bear. So many of us, present company included at times, tend to do what we've always done to cope: avoid. As stillness invariably leads our attention to the finer, subtler details of the present moment, it can be overwhelming as we adjust to feeling *everything* more acutely.

Stillness can make life more challenging at first. This is normal and expected. When we start paying attention to the impulses, emotions and all the different experiences within our body that were previously below our conscious awareness, we *feel* more of *everything:* the good and the bad. Yet the peace, calmness and clarity we seek are savored only when we journey through the initial discomforts onto the other side of consistent practice.

Meditation is not some kind of magic trick. We don't get the rewards as soon as we sit cross-legged and close our eyes. Respite and relief require the patient and steady application of consistency. Once acclimatized to our newly increased sensitivity, stillness is what allows us to savor every delicious morsel life has on offer.

Yes, this might mean that we feel our sadness and pain more, but it also opens us up to the previously unknowable and delicious flavors of joy, love and peace. We can't have the latter while avoiding the former, though the mind wishes this was possible. Meditation, thus, is a putting down of the defenses and slowly opening the gates to allow everything back in. Reconnecting with the body means feeling everything, not just the experiences the mind prefers.

Instead of racing from one activity to the next, placing the state of busyness on a pedestal, stillness enables us to begin noticing the beauty present all along. We stop rushing and live life at the speed of appreciation. Stillness reveals the magnificence of life and empowers us to participate within it with more attentiveness and presence. These little moments begin accenting our day with joy and happiness. Feeling the warmth of the sun or the rush of a breeze against the skin, paying attention to how the taste of chocolate lingers on the tongue as it slowly melts, or the refreshing feeling of a cold glass of water on a parched throat. And nothing, and I mean absolutely nothing, compares to an extended period of an early morning embrace with a loved one.

Despite the practice of stillness, external challenges will remain. The difference is that we can face them more calmly because we see what's in front of us more clearly. The intuitive sense of our body has sharpened to the point that we can see an old trap coming up on the road ahead. We know what happens when we choose a partner for the same old reasons. We know what happens if we hang out with that particular group of friends. We know what happens to our mental and emotional states when we start scrolling through our social media feeds. With the practice of stillness, we wisely take a step in a slightly different direction to avoid a familiar reactive pitfall. We stop shooting ourselves in the foot because we take our finger off the trigger. We show up more fully and authentically to life, embodying stillness throughout.

Essentially, what's happening on the inside during 'meditation' is more important than what it looks like on the outside. It's not enough to sit, plan and fidget through some guided meditation. That might provide a bit of relaxation, but it's a long way off from reconnecting us with our body, assisting us on the path of self-discovery and paving the way toward authentic change. Stillness is the depth to which a meditation practice must venture. Stillness is the wrench that brings the massive machinery of conditioned reactivity to a grinding halt, which is why it is the catalyst for authentic change.

Chapter Summary Points and Key Takeaways

- *How* you meditate matters. When you practice stillness, you gain access to the transformational quality of meditation.

- Meditation can be conceptualized as a body-based practice rather than a mental exercise. Many of the benefits experienced by meditators can be explained by viewing meditation in this way.

- Practicing stillness involves three aspects: physical, mental, and an internal posture of stillness.

- The body speaks through physical sensation. You can begin listening to and learning the subtle language of sensation when you practice stillness.

Three Ways to Get Started with Practice

1. **Start getting comfortable articulating sensations**. Using the chart provided earlier in the chapter, begin practicing articulating what you feel in your body. Use words from the chart and be careful to describe sensations rather than perceptions and interpretations. For example, tension (sensation) vs. overwhelmed (perception).

2. **Morning breathing**. When you wake up in the morning, before you reach for your phone (or do anything for that matter), take ten deep breaths. This could be the beginning of a consistent meditation practice if you choose to progress toward one and add to your ten breaths. If you're new to meditating, try working with a teacher to get started so you have someone to guide and answer questions.

3. **Invite moments of stillness into everyday life.** Periodically during the day, take a moment to pause and check in with the body. Close your eyes. Focus your attention on the body. Take a few breaths. Notice what it's like to be in your body without trying to change your experience.

Chapter 4
Change through Stillness

"If most of us remain ignorant of ourselves, it is because self-knowledge is painful and we prefer the pleasures of illusion." – Aldous Huxley

"Pain in this life is not avoidable, but the pain we create avoiding pain is avoidable." - R.D. Laing

"The mind's first step to self-awareness must be through the body." - George Sheehan

I'm unsure whether coincidence or destiny inspired my doctoral research on male pornography addiction. From the coincidental standpoint, getting a PhD was the fastest way of getting a visa and living in New Zealand. My son, Jack – less than two years old at the time – needed a father, so no matter how I was going to get it done, I was committed to staying in New Zealand. No boy should grow up without a father. I should know. My dad was there, physically speaking, but he wasn't, as I've learned, what a father figure should be. I've learned and accepted that he did his best, but I'm a different father for my son. That's why I'll always be grateful for the academic studies that allowed me to be Jack's dad.

From destiny's perspective, it seemed fitting to study a behavior I had more than 25 years of personal experience with. I knew that an immersive academic dive into the subject would help me learn, reflect and understand more about my own experiences with porn. It's quite common for researchers to use their doctoral studies as an opportunity to investigate something they are curious about within themselves. This is where the term PhD *me-search* comes from. While studying pornography – scientific studies, not content, allowed me to examine how others experienced it, I was able to inquire about myself concurrently.

As I write this book, there is still no formal recognition of pornography addiction. Instead of identifying themselves as *addicts*, the men who volunteered for my study identified themselves as having a problematic relationship with porn. I was only a boy when I was introduced to porn, so I knew I could relate to the research participants meaningfully. I had walked in their shoes and saw myself in the various struggles they expressed during their interviews. But because moving away from pornography was a mountain I had successfully summited, I knew there was a way out. My experience made it possible to sit with each man unconditionally and non-judgmentally, knowing there was nothing inherently wrong with him.

A combination of life experience, scientific research and great teachers contributed to my understanding of the role of self-soothing behaviors in addiction and problematic use. Every self-soothing behavior – in my case, porn – represents a short-term fix for an uncomfortable emotion or experience. If we've never learned how to acknowledge, accept, manage and respond to challenging experiences – like unwanted thoughts or uncomfortable emotions – then leaning on self-soothing avoidance behaviors becomes habitual, even if the repetitive expression of the behavior comes with its own set of costs. The solution slowly becomes the problem without the conscious mind knowing when or how it happened. More accurately, 'problem' is the label the mind places on the self-soothing behavior.

The real problem lies in the mind's inaccurate perception that there is something wrong with a particular behavior when that behavior is, in actuality, a form of protection. Judging the protector gets us nowhere because we're focusing on the surface level of the issue. No matter how stigmatized, shame-ridden or destructive the behavior is perceived to be, it still originated as a form of protection. It's easier to demonize the behaviors than to recognize that they were once coping mechanisms when no other options were available to us.

For years, I held the belief that *porn is bad*. Without acknowledging and understanding the nuances that contributed to *why* I watched porn, I started to notice shame and guilt flooding my physiology soon after viewing. Judging and shaming myself only reinforced the continuation of the habit because porn was what I invariably leaned on when I felt the full weight of guilt and shame.

I spent my 20s quitting porn. I quit many times. My willpower carried me through several failed attempts. Whether it was three months, six months or sometimes nine, eventually, I broke. Without the necessary self-awareness and resources to manage the painful and uncomfortable experiences which triggered my viewing, porn was what offered me immediate relief from the discomforts of loneliness, fear, anger and stress. It was easy to empathize with the participants of my doctoral study as they shared similar and similarly numerous experiences of 'quitting' porn. There's only so much accumulated stress a body can carry before willpower capsizes and we reach for the only life jacket we have access to.

When the underlying source of our pain and discomfort remains unseen to the conscious mind, the self-soother and protector becomes the villain. To move away from porn, fully and completely, I had to ask myself *why* I was reaching for porn in the first place. It was against the backdrop of stillness that such explorations and reflections were possible.

Stillness broke the cycle of porn viewing that had been stuck on repeat for me since very early childhood. Porn disappeared from my life only when I stopped focusing on it as the problem and turned my attention toward the impulses, cravings, urges and emotions within my body that were triggering the habit. I took my attention away from porn and focused intently on what was happening in the body in the moment of craving and impulse. I turned away from my thoughts and toward my body because thoughts, by their very nature, are a reaction.

When we stay with the body in the moment of trigger, we don't get the mental thoughts, images and words of what we should do in response to the physical sensation and somatic trigger manifesting in the body. Instead, what we get is the *felt experience* of the trigger. It was uncomfortable at first, but each time a trigger was met with stillness, I watched with curiosity as it peaked and eventually passed away. This is the destiny of every sensation, emotion or feeling we ever come into contact with.

I stopped avoiding my discomfort, a key component of moving away from behaviors that no longer serve us. In fact, by going to the source of my pain and staying with the body, I found that the uncomfortable somatic experience almost always passed quite quickly. Had I stayed with the thoughts of porn, however, my mind would have continued ruminating until I eventually succumbed to the overlooked and unattended experiential state within my body.

Over time, triggers became softer, dampened and loosened their grip over decision-making because they weren't being reinforced and maintained by my conditioned thoughts, and eventual use, of porn. Through stillness, the reactive program for porn was slowly getting deprogrammed from my body.

The sacred space created by stillness allowed me to reflect on the situations and circumstances that regularly triggered me to reach for porn. I learned to pause, bring my attention to my body and *feel* what was happening. I'd ask myself questions like: *what am I stressed about? Is there something that's making me angry or upset at this moment? What feeling am I trying to avoid right now?* There was always an answer beneath the surface of the porn craving. There was always a message my body was trying to tell me. At times my body cried, spasmed, tensed, shivered or convulsed as it processed, released and integrated the real pain beneath the surface of conscious awareness. But then the uncomfortable experience passed. It always passed. And so did my craving for porn.

Over time, stillness makes it possible first to notice, and then stop, more significant cyclical patterns in life playing on repeat. For me, I became aware of the self-sabotaging relational pattern that was below the surface of my porn use.

I had started every romantic relationship in my life with an explosion of fireworks. Abstaining from porn was easy when I was high on relationship endorphins. After around six months, however, when the sparks of the honeymoon phase began fizzling out, I was left swimming (more like drowning) in relationship waters that I knew little to nothing about navigating. I didn't know how to communicate, be vulnerable, express boundaries, or assert my emotional needs. I certainly hadn't yet developed the capacity to listen and be present with another person.

When relational stress and conflict invariably arose, I retreated to porn because it was the only thing I knew. I kept my walls up, rebelled, didn't connect, didn't communicate and watched porn as a passive-aggressive form of rebellion (and to soothe my upset) because I didn't know how to communicate and assert my needs within relationship. At any sign of emotional distress, I disconnected and checked out, the same protective process I had used as a child when it wasn't safe to express my emotions.

The break in abstaining from my habit, coupled with the lack of resolution within my relationship, would kickstart the porn cycle that had been dormant for months. Of course, I'd keep my porn use hidden. As a result of my secrecy, trust wavered, connection severed, and resentment spread like a weed through the garden of the relationship.

Rather than facing the problems in communication with whomever I was with at the time, I avoided them by becoming distant and cold. Eventually, I would check out of the relationship and create, consciously or subconsciously, the circumstances that would inevitably bring the relationship to an end. By 30, I had collected seven relationships that followed similar patterns, most ending at, or right before the 2-year mark.

Free from porn, this cycle came into full view. So, too, did the realization that if I wanted to avoid the same trap in relationships moving forward, I had to start learning skills that were like a foreign language to me. At 30, I learned what an emotion is. I learned about boundaries and how to implement them. I learned to say 'yes' when I meant *yes* and 'no' when I meant *no*. I developed the capacity to connect with and articulate my inner world. And when I allowed myself to be vulnerable and practiced sharing my inner experience within safe environments, like magic, the tension and stress from my body washed away. I had thought that connection was forged through physicality and passion. I was so wrong. Vulnerability is the pathway to the most profound connections.

There is nothing inherently wrong with porn in the sense of adults consuming porn produced by and featuring other consenting adults (there are undoubtedly unethical manifestations of pornography, though these conversations are outside the scope of this book). And when I accepted that as truth, my porn use dropped away without having to expend the energy and effort that had characterized previous attempts at quitting. *I just didn't care about porn anymore.*

Every addiction, bad habit or problematic behavior is a symptom of something that goes far deeper. This inspired my desire to help other men struggling with porn, both within my professional work and in my academic research. I am now porn-free not because I consciously willed myself to quit porn but because

I got curious about the situations, contexts and emotions that triggered my use. I stopped avoiding the uncomfortable experiences that were beneath the surface of my behavior.

There is a way out of porn, just as there is a way out of all habits that no longer serve us, but the path doesn't present itself until we realize that the behavior is merely at the surface of a deeper experience and pattern. The problem we are trying to get rid of was once a solution for some other pain or discomfort. When we find and integrate what we've been avoiding, the solution won't be necessary anymore.

Everybody is Doing the Dance

We're all avoiding pain and discomfort. Who isn't running away from an internal state and trying to fix and heal inner turmoil with an endless variety of external *doings?* It's only a lack of self-awareness, an unconsciousness, that prevents us from seeing that those who are shamed, ridiculed and then blamed for their behaviors and predicaments in life are not so different from the person looking back at us in the mirror.

We've grown accustomed to avoiding our problems, distracting ourselves from the bitter truth of the present moment. As a result, we cannot stand the slightest discomfort. We think life is about creating safety and security and pursuing contentment. But life comprises a combination of pleasure and pain, satisfaction and suffering, delight and difficulty. We need both.

By focusing only on comfort, we cut ourselves off from the full range of human experiences, as well as the knowledge, skills and qualities that blossom when embracing the full spectrum of emotions (more on this in a later chapter, *Radical Self-Acceptance*). We prevent ourselves from experiencing the true beauty of life *precisely* because we've cut ourselves off from the other side of the spectrum, the side the mind has deemed uncomfortable, unpleasant and unacceptable. We're never truly at peace because anything that deviates from comfort keeps us in a constant state of agitation.

We are all doing the dance of avoidance. We are doing anything and everything to avoid the dark void that becomes all too palpable and obvious when we stop being busy for more than a moment. If we're trying to create change, especially moving away from a particular behavior, and we focus only on the behavior we use for coping, soothing and avoiding, then we miss the target.

We know we've missed the target because another pops up in its place not long after we ditch the so-called 'problem' behavior. And regardless of the external behavior we use as a substitute, the painful and uncomfortable triggers remain underneath and outside of conscious awareness. The discomfort beneath the surface of the self-soothing behavior allows the dance of avoidance to continue with new dance partners

***

We avoid pain because we don't understand it. Understanding the experience of pain and discomfort more objectively (i.e., focusing on the physiological experience of pain within the body rather than believing the mental stories about our pain) makes it easier for the mind to stop avoiding it at all costs. Understanding pain is essential because if the mind doesn't have buy-in with the process, it won't willingly step aside and allow the body to lean into an uncomfortable experience.

Awareness gives the mind an understanding of what it is ceaselessly attempting to avoid. For that reason, the first step to ending the dance of avoidance is to bring conscious awareness to what's been unconsciously avoided: pain.

Pain is intended to be an output from the brain when the body is in danger. Pain is the near-instantaneous decision only the brain can make after processing all the relevant informational inputs. We can break a bone, sever a nerve or tear a muscle, but we won't experience any pain whatsoever if the brain doesn't interpret the event as dangerous or harmful. Interestingly, a single genetic variant determines whether we perceive any pain at all. While not feeling pain might sound enticing, *Congenital Analgesia*, a rare genetic disease in which a person can't feel physical pain, is dangerous because those who have it can't accurately determine if what they are experiencing is a serious injury or if it requires medical attention.

The biological function of pain is meant to motivate us to act against external threats, regardless of whether that pain is real or imagined. The distinction between real and imagined makes pain a head-scratching concept because it implies that pain is largely a mental perception. Indeed, many spiritual teachers have proclaimed that pain is nothing more than a construct of the mind. To the mystic, pain is an illusion, a label the mind gives to a sensation in the body deemed uncomfortable, unfamiliar or one that we have been conditioned to avoid. Stoic Philosopher Seneca said: *we are more often frightened than hurt, and we suffer more from imagination than reality.* In other words, what we *believe* about pain, whether consciously or unconsciously, impacts how we experience it.

Experiencing pain doesn't necessarily mean that we're hurt or injured. A paper cut may feel immensely painful, but the relative harm caused by a paper cut is almost always minimal. This is because pain involves several interconnected physical, mental and emotional factors.

Recurrent or chronic pain, for example, is often protective in nature and doesn't mean the body is experiencing continuous insult or injury. Additionally, the interplay of the autonomic nervous system (where the fight-flight-freeze response is triggered or overactive), the endocrine system (where excess cortisol or adrenaline is produced, which intensifies the experience of pain), and even the immune system function (which produces high levels of pro-inflammatory metabolites that can be very painful to experience) all contribute to our experience of pain. Other factors that play a role in how we experience pain include increased stress levels, a medical diagnosis, early childhood experiences of pain, and daily movement and activity levels. Our emotional stability and perceived sense of safety within our relationships also influence how we experience and adapt to chronic pain[94].

Whether physical, mental or emotional pain, there is a substantial overlap between how the brain and body process and experience pain[95]. In other words, emotional wounds can *feel* the same as physical pain. Or, as Ancient Greek Comic Poet, Antiphanes, put it: *all pain is one malady with many names.* Broken hearts really do hurt, and being rejected can feel like being punched in the gut. This implies that all pain, regardless of context or source, shares an underlying felt structure within the body[96]. All pain is felt and experienced similarly in the body.

The point is that pain is commonly thought to be merely an impulse that warns us of a threat or harm, but it is not that simple. While something may hurt, it may not necessarily harm the body (for example, our papercut example mentioned above). There's a difference between hurt and harm, and understanding the variables contributing to pain is helpful for learning how to relate to it. This understanding can empower us to choose something other than automatic avoidance. And when we stop avoiding pain, we begin appreciating some of the messages and lessons only pain can teach.

Pain as Teacher

I visited Sri Mooji, a non-duality and self-awareness teacher, during my travels for *A Million Ways to Live*. He was the subject of my episode in Monte Sahaja, Portugal. The first question I asked him was why the path of growth and healing is laden with pain and discomfort. His answer: *pain is an essential part of life*. It may have been an interview, but it seemed as though Mooji's words were meant more for me than my camera given the many pains that I had been experiencing during the filming of my documentary project.

We need pain and suffering to mature as human beings. My lived experience has revealed the truth and validity of this statement. We don't reflect, learn or grow in good times. We don't stop in the middle of having enjoyable sex or a delicious meal and start paying attention to our inner world, questioning life and wondering why we're feeling so great. We don't stop and ask ourselves, *hmmm, what's going on here that's causing me to be so happy right now?* The pain of breakups, job losses and tragedies – coupled with courage – prompts reflection, inquiry and introspection.

We can accumulate knowledge and information about pain, but it's the experience of it that makes pain a great teacher. It's easy to accept literature and teachings on pain at face value. It's a different story when we come into contact with the real experience of pain.

What we *think* about pain fades into the background when we actually *feel* it and our programmed instincts to avoid pain kick in. We can tell ourselves that pain is an illusion as much as we would like, but until we learn how to be with pain and relate to it differently, we will react to it based on our beliefs about pain and the conditioning of our body's nervous system. It's direct experience that transforms information into *wisdom*, knowledge into *knowing*. It was Vipassana that provided that experience for me.

One of the common threads connecting Vipassana meditators, especially the first sittings, is the experience of pain. *A lot of pain*. Pain and discomfort in areas of the body that we would expect to feel after sitting cross-legged for hours at a time. The knees, midback and hips are the usual suspects.

Though meditators are tasked with focusing on the breath as it naturally passes through the nostrils, the mind begins to see how difficult this can be as it becomes increasingly preoccupied with the ever-intensifying aches and pains in the body. The pain becomes so great that many try different ways of diminishing it or buffering against it.

Some jam several small cushions under their knees to keep their knees elevated off the ground. Others stack several cushions under their butt, thinking their backside will be more comfortable this way. Some request a backrest or sit in a chair either because the pain intensifies too much or because of a medical reason. All of these strategies, however, are attempts to escape from pain that is unavoidable, inevitable and, at first, incomprehensible.

Teachers and discourses urged me to accept the pain because it was *just a sensation, nothing more*. The teachings were impossible to believe at first. My first few days of sitting and observing pain in my body were remarkable failures. No matter how many affirmations I mentally rehearsed, the pain only increased with each sitting.

It didn't matter how empathically my mind proclaimed, *this isn't pain. This is just a sensation. This is just an experience my mind is labeling as pain*, it didn't work. They were just words of a mental story my body wasn't buying. My body responded with more tension, avoidance and rejection in relation to the pain. Essentially, I was fighting tension with more tension because my mind was still unequivocally fighting, resisting and avoiding the experience of pain. It was an unconscious reaction that I had no control over.

Then something unexpected happened. After days of sitting, experimenting and observing the petri dish of pain within my body, there came a moment when my mind gave up its efforts to fight, struggle and avoid the pain. My mind accepted the present moment *as it was*. When my mind gave up control, the tension in my body dissolved instantly. The pain vanished. I now *knew* what acceptance *felt* like. Until then, I had only had an intellectual understanding of acceptance. They were just ideas and concepts without the experiential reference point of what acceptance and surrender feel like in the body. They were a story. I needed to experience surrender in the body to understand the word's meaning.

In that moment of pure surrender and acceptance, as if a magician had snapped their fingers, the internal fires of perceived torture were extinguished, replaced with waves of euphoria that rushed and surged through my body. The tension in my hips spontaneously released, allowing my knees to drop lightly toward the floor. My spine straightened without any seeming effort. I felt the muscles of my face soften into a smile I didn't put there. My mind reacted with a single thought of confusion: *What the hell was that?* Insurmountable pain transformed into pure bliss in a single moment. Nothing changed in that moment except how I was *relating* to my pain.

After each session, I would open my eyes and curiously look directly at the parts of my body where I had felt these profound pains. I expected to see a protruding bone given the intensity I had just experienced. Surely with sensations so strong, I would be able to see *some* residual imprint on my physical body. And yet, as soon as I opened my eyes to look, the pain disappeared completely, as if it were never there.

After every course, after countless hours of sitting, my body always feels incredibly spacious, open and relaxed. After each sitting, there's no tension left in my body. It's like a towel being wrung so tightly that every last bit of water squeezes out of it. While my mind was screaming that Vipassana was torture, it was evident that my body welcomed it as a miracle of healing.

***

My experiences during Vipassana can be explained by science, which has revealed some interesting things about meditation and the experience of pain. Meditators experience less pain and demonstrate a greater ability to cope with it[97]. Another study showed that when we turn toward our pain (rather than avoiding it), we experience less of it[98]. Other researchers found that as we learn to observe our experience with a calm acceptance – another way of describing still-ness – our sympathetic nervous system becomes less activated and sensitive[99], and the parts of our brain responsible for regulating and reacting to stress are strengthened[100].

The findings of these studies all contribute to explaining what happened to me during my Vipassana experience. While science offers some insights, I believe my experience with pain is more accurately understood as a result of the altered state of consciousness that meditation can induce. Just when the pain had reached unbearable thresholds, a shift in my consciousness wiped my perceptual slate clean of pain, leaving only the subtle, electric vibrations of the body underneath in its place. This is a common experience reported to me by many of my fellow Vipassana meditators.

I could have read a thousand books about the illusion of pain or altered meditative states and it wouldn't have changed the fundamental conditioning related to how my body reacts to the experience of pain in real-time. I had to jump into the deep end of pain to *know* pain isn't what the mind *thinks* it is.

I had to keep tasting pain and adjusting the internal recipe of how I was relating to it until it tasted just right. I also learned not to automatically trust my mind's initial interpretations of what is being experienced in the body. Seneca's quote – *we are more often frightened than hurt, and we suffer more from imagination than reality* – had transformed from words to embodied wisdom. When it comes to our lived experience, there is more to consider than the mind's story. There is more to consider beyond our fear of pain.

Life has taught me that any time I've stopped dancing around an issue and faced the painful experience with conscious intentionality, I've emerged on the other side with renewed strength, resilience and clarity. Feeling pain is often the indicator that something is shifting. *Pain initiates healing.*

Personal growth always involves some kind of ability to stay with discomfort. It's uncomfortable growing beyond the confines of the shell we live in. It's also uncomfortable taking off our shell and vulnerably exposing ourselves as we find a new and bigger shell to continue our growth. If we need one at all. Whether spiritual or material, facing pain and discomfort is a requisite skill if we want to grow and mature in any aspect of self or life. If pain is truly one of our greatest teachers, I am a devoted student.

Stillness Unravels Reactivity

When pain and discomfort are blindly avoided and intellectually misunderstood, they become the subconscious triggers that catalyze reactivity. Pain and discomfort are the notes in the song that cue the dance of avoidance to continue. Most don't comprehend or appreciate just how strong the impulse for reactivity truly is. A quick exercise demonstrates the strength of the body's automatic reactions.

This exercise is quite simple. Take a reading break and wash your face with some cool water. Use a towel to gently pat dry the face without drying it thoroughly. For this exercise, you won't want your face completely dry. Next, as you return to your reading space, sit in a comfortable position. Set a timer and practice stillness for 5-10 minutes.

You'll notice that with your eyes closed and attention directed inward, you will acutely feel the water molecules on your face drying away. What you'll also notice is that the drying process can be very, very uncomfortable. Notice the body's urge to scratch, wipe or otherwise avoid the experience of water drying on your face. Remind yourself that the intense sensations you may be experiencing are nothing more than evaporation. See if you can stay in the container of stillness to witness what happens after the experience peaks and passes away.

Did you last the whole 10 minutes? It's okay if not because this exercise was intended to provide context, reflection and insight into the strength of conditioned reactivity. If it is this challenging to remain still in response to water drying on the face, imagine the subconscious impulses to initiate and efforts required to resist our automatic reactions and conditioned behaviors.

***

Everyone likes the idea of authentic change. We want to be more present with our partners and children without our minds thinking about work. We want to respond calmly when we get triggered and angry. We want more peace and ease in our everyday relationships. We want to courageously embark on journeys of personal growth and self-discovery. These were all the things I wanted for myself as well, but attentively listening to our partners, being present with children, not reacting to anger and facing our deepest fears invariably require that we learn how to be comfortable with discomfort.

When we set intentions or goals for ourselves and put in place strategies and plans to get there, we have to experience various degrees, layers and flavors of pain and discomfort en route to authentic change. We have to face and move past our programmed reactivity.

If we don't make friends with pain, explore how our body experiences and reacts to it, and get to know it intimately, it will always become the wrench thrown in the gearbox that sabotages movement toward deeper purpose and meaning. We must bring the light of conscious awareness to our subjective experience of pain so that we can learn how to relate to it and subsequently pass through it. Consciously facing discomfort is so important that the next chapter is dedicated to the topic.

Stillness is the birthplace of insights and choices aligned with our conscious intentions. With stillness, we can mindfully reflect, consider and give our bodily intuition a voice to be heard and listened to. This is because the body speaks to us in subtle ways, imperceptible to us because we're constantly on the go and moving.

Stillness is a confrontation with the truth. It is a confrontation with the long-avoided, unwanted and uncomfortable thoughts, emotions and body sensations that trigger our reactive behaviors. These experiences are essential to face and become intimate friends with.

It is often humbling to witness the true extent of the deeply rooted reactivity in our bodies. I was amazed it was even possible to access and be with my impulse to react when I experienced the intensity of it within myself. But, with consistent practice, I learned to observe and unpack moments of reactivity using a steady and consistent application of stillness.

Stillness creates the space between stimulus and reaction that Victor Frankl has famously described as *the space which empowers us to choose growth and freedom*. There is a space between feeling stressed and reaching for porn, between feeling sad and reaching for sugar or a glass of wine, and between feeling pain and reacting with anger. Stillness makes us aware of this space and empowers us to choose a different response. We can choose something different. *We can change*. This is why at the very core of authentic change, we find stillness.

Settling the Snow with Stillness

When I teach clients to meditate, I sometimes use a snow globe as a teaching prop to explain how stillness serves as the catalyst for change. We can't see the object at the center when we shake up a snow globe. Firstly, our eyes can't focus on something when it's being vigorously shaken. But even when the globe stops moving, the view of the centerpiece continues to be blocked by the snow floating in front of it. If we want to see the details of what's inside, we must wait for the snow to settle at the bottom of the globe. Once the snow settles, we can appreciate the intricacies and finer details of the centerpiece. Stillness enables this distinct clarity.

We see and engage with the world like a shaken-up snow globe. The centerpiece of our life's snow globe is the object in front of us. This could be a work project, a meal or a person, such as a stranger, friend, child or spouse. The snow represents the many internal experiences – thoughts, beliefs, emotions and body sensations – that prevent us from seeing what's in front of us with clarity. Instead of seeing what's in front of us, we see our thoughts, beliefs and emotions. We see the snow.

In the world of collectible souvenirs, having an accurate take on the centerpiece is inconsequential. Our life won't be too impacted if we don't notice the hand-painted rails on the Golden Gate Bridge of the snow globe we purchased at the Fisherman's Wharf while visiting San Francisco. In everyday life, however, differentiating between snow and reality has real consequences. If there's a person in front of us that we're trying to listen to, be present with and understand, then snow gets in the way of *seeing* them clearly.

Our thoughts about a person aren't an accurate representation of the person. Several things distort our experience of the person we are in relationship with, such as our memories of and with them. It's why our parents will often, maybe always, speak to and treat us as if we are still young children.

When we rely on our past experiences of another, the mind's assumptions may be inaccurate representations of who and how the person in front of us is showing up in the present moment. Leaning too heavily on assumptions can quickly cause tension, disconnect and conflict in the relationship.

When the body experiences fear, jealousy, sadness or anger when with another person, then too, the mind creates fantasies that don't represent reality. We imagine betrayals, abandonment, affairs, arguments and slights, and then treat the other as if they had already committed the crime. This is how unprocessed traumatic experiences from our past manifest and make themselves known in the present moment. We project an identity onto someone. They then become a living representation of the past hurt. We react as if they are the original players in our past trauma. While this is the mind's attempt to protect us from being harmed again, the result is a failure to see people and situations clearly.

One way of relating to distressing thoughts that *feel* real is to consider them as only a single data point that can help us assess and understand the person or situation in front of us. This means that we don't have to immediately discredit the thought as false (which is admittedly hard to do) and gives us space to assess the situation more deeply. *Is my thought about this person and situation accurate? What is my evidence? Can I ask this person something to help me see things more clearly and accurately? When has my mind been correct about this specific situation and person? What is happening in my body right now that is leading to these thoughts? Are my body's needs for support being projected outward onto the other?* Stillness is the quality that allows the other snowy thoughts to settle so that these thoughts – this reflective process – can occur. With practice, it becomes easier to differentiate what we're imagining to be true from what is really happening.

Snow doesn't just prevent us from seeing the person and situation in front of us, it also prevents us from seeing *ourselves* clearly. The snow blocking the view of ourselves is the beliefs, harsh judgments and criticisms we routinely punish ourselves with. The inner critic seems to always be on the loudspeaker broadcasting messages such as *I'm not smart enough, I don't make or have enough money, I am unlovable, I don't deserve to be happy,* or some other iteration of the Original Sin of limiting beliefs: *I'm not good enough.*

Until we learn how to relate to our beliefs more compassionately (explored in detail in a later chapter, *Radical Self-Acceptance*), the beliefs we hold of ourselves keep us stuck, static and suffocated. Every time we manage to take one small step forward toward our intentions, those limiting beliefs we have of ourselves activate to send us two steps back.

Through the consistent, steady and patient application of stillness, what emerges as the centerpiece of the snow globe is our authentic Self, what we naturally and inherently *are*. Just as the snow globe displays something beautiful to admire, what we find at the core of who and what we are is equally beautiful.

We often don't see ourselves as the complete and whole beings we fundamentally are because snow obstructs the view. We never give the snow a chance to settle because we constantly keep ourselves busy, moving and shaking up our inner worlds, mostly reacting to the snow itself. As we allow those layers and layers of snow to fall to the ground and melt away, we see more and more of our authentic Selves.

***

When we are in a constant state of moving, we end up in relationship with snow, not with the real world. A lifestyle characterized by perpetual busyness means the snow never has a chance to settle. We never get to see ourselves or the world with clarity, free of – or at least freer of – the conditioned perceptions we overlay atop our sensory experience.

On the windy path through change, taking time to create detailed plans and strategies might be worthwhile. However, the cycle of self-sabotage and reactivity continuously repeats without the capacity to become still. These cycles make it seem like a blizzard rather than a few gently falling snowflakes.

Mike Tyson, one of the most famous professional boxers of all time, said it quite poetically: *everyone has a plan until they get punched in the mouth*. Tyson was referring to how quickly reactive conditioning will take over when we get physically stressed or triggered, no matter how well-prepared or planned the mind's strategies might have been.

It's snow that gets in the way of our intentions for change and can feel like the proverbial punch to the mouth. In this sense, stillness provides the practical training ground for rehearsing non-reactive observation of the cravings, urges and unwanted thoughts[101]. Stillness is the preparation for life's punches. And preparing for life's inevitable punches is critical on the path toward change because it's life's punches that trigger habitual reactivity. Regardless of behavior, substance or intention, relapses originate as unpleasant and uncomfortable internal experiences[102].

The discomfort of unwanted thoughts, challenging emotions and uncomfortable sensations automatically trigger the impulse to reach for the self-soothing behaviors and substances that we are most familiar with. Frequently, these are the behaviors that no longer serve us. Even the experience of succumbing to peer pressure – considered an external force – is experienced internally, reinforcing the notion that our relapses originate as sensations in the body. In other words, and in summary, snow triggers relapse.

This is why I chose meditation as the addiction intervention for my pornography research. I anticipated that getting participants to spend time in stillness would help them cultivate a capacity to sit and be with their painful or uncomfortable experience instead of reacting to it[103]. Rather than passing through and out of the discomfort of unwanted thoughts, negative emotions and uncomfortable body sensations, these men reactively turned to porn[104]. I wanted to see what would happen if they gave themselves a chance for the snow to settle. What would happen after? Would they choose a different behavior or response? What insights and responses would replace reactivity? Essentially, I was curious about the possibilities that would arise when compulsive thoughts of porn were given a chance to fall to the ground.

Change requires us to perceive the possibility of choosing something different. We don't *have to* react. We can follow the impulse inwards, back to its origin within the body, only to discover that it's nothing more than a sensation in the body. The mind provides the label, thought, belief, projection and narrative *about the sensation*. The mind tells stories, the body speaks the truth. When we stop believing the story and wait for the impulse within the body and subsequent activation of the nervous system to arise, peak and pass away, the snow settles.

***

Stillness empowers us to choose a different path because it cultivates the fundamental capacity requisite for change: self-awareness. We cannot self-manage, self-regulate or consciously move in any direction without a deep understanding of ourselves and the internal experiences that drive our external way of living. These self-management and self-regulation skills are at the heart of behavioral change[105].

Stillness creates the conditions necessary to choose different ways of responding to impulses toward reactivity[106]. Understanding the specific contexts of our behavior – along with why we use it, when we started, the benefits it gave us then, the challenges that come with it today, and the judgments we hold about it – leads toward permanent shifts rather than fleeting and temporary fixes.

The deeper we look, the more we realize that the uncomfortable experiences we're avoiding and running away from have been there for a very long time. We can prepare the best possible plan alongside the world's most prominent experts, but only a few steps forward through time reveals that the stresses of life prevent us from clearly seeing what's in front of us and responding non-reactively. We react as quickly as we get triggered.

The self-regulation and self-management skills necessary for a life characterized by ease require us to look under the hood of our behaviors to see 'how' and 'why' we operate in the world. If we don't understand ourselves, we're destined to encounter the same pitfalls, wondering *why does this keep happening to me?* I'm not trying to scare but rather to humbly acknowledge the intensity, strength and propensity of the subconscious mechanisms deep within the body that initiate reactivity.

Stillness breeds the kind of wisdom that helps us navigate the challenging terrain of our individual lives. Each person will invariably make their own discoveries through stillness as they engage with the practice. I've shared a few of my discoveries already. Your discoveries will be your own.

With each new layer of meaning and teaching, stillness reveals highly personal and increasingly profound lessons relevant to the uniqueness of our respective lives. Regardless of the specific lesson, there isn't an aspect of life that doesn't benefit from an improved capacity to acknowledge, observe and non-judgmentally accept the present moment.

Ultimately, the journey of stillness helps us take responsibility for the quality of our individual life experience by cultivating a more conscious way of relating to the present moment. It's possible to feel more at home in the direct experience of living, even when the mind tells us that life is messy and challenging. We get there by practicing being in our body in the present moment, without trying to change, control or adjust our experience in any way; watching with an attuned sense of naïve curiosity as the snow settles. While this process requires patience, honesty and courage, it starts with stillness.

Precious Little Moments

While the mind is looking for magnificent, earth-shattering, 'light-shining-down-from-heaven' transformational events as evidence for change, the truth is that change is boringly slow. Examples of these seemingly dull moments include: choosing to meditate in the morning rather than checking our phone's notifications, saying 'yes' when we mean *yes* and 'no' when we mean *no,* or closing the pantry and walking away when we feel stress, boredom or agitation in the body. Change happens gradually over time, alongside seemingly small momentary decisions. I witnessed this gradual process of change play out in relation to my inability to trust women.

Relationships are built on trust. While my mind wanted to believe that it trusted the woman I was with, whenever I got triggered in contexts and situations that activated fear, insecurity and jealousy, my body let me know that trust was clearly *not* present. I *believed* the fear-based thoughts of cheating, dishonesty and abandonment that my mind conjured and reacted to them as if they were real.

Sometimes I'd check a partner's phone as I searched for evidence to confirm my neurotic suspicion or punish her with passive-aggressive words and actions as if she had already been caught. It was strangely fascinating to observe my mind *seeking* confirmation of mistrust and thus pain. Mistrust was my mind's default and what it had learned from the scripts propagated by mainstream pornography. The state of mistrust was my mind's safe space, where it felt comfortable and in control, but I wanted something different regarding how I related to women.

The body doesn't lie, and it showed me how often I wasn't trusting within relationship. I began working with my inability to trust in the same way I had approached my use of porn: one moment at a time. Seeing my partner on her phone was one of the instances that would routinely trigger tension in my body. My mind created stories about whom she was talking to and what she was saying.

In moments when I could have checked without anyone in the world knowing – like when she was in the shower – I developed my trusting muscle by sitting with the fear and discomfort of the unknown contents of her phone. Despite the immense impulse in my body urging me to check and satiate an inner need for *knowing*, I showed myself there was a different way of being. In a single moment, I changed my destiny with a small dose of stillness.

In these precious yet seemingly inconsequential moments – when no one is watching and no one will know – we can choose a different belief. We can choose a different way of being and move down the path toward freedom. I had to *choose* not to believe my distressing thoughts of, and intense emotions associated with, cheating, as well as the narratives I had acquired from a combination of life experience and mainstream porn. Every time I resisted the urge, I changed. Just like porn, the impulse softened over time.

It should be noted here that learning how to trust was made easier because, objectively speaking, there wasn't a shred of evidence against my partner that my mind could use to prove the distressing narratives true. In my case – and every case is different – my strong emotions expressed a different reality than my gut instinct, intuitive sense and external world. Learning to differentiate between strong emotions and sensations and the 'knowingness' provided by intuition is one of the subtle skills we can only learn when we are connected with the body.

Through stillness, my understanding of trust evolved as well. I learned that trusting others doesn't have to rely on their actions. When trust is dependent on the behavior of others, it can be a subtle way of masking subconscious attempts to control. Trust in this sense is like saying, *I expect you will always act in a way that will be in my best interests.* The more I sat with myself in moments of a trigger, the more I realized that it was *in myself* that I had to learn to trust.

Trust became the practice of sitting with the discomfort of the unknown, showing the part of me that was scared that it was safe and okay. That very young part – the inner child – deeply feared abandonment and believed that he wasn't good enough. That part needed to be shown that he would be fine no matter the challenges or obstacles life presented us. In those moments, I had to be present and available to him.

We can meditate, practice and prepare for countless hours. We can even surround ourselves with teachers, guides, experts and coaches. We can put thought, effort and intention into our strategies for change and print out, laminate and place notes throughout our surrounding environment. But when it comes down to it, change happens, slowly and incrementally, in tiny little moments. It 's *only* in the moment when actual change can occur.

There's no other time that change is possible because strategies, plans and intentions occur in the mind. Change isn't real at that point. Change doesn't happen in the mind. Until the change occurs in real-time, within the body, it's merely a thought.

Authentic change can only occur at the experiential level, in the body. And there is only one moment in which change can happen: *when we are triggered.* It's not until we are triggered and *feel* the uncomfortable impulse to react in old habitual and reactive ways that we are gifted with an opportunity to choose a different path. In the moment of a trigger, we can diverge from a programmed destiny and move toward a conscious choice.

Change comes down to a single moment. Magic happens when we begin unpacking those moments of change. First, we might notice an uncomfortable impulse in the body. We then meet the impulse with an embodied sense of surrendered stillness. Next, we get curious and lean in instead of running away. There might be some pain or discomfort. Okay, I won't lie. There *will be* discomfort. Instead of believing the automatic thoughts, which is the snow in our snow globe, we introduce a new solution: staying with the feeling.

When we don't follow the path of reactivity, we are humbled by the strength and intensity of the reactive impulse. It's unpleasant to step in front of a physiological wave of chemicals, hormones and activated neuronal pathways. The wave of feeling may intensify, but eventually, and always, it passes. All of us can reflect on this within our own lives and notice how nothing, and no part of our lives, has ever stayed the same. The same is true of the experiences in our bodies. Our stillness practice will always remind us of this fact.

While these moments of change can seem small, they are truly precious. Small moments that the mind considers to be insignificant change our destiny. Small shifts and deviations slowly unravel subconscious and deeply ingrained habits and patterns. A new future of possibility emerges.

Change is also a less daunting endeavor when we approach it moment by moment, one potential moment of change at a time. It's the slow, gradual and patient process of tiny changes that makes the overall change authentic and permanent. And when we connect with and pay attention to the experience within our body, we will see that these precious little moments of change are available to us and happen all the time. Every detail we notice is a piece of the self-awareness puzzle that helps us cultivate an understanding of ourselves.

While these moments may feel small, our choices in these moments are the first sentences of a new life story. One small decision breaks a cycle and creates a new possibility. This is the birthplace of authentic change, the accumulation of precious little moments of change that cumulatively create permanent shifts. Everything else is just mind games.

Chapter Summary Points and Key Takeaways

- Everyone is avoiding pain and discomfort in their own unique, individual way.

- When looking to change a behavior, don't judge the behavior. Look beneath the surface and explore *why*. Seek to understand, experientially and intellectually, the context that makes the behavior continue.

- The experience of pain largely depends on many internal and external environmental contexts that influence whether – and how intensely – we experience pain.

- Stillness settles the snow of the mind. When the snow – perceptions, emotions and sensations – settles and passes away, we can *see* what's in front of us more clearly.

- Change happens over time. Precious little moments of change may not be what the mind considers change, but they accumulate over time to create a new reality.

Three Ways to Get Started with Practice

1. **Establish a consistent stillness practice**. Whether it's 30, 15 or 5 minutes, practice being still daily. Remember that stillness isn't intended to be a check-the-box item, but rather practicing a different way of being.

2. **Unpack a reactive behavior**. Spend time reflecting on one behavior you want to move away from or change. Write an answer to some of the following questions: *When did I start? What feelings does it help me manage? What are the everyday contexts that trigger that behavior? What resources could I lean on other than this behavior to achieve the same relief?*

3. **Acknowledge a moment of small, incremental change.** No matter how big or small, celebrate yourself when you notice a precious little moment of change.

Chapter 5

Conscious Discomfort

"What if pain - like love - is just a place brave people visit?"
- Glennon Doyle Melton

"He who is not every day conquering some fear has not learned the secret of life." - Ralph Waldo Emerson

"Discomfort is the price of admission to a meaningful life"
- Susan David

It's one thing to be scared and quite another to be aware, present and attentive to fear as it courses through the body. My first conscious confrontation with fear, and the pain and discomfort that accompany it, was at the age of nine. It wasn't the first time I felt fear, but it was the first time I leaned into and curiously surrendered to it.

I was lying in bed trying to fall asleep when I started ruminating on thoughts about death and dying. As my mind imagined what dying might be like, it wasn't until I began thinking about *how long* death would last – *forever* – that my body had an intense visceral response.

The prospect of being dead for an infinite amount of time triggered a contraction deep in the pit of my belly. As if I had been punched in the stomach, fear sucked the air out of my body. The abstract conceptualization of infinity scared me to the point of crying. My body convulsed as I felt the full force of fear surge through it. Subconscious avoidance instincts quickly kicked in. I rolled over in bed and tried to distract myself from the terrifying cognition of infinite nonexistence. Avoidance is, after all, the most popular coping strategy.

I was about to turn on the TV to distract myself further. Instead of watching cartoons, however, I rolled back over. Something, or some part of me, felt called to return to my exploration and face my fear. Curiosity got the best of me. I allowed my body to fall back into a state of stillness. I gave my mind permission to continue unpacking the petrifying thoughts of death. As expected, fear seized my body again. My breathing became jagged and staggered. The flow of tears streamed down my cheeks again. This time I didn't roll over and distract myself. I didn't turn away.

I chose to stay with my mind's perception of the terrifying endlessness of death. The second time was painful but not as bad as the first gut shot. I remember finding it strangely satisfying to notice fear expressing itself through my body.

I question whether I was unintentionally cultivating masochistic tendencies. I don't think that was the case because I didn't enjoy the fear, pain and discomfort I encountered. I didn't then, and I don't now. Pain and discomfort aren't pleasant experiences. They're not meant to be. What overwrote my instinct to avoid fear was a deep sense of curiosity for what was on the other side of the experience.

Leaning into discomfort, instead of turning away from it, was either an inherent personality characteristic I was born with or something I developed myself over time. Regardless, the conscious choice to lean into pain is what empowers us to live a life of meaning. Indeed, *leaning in* is the quality required for reconnecting with the body and doing the deepest aspects of inner work.

Maybe my early experience set the stage for a life of bold, sometimes risky, experimentation because facing fear became a ritualistic part of my life. I learned how to feel fear and do something with conscious intentionality. I still remember a mantra from my early teenage years: *fuck it. I'm going to die anyway. Let's do this*. I never stopped living by those words. Some of the best and worst decisions of my life resulted. Regardless of the outcome, there was always a lesson to be learned.

If we intend to avoid pain and discomfort at all costs, we also choose to renounce the experiences that make life worth living. The surest way to prevent a broken heart is to avoid putting it on the line by falling in love. The easiest way to avoid failing at a business venture is to avoid pursuing it altogether. We won't have to feel uncomfortable exploring foreign lands and cultures if we never leave our hometown. But staying in a bubble to inoculate ourselves from the unavoidable fear, pain and discomfort in this life requires a lot of effort and will be unsuccessful.

We'll still encounter fear and discomfort whether we play it safe in our hometown or explore the farthest edges of the world. The difference is whether our experience is rooted in reactivity and fear avoidance, or a conscious choice. In other words, we get to choose the ground where we experience fear, pain and discomfort.

Facing discomfort is also an essential step to becoming *Somawise*, becoming attuned with and sensitive to our body's experiences and understanding the message the body is trying to tell us. As we learned in a previous chapter, pain is a great teacher. While reconnection with the body allows for the experiences of authentic peace, happiness and joy, it also means letting uncomfortable experiences in. We can't have one without the other.

It's the seeking of pleasure alone and the avoidance of pain and discomfort that shuts off the body's capacity for feeling anything at all. The result is a limited experience of life because, in that case, our conscious mind only perceives the extremes of the body's experience. Everything in the middle, aka life, we become numb to. Often, the only emotional states able to break through the barricade between the felt sense and conscious awareness are the intense expressions of anger, sadness and panic.

Reconnecting with the body is an uncomfortable process. That's because when we reconnect with the body, we begin to feel. We feel *everything*. We feel everything *more*.

This is because meditative stillness allows individuals to be more sensitive to their surroundings[107], specifically improving sensitivity to internal and external environments[108]. However, when the shell of protection comes off and sensitivity increases, it takes time for our new skin to acclimate to its new sensitivity and surroundings.

Once acclimatized, however, we enjoy an enhanced capacity for information gathering, developing insights and adapting to the ever-changing variables of life[109]. Moreover, we open ourselves up to finally being able to savor the positive emotions and experiences that have previously seemed just out of reach.

Of course, relating to pain and discomfort as a close friend is easier said than done. The process requires immense amounts of patience, acceptance and surrender. But what provides the mind the evidence it needs to convince it to step aside and let the process of healing happen is the knowledge that pain in this life is inevitable.

Pain and discomfort are universal and inescapable. What we do have control over is the choice of how we face and relate to pain and discomfort. Like meditation, *how* we practice is more important than the practice itself. Pain and discomfort, too, can be met with the quality of stillness.

Consciously facing discomfort turns the intellectual concept and trendy buzzword of acceptance into something palpable and real. The practice of meeting discomfort with stillness gives us an experiential reference point to use in everyday life. We can determine for ourselves, as if our bodily experience is a litmus test, whether we are genuinely in a state of acceptance or if the mind is fooling us. We will *know* what acceptance *feels* like in our bodies.

The mind can say the word as often as it would like, but the body doesn't lie. When we accept something, the body is relaxed and isn't resisting the experience. Tension is absent.

Learning how to relate to discomfort is an essential prerequisite for authentic change. Choosing to be ourselves, choosing authenticity, is an uncomfortable process. As a result of our choice to consciously face discomfort, we build the resilience that helps us meet the stresses of everyday life and move toward a life of meaning and purpose. This chapter is an invitation to *practice* feeling uncomfortable.

Conscious discomfort practices address the big picture that is our life. Conscious discomfort teaches us that it's possible to turn toward and lean into our discomfort instead of avoiding it. If we want to influence and impact some of our most deeply rooted conditioning and how our nervous system has been programmed, then the path forward is one where we are willing to curiously and objectively observe the complex phenomenon of pain and discomfort within the framework of our respective bodies.

Those few moments of perceived suffering are the nurturing soils for confidence, patience, focus, fearlessness and surrender. In this sense, conscious discomfort makes the rest of our life easier. While the confrontation with pain and discomfort is not always easy, the relaxation and peace that follow provide the experiential wisdom that demonstrates that conscious discomfort works.

Let's Get Funcomfortable

While Vipassana provided my comprehensive introduction to the world of pain and discomfort, many practices assist us in developing the capacity to face, embrace and explore discomfort. Conscious discomfort practices bring our conscious awareness to the internal states of tension, agitation and discomfort that we've subconsciously been numbing, sedating, repressing or avoiding. With conscious discomfort, we tune into the uncomfortable experiences arising within the body instead of attempting to tune out.

The trickiest part of conscious discomfort is convincing the mind to relax, accept and surrender amidst the bombardment of protesting thoughts. It requires a connection with the body to assess, calibrate and meticulously recalibrate how we relate to discomfort as it arises in the present moment. When we are in the midst of an ice bath and the sensations of intense cold rush through the body, staying connected to the body is the key to not experiencing overwhelm or immediately jumping out of the cold water. Connected to the body, we can observe the body's response, watch our breath, and calmly wait for the initial wave of the cold exposure experience to pass. For those who may already hear protests in their mind, here's the anchor for the mind to help settle its hesitancy: *conscious discomfort practices are healthy for the body.*

No matter how much the mind may initially scream out in fear, science has provided robust evidence for the following practices' capacity for healing the body, making it stronger, supporting mental health and building resilience against stress.

The concept of *hormetic stress* explains the physiological health benefits of conscious discomfort. The phenomenon of hormesis, whereby small amounts of a potentially-harmful stimulus are applied to positively impact one's health and lifespan, is well documented[110]. Conscious discomfort triggers the body's natural recovery mechanisms, improves the healthy functioning of recovery systems[111], and increases antioxidants and oxidative stress protective mechanisms[112]. Hormesis explains why children who play in dirt, mud and sand have healthier immune function compared to those who grew up in sterile environments. The low-grade hormetic stress on the immune system provides precisely what a developing body needs to build robust immunity.

It's possible to allow just enough stress to elicit a healthy and adaptive response while not enough to injure or harm. The phrase "the dose makes the poison" – coined by 16th-century chemist and physician Paracelsus – sums up the difference between the beneficial and deleterious effects of a stimulus, activity or substance. We need little doses of hormetic stress to throw the mind and body out of balance to build physical, mental and emotional resilience as it moves back toward homeostasis. As a result of this process, our stress threshold grows wider and we become capable of facing stress more calmly.

Conscious discomfort is Funcomfortable. Yes, conscious discomfort practices can be *fucking* uncomfortable at first, but they can also be fun. Conscious discomfort gets easier as we learn to accept and settle into our experience. Over time, and after consistent practice, conscious discomfort can begin to feel normal, natural and, yes, even fun.

Conscious discomfort is an intimate confrontation with fear, pain and discomfort. We get to consciously explore these states, see how the body experiences them, and observe the thoughts that arise alongside their expressions. Then we learn how to settle into discomfort without avoiding it, befriending it so it doesn't subconsciously control us. Conscious discomfort is an opportunity to reflect and learn about the finer details and nuances of our reactivity and programming.

The following are the stable of conscious discomfort practices that have supported my journey of becoming more comfortable in my skin: *Thermal Stress Exposure, Yin Yoga, Fasting, Breathwork* and *Ayahuasca*. This list is anything but comprehensive or exhaustive, not just for me but also for conscious discomfort practices in general. These are just the evidence-based and scientifically backed conscious discomfort practices I have regularly experienced significant changes from.

As conscious discomfort is an experiential journey more than merely intellectual stimulation, remember that *how* we practice is as important as the practice itself. The invitation is to embrace stillness and cultivate acceptance as we practice. White-knuckling through an experience indicates we're not developing an internal capacity to observe our discomfort objectively. Embody the quality of stillness. Trust the body. With that, let's get *funcomfortable*.

Thermal Stress Exposure (TSE)

Throughout our millions of years of evolution, our primate ancestors had to endure physiologically demanding stressors – such as extreme hot and cold temperatures – as part of everyday life. Times have changed. Central heating and air-conditioning ensure that our home temperature never strays into even remotely uncomfortable territories. While it's human nature to seek comfort, this lack of thermal exposure might be more detrimental to the body than the discomfort we've sought to avoid.

Thermal Stress Exposure (TSE) involves embracing brief changes and disruptions to the body's homeostasis that contribute to overall health and wellbeing. TSE practices take advantage of the body's natural reaction to temperature changes to make it more resilient. TSE practices – like ice baths, cold showers, saunas and geothermal spas – increase the body's capacity for managing physiological stresses and life's many other challenges.

Ice baths have been used for thousands of years for various health concerns. Russians, Scandinavians, Finns and even the Japanese still practice 'polar bear plunges' to improve circulation and help fight fatigue. The world can thank Wim Hof, internationally known as The Iceman, for the revitalization of research into the field of TSE, namely cold exposure. Hof has garnered international attention for his seemingly-superhuman ability to withstand freezing temperatures.

While I celebrated my summit of Mount Kilimanjaro on the 6th day of a guided trek, it was Hof who leisurely summitted the tallest free-standing mountain on Earth in two days wearing nothing more than a pair of shorts and hiking boots. When researchers stopped dismissing Hof's abilities as scientifically impossible, they began unearthing the physiological mechanisms that made such feats possible. To various degrees, everyone can activate the very same physiological mechanisms.

When first moving to New Zealand from the perpetual summer of Santa Monica, California, I found myself bedridden with a cold four times in six months. My body and its immune system weren't ready for the drastically different and constantly changing weather patterns of Auckland, a stark contrast for this Californian. To train my body to adapt to temperature shifts, I was led down the path of contrast therapy, which combined cold showers with a sauna. My cold showers eventually evolved into daily at-home 'chest-freezer-turned-ice-bath' dips.

My efforts were met with immediate results: I stopped getting sick. TSE practices soon became, and continue to be, an essential part of my holistic wellbeing routine. Anyone can experience the benefits of ice baths and cold showers. Unless someone has preexisting heart problems or plans on taking an extended nap in the ice bath (thus inducing hypothermia due to overexposure to the cold), most people can safely 'enjoy' ice baths and cold showers as an effective conscious discomfort practice.

Aside from the physiological benefits (there are many), one of the gifts of cold exposure is the opportunity to explore challenging emotions, namely fear. I'm surprised at the palpable levels of fear I continue to feel in the moments leading up to chilly dips. The hardest part of ice baths continues to be the moments *before* submerging.

Sometimes I find myself folding laundry, putting away equipment in my home gym or trying to find the perfect song on Spotify to temporarily postpone the inevitable plunge. But what a beautiful opportunity this is to acknowledge, face and fully embrace fear and angst as they arise, peak and pass away within the body.

I never expected cold water to provide the laboratory for examining emotional states, especially the ones that often hold people back from being authentically themselves. This is also why many of my clients invariably end up in an ice bath after some convincing. Before many courageously take a cold dip, I have to spend some time convincing the voice in their head screaming '*hell no!*' to try one by first explaining the many benefits of cold exposure.

While the mind is preoccupied with fear-laden thoughts moments before submerging into the icy water, it quickly forgets that a few conscious moments of chilly discomfort increase the production of anti-inflammatory mediators, help regulate chronic inflammation – one of the primary factors in autoimmune diseases such as diabetes, MS and psoriasis – and suppress an overactive immune system[113].

When the initial shock of the cold hits the body and we instinctively gasp for air, our blood vessels constrict in unison and pump vital nutrients and oxygen throughout the body. This process simulates a pumping action for the circulatory system and helps flush metabolic waste out of the body. This circulatory pump helps flush the stagnant fluids in the lymph nodes since the lymphatic system has no contractile properties to initiate such an action. As the cold immersion continues with waves of tingling and prickling sensations rushing over the skin, the immune system is bolstered with increased production of white blood cells[114] and cancer-fighting cytotoxic T-cells and NK cells[115].

As the body settles into the chilly water and we begin noticing how the mind interprets sensations of cold, the body is activating and producing brown fat[116], a type of fat that generates heat, which helps burn fat and supports a healthy metabolism. When we emerge from an ice bath with red-tinged and taut skin and a whole-body electric buzz, the sympathetic nervous system has released powerful endorphins and catecholamines such as noradrenaline, which has been boosted by up to 530 percent[117]. When these neurotransmitters flood the nervous system, they reduce feelings of pain, sharpen our mental focus and improve our mood[118]. This is why people with chronic pain use ice baths and cold therapy to manage their pain symptoms.

Finally, when we can observe our cold plunge with stillness, we consciously stimulate the *Vagus Nerve*[119]. The Vagus Nerve, one of the vital cranial nerves of the body's nervous system, connects to many body systems and helps the body switch back and forth between the flight-or-fight response and the more relaxed parasympathetic mode. Stimulating the Vagus Nerve can treat many signs, symptoms and diseases related to systemic inflammation[120].

The cold temperature triggering the body's parasympathetic mode makes everything else we face during the rest of the day easier to respond to and manage. Knowing that we've successfully faced and overcome a challenge also leads to a cascading release of opioids, cannabinoids and neurotransmitters that further enhance the feelings of wellbeing.

Cold exposure furthermore serves as a playground for exploring uncomfortable emotions and insights that can be applied to everyday life. To illustrate this,

I'll share my own experience of cold exposure. When my body is exposed to the shock of the cold, it experiences a rush of fear and angst. The mind automatically tries to identify something as the source or cause of the fear and panic induced by the cold.

Since I've already convinced my mind that my body is safe within the confines of my ice bath, the only thing my mind can attach these sensations to at this moment are the bits of ice harmlessly floating in the vicinity of my neck. And so, during my first few ice baths, my mind perceived these tiny bits of ice as murderous daggers about to slice or impale my throat. I pushed them aside in reaction to my thoughts, even though the ice posed no danger as they harmlessly floated in the water. The ice was the external object my mind could attribute to the fear and panic in my body.

A profound lesson emerged with this seemingly insignificant moment of ice floating around my neck. I laughed in the ice bath because I realized this same dramatization must also happen in other life contexts. The mind tirelessly and endlessly seeks to find external explanations and reasons for an experiential phenomenon that is purely internal. Essential to practicing cold exposure then is adopting a *witness mindset*, aka stillness, where we watch and observe our reaction.

I've used this insight as evidence and as a reminder during moments in my life when flooded with thoughts that don't have any substantive real-world evidence. The mind will *always* try to find the source of the body's discomfort by looking outwards. Unfortunately, this assessment isn't always accurate. When emotions like jealousy, anger, sadness, fear or insecurity have us pointing a finger in blame, the cold can serve as a beautiful reminder to own our experience without immediately projecting discomfort externally.

Cold exposure is only half of the TSE equation. When we challenge the body with heat exposure, we begin to unlock the body's healing processes in different ways. There are few things more invigorating than a healthy sweat in a sauna. Again, and like ice baths, the mind may not like sitting in the discomfort of the heat. However, the body's response to gentle, persistent heat is well-documented throughout history, both in terms of traditional cultures and scientific literature[121].

Saunas, one of the ways to consciously expose the body to therapeutic heat, don't just feel good as our body tension releases and we relax, sauna bathing also flushes toxins out of the body and aids recovery after exercise via sweating and detoxification processes, improves brain function and may even represent a preventative practice against neurodegenerative disorders like Alzheimer's Disease and dementia[122]. The deep sweating characteristic of sauna sittings also cleanses the skin, helps the body fight illness by substantively inducing an artificial fever, and induces deep therapeutic sleep[123].

Sauna bathing can be conceptualized as the yang to the Yin of ice baths. By practicing both, we experience the complementary therapeutic benefits of both worlds. It's when we combine and contrast hot and cold TSE practices that we experience collective benefits greater than the sum of the two individual parts.

The body's circulatory systems benefit from the alternating experiences of constriction and dilation, with the cold moving the blood and nutrients from the extremities to the core. At the same time, the heat helps move blood, oxygen and nutrients away from our body's center, thus cleaning out the core.

The contrasting hot environment creates a physiological pumping action that promotes detoxification, circulation and lymphatic drainage. When combined, TSE practices come with many real-world benefits, like decreasing the number of sick days taken from work, improved self-perceived quality of life, and work productivity[124]. Whether it's cold or heat (or both), TSE practices tap into the body's natural and innate capacities without the common side effects associated with pharmaceutical drugs[125].

For those new to TSE practices like cold showers, ice baths or sauna bathing, it's best to start slow and gradually move toward more intense and demanding environments. Remember that the intent is to remain calm, keep the breath flowing freely, and embody the quality of stillness.

The intention is to really sink into the moment, allowing the eyes to close and resting our attention in the body so we can observe how the body responds to these temperatures. We don't have to fight the experience of cold by tensing the body or constantly fidgeting and adjusting away from the heat or cold. We can relax into the experience and remind ourselves that it only lasts for a few seconds or minutes.

Yin Yoga

We've become so accustomed to the perpetual state of doing, that sitting and relaxing usually involves endless scrolling on a smartphone. However large or small, essential or useless, we desperately fill any available gaps of time to maintain a constant state of busyness. As much as we think we want to unwind and rest, even the smallest doses of inactivity are viscerally uncomfortable, so we reach for some form of self-soothing stimulation. Over time this go-go-go way of being becomes physically, mentally and emotionally exhausting.

As a much-needed and stark contrast to constant activity, Yin yoga can help restore equilibrium to the intimate relationship between the physical, mental and emotional aspects of ourselves. Yin yoga involves more prolonged, gentler and sustained stretches that activate the body's restorative parasympathetic nervous system, responsible for digestion, eliminating toxins, healing and repair, and it helps alleviate psychological problems such as stress, anxiety and depression[126]. The profound physical benefits of Yin yoga include more than lengthening connective tissue, increasing flexibility and improving circulatory function. Yin yoga poses, however, stretch more than just the superficial layers of the body's muscle tissues. To truly appreciate how Yin yoga benefits the body, we must briefly visit the fascinating world of *fascia*.

Fascia is a system of connective tissue that runs throughout the body and wraps all our muscles, internal organs and joints. The primary functions of fascia are related to movement. Fascia transmits muscle forces throughout the body, coordinates complex movement, plays a crucial role in positioning the body in space and holds us together so that we can communicate and live independently[127]. The intricate fascial web of inseparable interconnections allows athletes, dancers and performers to move their bodies gracefully and powerfully in seemingly impossible ways as a single, connected whole.

It's within this system of fascia that Yin yoga truly displays its magic. Fascia doesn't stretch because it's made mostly of collagen fibers. Instead, it responds to how the body regularly moves or doesn't. When our body does one thing repetitively and over time, like sitting at a desk, the fascia adapts to this environment to help the body maintain its shape. It's a bit of a double-edged sword.

On the one hand, the body adapts to its external environment, making it more energy efficient. In terms of sitting, the body doesn't have to expend energy to stay in a seated upright position as the hardened fascia holds the body in place. On the other hand, the body's improved ability to sit invariably means it's not ideally prepared for other movements and positions. When we abruptly stand, run or stretch, the adjusted shape of the fascia can make it a difficult or painful experience. Minor injuries might result, such as slight strains and tears.

In addition to moving our bodies regularly, Yin yoga gently changes the shape of our fascia by lengthening it because we must use greater ranges of motion in Yin postures than in everyday life. Profound changes occur as the fascia is stimulated and manipulated during long Yin poses, creating an improved circulatory flow through the body that makes us feel more spacious and well. In essence, we are making our body more responsive and capable of handling our life's many diverse movements.

While the traditional mechanistic model of anatomy has suggested that fascia, and its functions, is solely proprioception and movement-related, emerging science is equally inspiring and confusing. It seems that fascia may additionally play a crucial role in immune function. A significant component of the body's immune response takes place in the fascia as the initial immune system defense mechanism is a more generalized response in which the area of infection is isolated in the fascia. Compromised fascia – such as when fascial tissue is dehydrated, chronically exposed to any form of stress or stiff due to a sedentary lifestyle that lacks varied movement patterns – can lead to a weakened immune system response[128]. Fascia's overarching role in immune function might also be related to maintaining an optimal lymphatic fluid flow throughout the body, which is hindered when fascia becomes stiffened or hardened. We are only beginning to scratch the surface of why it is so vital to maintain healthy and hydrated fascia.

Fascia may also contribute to mental and emotional states, as a dysfunction within the fascial system perpetuated in everyday movements stimulates emotionality[129]. In other words, hardened and compromised fascia could reinforce positions and postures of the body, such as a slouched and rounded back, that are associated with low mood, low self-confidence and low self-esteem[130]. This means that the state of our fascia impacts how we *feel*.

The fascial web is one of the potential sites in the body where implicit memories might be mechanically, chemically, neuronally or energetically embedded or stored in the body[131]. If the body is indeed our subconscious mind (see *Introduction: The Wise Body – Who's in Control?*), and we do store our experiences in the fascia of our body, then there are therapeutic implications for accessing, recalling and processing such memories through activities such as Yin yoga.

Yin yoga provides a safe environment for the body to move through poses that stimulate and manipulate the fascia through broad ranges of motions that could trigger memories to resurface to conscious awareness. This phenomenon seems plausible because when someone experiences something traumatic in their lives, this impacts their thoughts, movements and behaviors as they attempt to protect themselves from further exposure to pain. For example, if touch to a specific part of the body activates a conditioned self-protective reaction, then that body might adopt positions, postures, movements and, indeed, an entire lifestyle, that prevents this part of the body from being exposed to touch. Over time, these attempts at physiological protection could manifest as unique adaptations within the fascial network that emerge as an outward expression of posture or movement pattern. We subconsciously sacrifice our body's range of motion to protect ourselves from experiencing pain buried in our body's fascia.

When Yin yoga stretches access deeply rooted tensions within the fascial network, it could trigger the neurophysiological pathways for recalling memories that daily movement patterns protected against accessing in everyday life. This phenomenon explains the common scenario of individuals in a Yin yoga class experiencing sudden waves of grief, sadness and tears. These moments of intimate connection with deeper aspects of the body can be profoundly therapeutic as the body integrates and releases the energetic signature (i.e., the sensations, emotions and felt experience attached to the memory) without the mind's reactivity interfering with the release.

While Yin yoga may seem gentle, I quickly realized why it qualified as a conscious discomfort practice when I was introduced to it. As the body is marinating in releasing postures, the mind is allowed to face two of its greatest discomforts: stillness and silence. Only by slowing down can we begin to appreciate how such a seemingly calm and restorative practice can help us consciously embrace discomfort. When we become silent and still, what we've been running from and avoiding comes to meet us. When our eyes are closed and our external doings come to a halt, the mind becomes acutely aware of its inner world. When we gaze inwardly for the first time, it's common to encounter tension, agitation and discomfort.

My introduction to Yin yoga was accompanied by the realization that I couldn't settle into a sense of stillness. Being in my body for more than a few breaths was too uncomfortable. Jolted and agitated thoughts kept my body in a constant state of fidgeting and adjusting away from the cascade of uncomfortable sensations that arose in my body. It took several classes to notice that the angry, judgmental thoughts directed at the Yin yoga teacher, whomever it might have been at the time, were merely outward expressions of the tension within my body.

To help with my intention of disconnecting from mental stories, Yin yoga provided me with an effective tool: the breath. Slow, deep and conscious breaths are a key component of Yin yoga practice because breathing provides the mind something to focus on when it invariably becomes swept away by thoughts or entangled by challenging body sensations and emotions.

When we notice the mind getting distracted, we can gently refocus and anchor our attention to the breath. When we observe physical sensations, those stories that have outlived their usefulness begin to unravel and lose their grip on our identity. It costs the body a lot of energy to keep stories going and emotions suppressed, so the release we feel from letting it all come up can be just as big as the effort to hold it all in.

Yin yoga is arguably one of the best practices for reconnecting to the body. It serves as the training ground for cultivating *interoception* (see *The Wise Body – The Body Speaks the Truth*) and body awareness. Through the practice, we tune into our inner workings, connecting to respiratory and circulatory functions, internal organs and sensations within the muscles and joints. When we allow ourselves to stay present and experience the subtle, nearly imperceptible shifts that occur while holding a Yin yoga pose, we improve our ability to understand the body's language of sensations. This heightened awareness of physiological processes and body sensations helps cultivate a greater capacity for self-awareness. Like with meditation, we become better at detecting subtler changes to mental and emotional states before they reach levels that make them harder to regulate.

Yin yoga taught me to be gentle with and nonreactive to my arising experience. It continues to soften me. Through Yin yoga's gentle movement and invitation for profound stillness, trapped energy has regularly bubbled up to the surface of my conscious awareness. I've then learned to acknowledge, accept and ultimately release it.

My practice prompted reflective processes around how I relate to my present moment experience. *Am I meeting my body where it's at, or am I forcing it? Why do I judge myself when my body can't reach a specific angle or posture? Where is my body resisting and avoiding the stretch? Can I trust that my body and this pose are exactly as and where they're meant to be? Can I be present with my breath without overlaying my experience with unnecessary layers of judgment? Can I be still?* Every pose represented a worthwhile exploration that gave me feedback, insight and valuable wisdom for everyday life.

When life gets tough, a few poses on the mat reveal that maybe there isn't anything wrong with the world, but rather an interpretation that often stems from a body fraught with tension, anxiety, worry and fear. When we are mentally stuck and the desire to walk away is overwhelming, our gut instinct might be to fidget, adjust or get out of the pose altogether. Yin yoga teaches us that staying still and dealing with whatever comes up, one breath at a time, will help us grow.

Adapting to the many ups and downs of life and managing change with grace can dampen and soften our reaction to stress. Yin yoga teaches us to find a place of comfort in the uncomfortable space of stillness and silence. Resilience can be built upon a foundation of gentle surrender.

Fasting

We all know how uncomfortable the feeling of hunger can be. People sometimes proclaim they're *starving* just 3 to 4 hours after a meal. Whatever emotion, sensation or experience may be present, *starvation* isn't an accurate description of what is happening in the body after a few short hours between meals. If our ancestors had required three to six meals daily for survival, humans would have died out long ago.

Social conditioning, along with ready availability of food and effective marketing, has ingrained into the modern-day human psyche that three meals, plus some snacking in between, is how we are meant to eat. The psychological drives toward constant food consumption have become so embedded in our psyche that breaking the habit often requires Herculean efforts of willpower and discipline. These qualities are in short supply compared to the food we have access to.

Disconnected from the body, people have different reasons for eating food other than hunger. They eat out of boredom, because food tastes good (sometimes too good, and thus addictive, due to the artificial flavorings and additives) or because people around them are eating. Often uncomfortable emotions and stressful situations trigger us to automatically reach for those *oh-so-delicious* comfort foods without the conscious mind even noticing[132]. It seems that whatever impulse, sensation or emotion *does* trigger food consumption, it isn't the physiological experience of hunger.

Enter fasting.

Fasting is the conscious discomfort practice that requires us to enter into and embrace the physiologically and psychologically challenging experiences of hunger. Through fasting, we can connect with our body by familiarizing ourselves with one of its most uncomfortable states. Voluntarily abstaining from food, and sometimes food and drink depending on the context, for periods of time has been practiced since ancient times by people, cultures and religions around the world.

Like every behavior or technique, our intention is the thin line that separates fasting as a conscious discomfort practice and fasting as an unconscious eating disorder. The former is a practice laden with remarkable health benefits, while the latter is potentially extremely harmful. Ruthless honesty and authenticity are our best allies in examining our intentions and motivations for choosing a conscious discomfort practice that is far more than a weight loss strategy. Know that if we are a person who struggles with disordered eating, then this conscious discomfort practice may not be an appropriate choice.

The renewed interest in and popularity of fasting regimens results from a plethora of evidence supporting the practice and its physiological benefits. Fasting elicits evolutionarily conserved, adaptive cellular responses that improve sugar metabolism, increase stress resistance, lower blood pressure levels and suppress inflammation, thus contributing to improved health and longevity[133]. Most, if not all, of the body's organs and systems respond to fasting in ways that enable the body to tolerate and overcome the challenge of fasting and subsequently return to a healthy homeostatic normal. The anti-inflammatory effects of fasting assist in managing and treating numerous chronic, non-infectious diseases, such as multiple sclerosis[134], Alzheimer's disease[135], Type 1 and Type 2 Diabetes[136], Parkinson's disease[137] and cancer[138].

Some experts believe that the therapeutic implications of fasting are linked to supporting the body's natural circadian rhythm, its internal clock. Eating during the day (while the sun is up) and letting your body rest and digest at night (after the sun goes down) improves physiological markers, such as hormonal secretion patterns, physical coordination and sleep[139], while also impacting insulin sensitivity, lipid production and blood-pressure control[140]. Fasting is thus a prime example of how the body can naturally heal itself if we get out of its way. We don't have to take any medicine or pill, just give the body a rest and let it do what it has evolved to do: survive and thrive.

I first experimented with fasting to improve focus and productivity. When I considered the time saved by skipping breakfast, coupled with the cognitive benefits I experienced[141], it wasn't long before breakfast disappeared altogether. When my body adjusted to 16-hour fasts, I began reading about prolonged fasts and their impact on the body's innate healing potential. While medically supervised fasts can last between 5 and 40 days, research suggests that the magic number for a safe fast that leads to a cascade of health benefits is 72 hours, or three days. I'll recap, step-by-step, my first fast to highlight the physiological health benefits that unlock with each passing hour and day.

Regular intermittent fasting had prepared me for the initial 16 hours of my first fast, which is when the metabolic switch from glucose-based to ketone-based energy, called ketosis, begins to be triggered. In ketosis, the body starts to break down and burn fat[142]. Ketones serve as an alternative energy source for the cells of the heart, muscle and brain when energy from sugar isn't readily available. More interestingly, the brain's switch to ketone utilization is one of the reasons that fasting is often claimed to promote mental clarity and positive mood since ketones produce less inflammation and even kick-start the production of beneficial proteins in the brain[143].

For anyone who can't remember ever skipping a meal, then the first hurdle of discomfort you'll likely face is the body transitioning from using sugars as energy to using fat. And for those who have never accepted the notion that sugar is an addictive drug, you'll reconsider when you experience sugar withdrawal. Energy levels come crashing down, mild headaches kick in and our mood swings drastically. Anyone within arm's length of us will learn what the word 'hangry' means if they accidentally or unintentionally trigger us. It usually doesn't take much.

While it might feel like the end of the world, this uncomfortable shift into a fat-burning state is accompanied by important bodily health benefits, including increased stress resistance, increased longevity and a decreased incidence of disease. When fasting, some of the body's fat gets turned into ketones that appear to reactivate genes that lead to fat metabolism, stress resistance, lowered inflammation, antioxidant processes and damage repair[144]. Like all conscious discomfort practices, the mind's reaction of aversion starkly contrasts with the therapeutic benefits experienced by the body.

As I overcame my first fasting hurdle, my intention was to keep my daily routine unchanged. I assumed that keeping busy would make fasting easier. Sitting around doing nothing would make any experiences of hunger my mind's sole focus. My first day thus included a somewhat normal workload and life responsibilities: a few hours of working with clients and an afternoon with my son after picking him up from school. Everything went smoothly until sunset, roughly the 24-hour mark of the fast. It was then that my mind became convinced I was *starving*.

As I was clearing my first full day of fasting, a pounding headache, low energy and grumpy mood meant that I was supremely unpleasant company for my fellow men's group members that evening. Thankfully, sharing, venting and complaining during that meeting gave me some semblance of relief and resolve that allowed me to go to bed that night without prematurely pulling the parachute. *One day at a time,* I told myself. I ignored the sensations of hunger deep in my belly as my head hit the pillow and drifted off to sleep. The first night ended up as the most challenging part of the fast. That has also been the case with every fast I've done since.

I was genuinely surprised when I woke up the following day with no hunger. Not even a sliver. I was wide awake and ready to take on my day. After my morning tasks finished, it was time for a workout.

There are different perspectives on exercising while in a fasted state, and I was curious to explore the debate experientially. I decided to stick to my workout regimen as planned: 20-30 minutes of high-intensity interval training. Completely abstaining from exercise was never an option as I wanted to take advantage of the increased growth hormone levels reaching their peak during the second day of fasting.

At the 48-hour mark of a fast, the body's growth hormone levels are up to five times as high as at the beginning of the fast due to the combination of ketones and *ghrelin*, the hunger hormone, both triggering increased growth hormone production[145]. While growth hormone is a crucial protein that plays a role in healing and longevity, I'd be lying if I didn't say I was excited about the impacts of growth hormone on preserving lean muscle mass and developing muscular strength[146]. I was also curious about how and to what degree my strength and endurance would be impacted by fasting.

I also knew about the connection between fasting and exercise relating to autophagy. We'll get to autophagy and what it means for health and longevity shortly. For now, it's only important to note that combining exercise with fasting increases autophagy[147], the body's natural recycling process, which gave me additional incentive to continue exercising.

I let my body guide the session as I tuned in and listened to what I felt throughout the workout. My body determined whether and how much I pushed myself during the workout. That I handled the workout easily wasn't as surprising as how amazing my mind and body felt in other ways.

The usual aches and pains of past injuries – my surgically-repaired right ankle, torn tendon in my left wrist and strained lower back – vanished. With the rush of endorphins surging through my body, I celebrated with a sauna session and cold shower.

The remainder of the second day was like a lucid dream. My focus seemed laser-like, with signs of hunger nowhere to be found, which was expected given exercise's role in appetite regulation and suppression[148]. Noticing the impact of movement and exercise on hunger was a little nugget of wisdom that I tucked away in my back pocket for future fasts. Without fail, the days that I exercise during fasts are always easier to get through.

As my body passed 60 hours of fasting, I spent most of the time in a highly concentrated mental state. The absence of the usual stream-of-thought roller-coaster meant I could indulge in a few enjoyable deep inquiries. I reflected on the sensations that were present in my body. It would have been easy to label them as hunger and move on. I dropped the label and curiously examined the uncomfortable sensations arising deep in the pit of my stomach. Stripped of story and narrative, I noticed that my thoughts of reaching for food were a reaction to fear, not hunger. *I was scared.*

Even after 60 hours of fasting, it was more accurate in that moment that eating would have been more about soothing fear than satiating hunger. I could soothe and relieve my discomfort by eating. By not eating, however, I was letting my mind remain in a state of uncertainty about the unknown experiential states of what would happen if I stopped eating for extended periods of time. I sat with the discomfort of not knowing and not controlling, which seemed like an important life lesson to experience. I smiled.

Meanwhile, with my mind amusing itself with explorations of its innermost contents, my body's insulin levels reached their lowest point since starting the fast, thus making my body increasingly insulin sensitive[149]. Lowering insulin levels comes with many health benefits, most notably improved insulin sensitivity, which is protective against chronic disease[150]. Lowering insulin levels also contributes to activating the body's natural recycling process called autophagy, which means *self-eating*. The only appropriate word to describe autophagy is *incredible*.

Autophagy is a critical metabolic process that is essentially the human body's well-preserved 'starvation program' designed for self-protection. In the simplest terms, autophagy involves cells hunting out scraps of dead or diseased cells and gobbling them up to use the resulting molecules for energy or to make new cell parts. This cellular and tissue rejuvenation process was essential for survival when food wasn't so readily available and energy-dense, which was most of human history.

Fasting and autophagy go together as the body cannot activate this incredibly healthy recycling process until glucose stores have been substantially depleted and insulin levels are sufficiently low. In a well-fed state, when insulin levels are normal or high, the body is in growth mode. Cells grow, divide and synthesize proteins. While this is undoubtedly beneficial, it could have metabolic implications for cancer growth when these processes are overactive.

Well-fed cells aren't worried about being efficient and recycling their damaged components because they are too busy growing and dividing. When fasting triggers autophagy, however, a recycling and cleanup process is triggered that breaks down fat, removes damaged cellular components and rids the body of misfolded proteins[151]. While autophagy is difficult to measure, many experts agree that it initiates after 18 to 20 hours of fasting, with maximal benefits occurring once the 48 to 72-hour mark has been reached.

Autophagy can lead to immune system rejuvenation. Some researchers say fasting flips a regenerative switch, prompting stem cells to create brand-new white blood cells, essentially regenerating the immune system. It's only after roughly 72 hours of fasting that the body turns on these cellular survival pathways that lead to the breakdown and recycling of old cells and proteins. This is also why many experts and fasting advocates say 72 hours is a useful marker for a prolonged fast.

It's impossible to discuss immune function without mentioning the digestive system. Taking care of our gut simultaneously maintains a strong and responsive immune function[152]. Not only does fasting improve gastrointestinal function and metabolic health[153], it may also influence gut microbiota by positively altering gut permeability and reducing systemic inflammation through bacterial translocation[154]. While I regularly attend silent retreats to give my mind and body a chance to rest and digest, I consider my prolonged fasts a much-needed retreat for my digestive system.

After 96 hours, I broke my first prolonged fast. Four days without food. Only water and unsweetened herbal tea. When I reflected on the difficulty of the first night, I never thought I would have crossed the finish line. The refeeding stage is the last and most enjoyable part of the fasting cycle. When we break our fast with a nutritious meal, we further improve the function of cells, tissues and organs that went through a cellular renovation process. Refeeding after a fast directly impacts neurons that promote synaptic plasticity, enhance cognition and bolster cellular stress resistance[155]. Each refeeding also triggers cellular regeneration of white blood cells that may have been depleted or recycled during the fast[156].

We're supposed to ease slowly into solid food after prolonged fasts over several days. Long-term medically-supervised fasts require a delicate and strategically-implemented refeeding process to ensure that the digestive system is not harmed. After a mere four days, I didn't heed any of that advice.

I kept it healthy but gave my body a refeeding fit for a 6-foot-5-inch frame. I snacked on seaweed, brie cheese and almonds while I cooked a delicious dinner of chicken breast, roasted potatoes, guacamole, pickles and sauerkraut. Dessert was a square of dark chocolate and half an apple. No bloating, indigestion, gas or pain. Just bliss. Never had food tasted so good, nor had food been more appreciated. It was a beautiful reunion.

While there's an abundance of evidence-based benefits that support fasting as a health-promoting conscious discomfort practice, I am always more interested in how someone subjectively experiences and relates to their fasting experience. I get curious about how fasting makes them feel, the affective challenges they are required to face, and the benefits they can palpably sense in their bodies.

After my first fast, I no longer needed scientific evidence to inspire my next fast. My body's joints and muscles felt freer, more open and pain-free. I consciously explored many sensations and emotions that make handling everyday life easier. My body and mind felt lighter, clearer and calmer. I had all the experiential evidence needed to do it again.

The unavoidable truth is that fasting for three days is hard. I'll repeat that: a 72-hour fast is really, really hard. There are also important considerations to determine for yourself: *Do I exercise? How intensely and how much? Do I work? How much? Do I involve health or medical professionals?* Without a baseline understanding of, and confidence with, our own body and its capacity for such an endeavor, it's safer to start with a shorter fast or one that is supervised. There are many different variations and approaches to fasting, which makes it easier for an individual to find the method that fits into their unique lifestyle. It's helpful for each person to experiment and find the type that works best for them and, more importantly, is sustainable.

As it turns out, we can still get many of the same benefits of prolonged fasting by adopting a more leisurely type of fasting, called Time Restricted Eating. While a prolonged fast of two to three days will induce the body to clean out old and damaged immune cells and switch on the production of new ones, time-restricted eating may work in much the same way, with science indicating similar health benefits[157].

With Time Restricted Eating, we essentially fast a little bit every day by keeping the entirety of our daily food intake within a 6- or 8-hour eating window. What this looks like in practical language is starting our food intake for the day at noon with lunch and ensuring to finish dinner by either 6:00 or 8:00 pm. We can move or shift the eating window to accommodate our lifestyle, but the intention is to try and time our last meal of the day so that it is 2 to 4 hours before bedtime. This ensures that we go to bed on an empty stomach and take advantage of the body's inherent restorative processes while sleeping.

Regardless of the type of fasting we decide is right for us, keeping water intake levels high is imperative. I include unsweetened herbal teas during my fasts because they provide various health benefits depending on the herb. Coffee is a 'no-go' zone for me, though some fasting experts and advocates suggest it is not only approved for fasting but also helpful. When I experimented with coffee during one of my fasts, the post-caffeine crash and intense hunger confirmed that my body, even when fasted, doesn't tolerate coffee well. Each person should assess coffee, and every aspect of a fast, for themselves to determine what fits within their personal and unique fasting equation.

Breathwork

Breathing is the most vital aspect of life. More than a couple of minutes without breathing reveals the fragility of life. How we breathe also impacts health and longevity[158]. Taking a moment to connect to the breath can be a spiritual act as it humbly reminds us of the connection we share with our surrounding environment and each other.

Breathwork is the umbrella term that describes any conscious breathing and breath-holding technique. The commonality shared amongst breathwork practices is the deliberate control of the breath instead of allowing the breath to flow with its natural rhythm. The specific pace and depth of the breathing pattern elicit different outcomes, such as deep relaxation, feeling energized or experiencing relief from mental, physical and emotional tension. Today, breathwork has become a means of therapy, self-healing and personal transformation.

Tuning into our breathing can give us valuable information about our mental state. When stressed or anxious, the body likely responds with a rapid, short and constricted breath. Breathing in this way can disrupt the delicate ratio of oxygen and carbon dioxide in the body, resulting in an increased heart rate, muscle tension, dizziness or a state of panic.

Taking long deep breaths from our belly, diaphragm and abdomen, however, reduces the symptoms of stress and anxiety[159]. By breathing deeply, we activate the parasympathetic nervous system, thus slowing down our heart rate, lowering blood pressure and cultivating a sense of relaxation and calmness[160]. When we use our diaphragm instead of our chest, we invite our neck and chest muscles to relax and counter some of the tension that typically accompanies the body's "fight-flight-freeze" response. Slow deep breathing has been one of the relaxation tips I always have tucked away in my back pocket whenever I notice I'm triggered and need a dose of relaxation and tension relief. This kind of breathing, however, is not the kind of breathwork utilized for conscious discomfort.

My introduction to consciously connected breathing, which I learned from Michael Brown's *The Presence Process*, concluded with two vitally important realizations. Firstly, I never thought breathing could be so hard! After years of dismissing the practice as fluffy, I was humbled by the challenge of sustaining a rapid breath rate for 20 consecutive minutes. My body became triggered, activated and disoriented as I passed through experiences of dizziness, feeling lightheaded, angst, panic, fear, nausea and even a mild headache.

Regardless of how uncomfortable my first breathwork session was, it resulted in my second realization, which kept me coming back for more doses of breathwork. When I opened my eyes after my first 20-minute practice, there was a short pause of peace and tranquility that I hadn't ever experienced before. I cried. For the first time in conscious memory, there were no thoughts in my mind.

The negative, destructive, angry, deluded voice in my head was somehow gone (for a few beautiful moments, at least). Pure and unfiltered gratitude flowed through my body. I hadn't known before that moment that identifying with the incessant voice in my head was optional. I was sold.

Consciously connected breathing is done using full, deep breaths without any pause between the inhale and exhale. The continuous inhales and exhales create a "circle" of breathing. Within only a few breaths, the body experiences myriad sensations. The robust list of potential discomfort includes, but is certainly not limited to, angst, fear, panic, heat, tingling, sweating, twitching, headaches, nausea, dizziness, buzzing, tears, yawning, tension, ache, pain, muscle spasm or twitch and racing thoughts. These experiences arise because the pace and rhythm of circular breathing activate the sympathetic nervous system. When the body's nervous system is aroused, it will express itself in different ways, some of which have been listed here.

When I work with clients, the first conscious discomfort practice they are introduced to is some variation of consciously connected breathing. I avoid layering expectations or assumptions on my clients as they begin their practice because I don't want my explanation to unnecessarily influence their experience.

A blank experiential slate, however, means they usually aren't prepared for the discomfort that meets them as they begin breathing. Without fail, clients report back on the uncomfortable and challenging nature of the breathwork at our following session: tingling sensations down the arms and hands, waves of heat washing over their face and body, headaches, disorienting sense of dizziness and feeling lightheaded, powerful emotions of angst, fear and panic simmer to the surface of conscious awareness, or tension seizing the body. When our eyes are closed, all these experiences are exacerbated because the mind is focused on the unfamiliarity of what is unfolding within. *Surely, this isn't what I'm supposed to be experiencing. Shouldn't I feel more relaxed when I meditate? Why the hell am I doing this?* The mind's judgmental reactivity to physiological sensations that are objective in nature imposes judgment onto them, adding more fuel to the flames of perceived discomfort.

The invitation offered by a connected breathing practice is simple: *be with what is, without judgment or avoidance.* For those who are only beginning their breathwork journey, the realization suddenly dawns on them that breathwork is not a peaceful and relaxing getaway. This can be profoundly triggering. *I'm already anxious, why would I want to experience it when I'm breathing? Why would I do something that makes my body feel so horrible?* The mind frantically searches for an Emergency Exit sign, but this only reproduces the same old song and dance of avoidance. With breathwork, we are invited to breathe *through* our experience.

I enjoy Wim Hof's variation of breathwork because it incorporates periodic breath retention. After a set amount of time of conscious breathing, we exhale entirely and hold the exhaled position until the body needs to take its next breath. It's within these moments of complete stillness that we can practice tuning into the subtlest of sensations of the body.

In complete stillness, we might be able to sense the waves that move through the body in response to each heartbeat. We can also pay attention to and differentiate between the body's need to take its next inhale and the mind reacting to the fear of not breathing. The longer the breath is held, the more likely the confrontation with fear and angst will occur. *Which am I experiencing, the body's instinctive gasp impulse for its next breath? Or are these fear-based thoughts, reactions of the mind?* And while the mind ponders the differences, the body senses when oxygen is in short supply and responds to this hormetic stress with physiological adaptations that make it healthier and better prepared for future oxygen shortages[161]. The human body is truly amazing.

Breathwork is uniquely practical because it cultivates our capacity to observe and accept the experiences of our everyday lives. *Can I be with what shows up? Can I accept myself, and any aspect of myself that emerges now, unconditionally? Can I calmly be with my angst so I am empowered to face it in everyday life?* One of Brown's quotes from The Presence Process that has never left me and that I frequently share with clients is this, "*the only way out is through.*" Only through acknowledging, accepting and embracing what our body perceives as discomfort can the body process and move beyond it. The mind might tell a story of punishment, but the body knows the truth that the practice is nurturing, not punishing.

The science behind breathwork supports it as a health-promoting practice. Wim Hof, and many others before him, have regularly utilized some form, type or iteration of connected breathing to tap into the immense benefits for physical, mental and emotional wellbeing. Neurons in the autonomic nervous system fire more during connected breathing practices, releasing epinephrine, which many commonly call adrenaline. The epinephrine surge causes the immune system to increase its anti-inflammatory activity and dampen its proinflammatory activity. This physiological response could have important implications for treating various autoimmune diseases[162].

The faintness that may sometimes occur during breathwork results from hypoxia, the bodily state of oxygen deprivation. Oxygen deprivation occurs through hyperventilation, and the reduced oxygen level is believed to induce a state of altered consciousness[163]. More importantly, this state of hypoxia, induced during breathwork that incorporates breath retention, alkalizes the blood and stimulates the creation of mitochondria, the formation of new red blood vessels and hormones responsible for creating new red blood cells[164]. With more intense applications of this style of breathwork, such as Holotropic Breathing, altered states of consciousness have been utilized within psychotherapy to facilitate deprogramming of avoidance behaviors and cultivation of self-awareness[165]. Connected breathing allows people to reconnect with their innate power and unlocks the potential for better physical, emotional and mental wellbeing.

It's normal to find breathwork practices challenging at times. The invitation is to settle into the experience as we breathe through the discomfort without reacting to it. As we remain still and allow the body to access deeper aspects of itself, conscious breathing reveals itself to be a powerful, self-healing and low-risk therapeutic modality that facilitates integration and the transformation of trauma, suppressed beliefs and unprocessed emotions[166].

When we open our eyes following breathwork sessions, we feel the palpable difference in our body: less thought and more clarity, alertness and presence. We smile as we calmly turn to face the day. As Brown puts it, this beautiful process of reconnecting to the body isn't about *feeling better*, but rather about *getting better at feeling*.

Ayahuasca

I had difficulty deciding whether or not to include this section. Including a topic as controversial as ayahuasca – a hallucinogenic drug, plant medicine or both, depending on one's opinion– in this book was accompanied by an internal debate that required some reflection to settle. A part of me, the rational part that feels like he must present himself as a competent professional, made the case to avoid diving into such a potentially divisive and polarizing subject that could discredit me in certain circles. This part of me feared being judged, labeled and ostracized. On the other hand, there is the part of me, the authentic part, that knows that my research into and experiences with ayahuasca can be helpful for those curious about it. As we can see, I am choosing authenticity.

Ayahuasca is a hallucinogenic plant mixture used to create a pharmacologi-cally complex tea that is utilized as medicine by indigenous cultures throughout South America. The psychotropic plant brew is created by combining two plants. Psychotria viridis is the first plant, rich in the powerful psychedelic agent *N,N-dimethyltryptamine*, commonly known as DMT. The other, banisteri-opsis caapi, contains the beta-carboline alkaloids that allow the orally-ingested DMT to sneak past our liver's metabolic defenses so that the DMT can reach the brain, where it induces its characteristic hallucinogenic effects. Both plants are necessary as the DMT by itself would be rendered useless due to the liver's potent metabolization processes.

Though hallucinogenic drugs like ayahuasca were historically used to treat substance dependence during the 1960s and 1970s, research came to a quick halt when all hallucinogens were deemed as having high abuse potential, had no accepted therapeutic benefits and lacked an acceptable level of safety for medical use[167]. These perspectives are now shifting and justifiably so.

Scientists are now exploring what many see as the substances' extraordinary therapeutic potential for many issues, from depression and PTSD to drug ad-diction and acceptance of mortality[168]. The re-emergence of psychedelic med-icine as a therapeutic paradigm has resulted in people from all corners of the world swarming to South America to try ayahuasca.

Despite the boom in Ayahuasca tourism, the potent substance should be treated with respect as it can tear down the walls of the conscious mind and reveal truths we may not be ready to see or accept. Intention matters, so when ayahuasca, aka *She*, does call, it might be wise to ensure our intention is aligned with the pursuit of a sacred space for healing.

Ayahuasca might be the epitome of conscious discomfort practices in terms of the level of discomfort experienced and the degree of benefit. For starters, each psychedelic journey is essentially an invitation for intense vomiting and immense physical discomfort, experiences the mind labels as uncomfortable. Beyond that, ayahuasca is often called a conscious death experience because the neurobiological effects of ayahuasca are strikingly like near-death experiences[169]. Despite the similarities to dying, the powerful hallucinogen may be a viable intervention for suicidality[170], though more research is ongoing and needed.

A closer look at the physiological experience of death within the body can help us understand the contributing role that the process of death plays in maintaining the body's health and wellbeing. Indeed, examining the physiological processes associated with cellular death – called apoptosis and discussed shortly – in the body results in a truth that differs vastly from the mind's many possible stories about death.

Death is one of the topics of conversation that universally activates the body and triggers many interpretations and perceptions. The discomfort that arises from thinking about and conceptualizing death – particularly one's own – is one of the reasons religions and belief systems attempt to explain what happens before, during, and after we die. The mind leans on these stories to reconcile the inescapable fact that what happens after death is unknown. The unknown is what scares the mind the most.

Recent scientific research and findings have resulted in a cultural shift from stories about death to truths about the body. The death of living beings is a necessary part of evolution, leaving space for other individuals, other species, and future possibilities. Since it is only through descendants that a new species develops, if organisms live too long, they become an obstacle to evolution. For example, the extinction of the dinosaurs allowed other beings, such as mammals, to evolve.

Death has only been considered a necessary life process for barely fifty years. Before that, it was thought to be simply a consequence of the passing of time, external attack or illness. Programmed cell death, or *apoptosis*, is a genetically regulated process of cell suicide central to the development, homeostasis and integrity of multicellular organisms, including humans. During its programmed suicide, the cell disintegrates and its entire content is swallowed up by neighboring cells. Millions of cells can die in a few hours without lesions or inflammation, without the conscious mind even noticing.

The regulated cell suicide pathways presently expressing themselves in our body have been selected as an adaptation during evolution[171]. At this very time, millions of our body's different cells are dying. White blood cells are being sacrificed so that we can survive an infection[172]. The hormonal changes in the female menstrual cycle induce the suicide of many cells in the uterus, bringing about menstruation. Indeed, when cells evade programmed cell death, the cell may start down the path of becoming cancerous[173].

Just like the death of organisms paves the way for evolution, apoptosis is the body's way of changing and adapting to align with its innate intentions of healing and thriving. As apoptosis destroys unwanted cells, mitosis, or cell division, is the process that makes new cells. While they may seem at odds, apoptosis and mitosis work together to keep the body healthy. Skin and hair cells are renewed via a continuous cycle of apoptosis and mitosis. So, too, are the cells that line our intestinal walls. Because new cells are constantly replacing old ones, our body's tissue remains healthy. Once again, the reason for exploring this tangent is to highlight the differences between the stories of the mind and the truths found within the body. When we examine the role and experience of death within the body, the body's truth differs vastly from the mind's stories.

It's difficult for the mind to imagine something more uncomfortable than dying – not necessarily the *actual* experience of dying, which research suggests might be relatively painless or even euphoric[174], but rather the *thought* of dying or impending death. The fear of death makes us avoid some things at all costs and do things we would never have dreamed of otherwise doing. The fear of death may be the most fundamental fear that all other fears stem from. But rather than preventing death, the fear of death prevents life. It isn't until many become acutely aware of their fast-approaching end – such as being diagnosed with a terminal disease – that they feel inspired to act on their bucket list and do many things that the mind was scared of experiencing, such as skydiving.

My fear of death made me initially scoff at the idea of taking ayahuasca. I was also puzzled by the vomiting or 'purging' aspect of the ayahuasca experience. *Why would anyone take a drug that induced vomiting?* It wasn't until my first ayahuasca experience that I understood that purging, in many more forms than just vomiting, is healing and therapeutic[175]. The more I read and heard stories, the more open I became to taking it. As it turns out, Mother Ayahuasca is said to call you when she feels you're ready for her medicine. I set the intention to wait for the calling, so I wasn't chasing or forcing the experience. I waited.

I eventually answered her call while sitting in a hostel in Sao Paulo, Brazil, planning an episode for A Million Ways to Live. The thought spontaneously emerged to reach out to ayahuasca treatment and retreat centers throughout Brazil and Peru to see if they might be interested in hosting me and being featured in the web series.

I left it up to fate to determine whether it was my time to take ayahuasca. Less than 6 hours later, I was booking flights to the Sacred Valley of Cusco, Peru, where I would spend five days at Etnikas Retreat Center in nearby Pisac. It was time to face my fear of death.

The ayahuasca psychedelic experience typically lasts between four to eight hours. The typical "transcendental circle" of the ayahuasca experience is divided into three distinct phases. After orally ingesting ayahuasca, it takes roughly 30 minutes for the effects of the first phase to be felt: unpleasant burning sensations in the stomach resulting from the acidity of the ayahuasca brew[176]. After having drunk several different mixtures of various kinds during my life, I can confirm that ayahuasca isn't particularly pleasant on the palate. I will say that some ayahuasca brews have been more drinkable than others. The closest comparable taste I can provide here is black licorice, which I find slightly less abhorrent.

During the first phase, there may be increased skin sensitivity, pins-and-needles sensations along the skin, and bouts of yawning, shivering or subtle body tremors. These experiences were pretty much standard for my sittings. As our conscious mind becomes aware of its apparent reality beginning to shift, completely justified and warranted feelings of confusion, paranoia and fear begin to surface because our perception of reality dissolves away.

This is the real point of no return. There's no turning back as we've already drunk the brew nearly an hour before, but it's in this moment that the conscious mind is gripping hard to any sense of familiar reality. This is the moment of surrender. This was when I had to face my fear and say, *okay, let's go,* and open myself up to whatever experience destiny had arranged for me.

All of my thoughts disappeared. I relaxed my awareness, and the journey began. As a side note, I don't find it surprising that in all of my life's significant moments and instances of personal growth, healing and transformation, the thoughts of my mind were absent from the experience.

As ayahuasca bulldozes psychological defenses, many come face-to-face with and re-experience traumatic memories that might have been consciously or sub-consciously suppressed or ignored. There's nowhere to hide when the conscious mind has been swept aside and the body summons what had been previously avoided to the surface. This might sound like a frightening experience, but it's during this uncomfortable journey into our deepest emotional wounds that we can properly attend to them. Our body can finally purge what is unnecessary and no longer needed.

We open ourselves to new insights as we process, integrate, and heal. We reconcile the personal challenges that are often too unbearable to face when the rigid walls of our thoughts, routines and beliefs are up. The purging that ayahuasca initiates makes change possible.

This is also around the time during the ayahuasca experience that nausea hits its most intense level, peaking with sometimes intense bouts of vomiting. As uncomfortable as it sounds (and it is), a good purge is often exactly what the doctor ordered.

I'll never forget my second ayahuasca sitting. I couldn't drop into my own experience because my attention was regularly distracted by the woman next to me. I'm not exaggerating when I say she continuously vomited for four hours. I felt terrible for her and could only hope she was okay as the shamans spent much of their time and attention tending to her needs. I didn't think I'd see her again as my mind assumed she would have packed her bags and left the following day.

The story in my head was incorrect. I saw her sitting quietly at breakfast the following day with a soft and subtle smile. We were supposed to process our experiences in silence, but there was no way I wasn't going to ask her about the purgative experiences from the previous night.

I sat in disbelief as she described vomiting as the most therapeutic experience she had ever had. She faced and reconciled her trauma-ridden relationship with her mother during her trip. With tears in her eyes, she said she could finally forgive her. She was finally able to forgive herself. She smiled as tears dripped down her face.

Given the right setting and circumstances, purging can be powerfully therapeutic as releasing bodily tension during such an intense experience creates an abrupt shift into a more open and expansive state afterward. When I asked her how she was feeling, she gazed into my eyes and softly said 'love' and nothing else.

There are countless testimonies of people visiting the spiritual world during their ayahuasca journey, encountering plant and animal spirits, or contacting a higher power. It's also not uncommon to experience feelings of oneness with the universe or to gain new understandings about life and death[177]. Based on my research, I wasn't surprised to hear about the woman's experience.

While I didn't get a spirit guide for my journey, I remember having a familiar figure guiding me through my first experience: me. As I began my trip, I was stripped of all my clothes, ideas and thoughts while the world around me melted away. To be stripped naked of my external layers seemed appropriate and symbolic. What was left was me, which I can only describe as pure, conscious awareness, and Naked Luke standing in front of me as my guide. Naked Luke, wearing nothing except Ray Ban sunglasses, pulled me forward as the fabric of reality began ripping apart at the seams. A jolt of fear permeated through my beingness. Naked Luke turned around, lifted his sunglasses just enough so I could see his eyes and gave me a wink as if to both acknowledge my fear and to let me know not to worry because I was safe. It was going to be okay. All I had to do was trust. And so, after turning back around and pushing on, Naked Luke navigated the nether realms of my subconscious mind in search of answers to the questions I had set out to find: *What is my gift to the world? What is the source of my anger? How do I forgive?* I received the answers I was looking for.

When it comes to ayahuasca, the visions, spirit guides and hallucinations usually garner all the attention. It's only because I've come to understand the wisdom of the body that I arrived at my own interpretation of how ayahuasca heals the body and how the mind follows.

During my last ayahuasca sitting, the facilitator offered a beautiful gem of insight to the group: purging takes many forms. As obvious as this sounds, it made me rethink everything I had thought about the healing ayahuasca provides.

My first sittings had been the stereotypical 'blasted out into space' experiences and highlighted by the characteristic visions, hallucinations and journeys through different realms and worlds. These experiences pique the curiosity of many who seek out Mother Ayahuasca in the first place.

However, when this particular facilitator started listing all the ways the body purges, I realized she spoke the somatic language I had become well-versed in. She said that vomiting is just one way to purge and that people shouldn't assume it's an automatic and inherent part of the ayahuasca experience.

Purging takes on many forms. Even thoughts are a form of purging. She emphasized not to place too much importance on the content of the mind's thoughts and visions. She said that it could be helpful to consider the possibility that many times the images that pass through our minds while on ayahuasca are merely another form of purging. We don't need to add meaning, yet another story, to them as they leave. Sometimes the mind needs to purge and clear our mental cache just as much as our body needs to vomit.

This made my fifth and final (so far) ayahuasca sitting the most transformational and also what separated it from the rest. I stopped following the thoughts, visions and hallucinations. Instead, I stayed anchored in my body. Essentially, I treated my ayahuasca experience as a meditation.

Every time my mind wandered away, I brought my attention back to my body to observe the different ways my body was purging and processing. I watched my body do a dance of healing. I didn't vomit. Instead, my body purged by shivering, quivering, yawning, sighing, jaw tremors, tears, sweating, hot flashes, spine convulsions, subtle sighs, twitches and spasms. If you speak the language of the human body, then you know that every subtle release of tension and energy has the potential to be therapeutic.

The way my body processed ayahuasca during this sitting was one of the most beautiful things I'd ever witnessed. I hadn't ever stayed so connected to my body while experiencing ayahuasca to appreciate the subtle shifts that it creates in the body. My final ayahuasca sitting confirmed that the real work of healing is done in the body, not in the mind.

The final stage of ayahuasca's transcendental cycle is characterized by the fading of visions, returning to the state of consciousness prior to consumption and experiencing general physical fatigue[178]. Tired? Yes. But beneath the superficial experience of tiredness is a vast undercurrent of profound peace, gratitude and love. I've heard people say that, after ayahuasca, they feel unconditional love for the first time. Many journal their experiences and meet with shamans to reflect on the insights gathered during their journey.

Ayahuasca creates the setting for our automatic habits, patterns, beliefs and concepts to be, at least temporarily, spliced, shredded and dissolved[179]. What's left is the possibility of examining ourselves from a different perspective that is less constricted and constrained. It is because we feel safe that we can temporarily let go of the rigidity of the defenses and beliefs that, while limiting and self-destructive, originated as a form of self-protection. When the straitjacket of our limited perspective of ourselves is removed, we open to different possibilities of who we are, what the world is and how we can relate to it. We begin to understand our true nature, patterns and fears, and receive messages and insights that help us heal and expand beyond the limited ways we view ourselves.

Ayahuasca's capacity for such healing is possible precisely because it is so effective at getting the reactive mind out of the way so the body can do its beautiful dance of healing. The setting and rituals created by shamans and facilitators help settle the mind and contribute to an environment that allows safety to be experienced. When the mind perceives safety, it can put its reactivity and defenses aside momentarily and let the body process and integrate what the mind habitually interrupts and intrudes upon. This is one of the many differences between consuming psychoactive substances within therapeutic contexts and under controlled circumstances, and recreationally taking illicit drugs unsupervised and without any meaningful framing.

For ayahuasca to be effective, we must surrender. As such, it's perfectly appropriate that ayahuasca is called *The Mother*. The sheer magnitude of safety and surrender necessary to pass through such an experience is made possible when we allow ourselves to feel safe and nurtured in a way only a maternal energetic presence can provide. Humans feel – or at least are supposed to feel – safest in the presence of an attuned, caring and nurturing mother. It is only because of unprocessed traumatic circumstances that have systematically overwhelmed the mothers of our world that this statement isn't universally true for all children. The mother's womb is intended to keep us safe and nurtured until we are ready to emerge into the world. Ayahuasca is the womb for our rebirth. Only maternal energy can provide that level of therapeutic holding.

Ayahuasca melts away the conscious mind so that the real work can be done on the subconscious level, in the body. This highlights the most crucial part of the ayahuasca experience: ayahuasca is not the healer. A mother's presence can be soothing and her calming presence of unconditional love can support us as we process and move through challenging times. Similarly, ayahuasca gives us a safe relational container so our body can pass through deeply rooted traumas and memories that we've never felt safe confronting. We cannot ever heal if we feel unsafe. Safety is the prerequisite to feeling and healing. Just as our mother is most often the person that held us when we were children and reassured us that everything would be okay, ayahuasca holds the same space for us. The Mother does not heal us, *she holds us as we heal ourselves.*

Ayahuasca can be a powerful catalyst for change. After ayahuasca, we may gain new and fresh insights, but what will we do *after* our experience? The choice is always ours. With each passing moment, we get to choose our destiny. I don't think ayahuasca is the answer, but it can be an essential step on our path. Nothing is the silver bullet. No external thing is the answer. The real work starts after we return from an ayahuasca trip. The work never stops.

Do I think Ayahuasca is for everyone? No. It is up to the individual to decide. Going through an ayahuasca session requires strength and determination, and drains the body of energy. Only we can determine whether the discomfort is worth the potential reward. Everyone should do their research. Read stories, news and articles from all angles and perspectives to have a balanced take on the subject.

Ayahuasca is a powerful way to clear our body's psychosomatic cache so that there's less obstruction and fewer barriers between us and the world. The feelings of unconditional love for ourselves and the world are some of the most profound experiences we can have as human beings. But the bliss we feel after ayahuasca is not enlightenment. It is an experience.

Every single moment is an experience imbued with spirituality. It is the mind – its perceptions and preferences – that labels those experiences as either spiritual or unwanted. When we realize that every moment is, in actuality, inherently and intrinsically spiritual, we've arrived at enlightenment. Ayahuasca is one of the practices that can help us understand this. Still, it can also trap us if we don't integrate these teachings into our life with awareness and responsibility. Tread lightly if or when She calls.

***

After reading this section, you might think I'm slightly masochistic. I believe the deepest depths of inner work require us to embrace at least a *tiny* bit of masochism. And if masochism is synonymous with learning how to face, embrace and befriend discomfort, then maybe all of us will embrace our masochistic side at some point during our healing journey.

Fear, pain and discomfort, in and of themselves, should not deter action. We can learn to face them, question them, lean into them and curiously explore what's on the other side. Make it a regular practice to dine with discomfort, so when it does show up in everyday life, it's like meeting an old friend for a new and exciting conversation.

In cognitive behavioral therapy, cognitive diffusion is a coping technique to help people create space between themselves and uncomfortable or unhelpful thoughts. Cognitive diffusion teaches people that they don't have to react to the contents of their mental world. Similarly, conscious discomfort can be conceptualized as *experiential diffusion* because the practices expose the individual to *experiences of discomfort*, so that when they face such discomfort in everyday life, they've already practiced sitting and being with it in a non-reactive way.

Conscious discomfort cultivates *experiential flexibility*, the capacity to know that we can pass through life's diverse experiences without being swayed or impacted. We become less reactive as a consequence. As we decrease sensitivity to external stimuli, we become less sensitive to sensations that would have triggered reactivity. As we get deliberately comfortable with discomfort and become less reactive to it, we learn to take the experience of discomfort more seriously and tune in when the body *does* experience it during everyday life. No longer is our body the boy who cried wolf.

When I notice myself resisting pain and discomfort in everyday contexts, conscious discomfort has shown me how to relax, soften and lean into my experience. I allow my body to subtly move and adjust itself of its own accord. I intend to do nothing except watch. The external circumstances may not change, but change is made possible because I am empowered to consciously choose rather than react.

How I calibrate internally helps me settle into the moment and be more present with what's in front of me, whether it's my son, a client or a daily task. Furthermore, the capacity to be present with my son, my partner and my clients as they sit with their pain is easier because I've practiced sitting with my own. This is because our capacity to be an unconditionally accepting, empathic and non-judgmental presence for another develops in accordance with the processing of our own pain. We won't habitually try making the other feel better or subconsciously attempt to make their pain go away because our practice has taught us that sitting with our pain can be beneficial and healthy. We learn to be present with and supportive of others while trusting that they can experience the same benefits.

It's important to note that practicing conscious discomfort doesn't make the difficulties and stresses of life vanish. I didn't think I'd stop getting angry, feeling insecure or jealous, or immediately stop watching porn if I practiced enough conscious discomfort. That's because conscious discomfort is not a substitute for the healing we may have been avoiding. Conscious discomfort is preparation for pain, not an avoidance strategy. This is what makes conscious discomfort fundamentally different than masochism.

Conscious discomfort gets us comfortable with discomfort, but the practice can't eliminate the body feeling the real thing, which is a necessary step toward change. We can't use conscious discomfort to avoid other pain or life challenges. Pain is an unavoidable aspect of life. Pain can hurt, be unpleasant and just plain old suck. But it can also transform.

Compassionate Conscious Discomfort

The purpose of conscious discomfort practices, and all practices, is so that the lessons seep into and permeate through other aspects of everyday life. What conscious discomfort practices are not intended to be are another form of avoidance. When we stay connected to our experience, we can check in with our experience to see if we are embracing discomfort for increased consciousness or inviting physical discomfort as a means of feeding unconscious avoidance. If we fall into a state of unconsciousness, we can quickly fall into the trap of utilizing conscious discomfort practices to avoid or soothe other uncomfortable emotions or experiences. Reflection and self-inquiry can help us see the intention beneath the practice.

Intention – our *why* and our *how* – is particularly important with conscious discomfort practices because we are meeting the experience of pain. Whether we are relating to conscious discomfort practices as a gift to the body or subtly punishing ourselves will influence how the many interconnected systems of our physiology experience the practices.

Specifically related to conscious discomfort, there's a thin line between conscious discomfort and self-flagellation. Intention matters. *Compassionately* embracing discomfort means we must be honest with our intentions and clear that we aren't cleverly and unconsciously punishing ourselves. If at the core of our practice is the fundamental seed of avoidance or disapproval of ourselves, then conscious discomfort will only take us so far before we realize we haven't truly escaped our limiting self-beliefs.

Rather than practicing to get rid of experience, conscious discomfort is a means of practicing a different way of relating to the present moment. In turn, we cultivate the capacity to meet whatever experience arises, regardless of whether the mind labels it as pleasant or unpleasant, comfortable or uncomfortable. Compassionately practicing conscious discomfort implies that, yet again, *how* we practice conscious discomfort matters.

There are two vital considerations for compassionately practicing conscious discomfort. First, when starting any conscious discomfort practice, it's helpful to experience small doses at a time. In the world of healing trauma, this is known as *titration*, or slowing and portioning. Titration is a technique that originated within chemistry and medicine but is also used to approach psychological contexts. With titration, small amounts of a stimulus or substance are added and adjusted until the right balance is found.

Within the world of conscious discomfort, titration refers to adding just enough of the hormetic stress to get a physiological and psychological benefit, but not so much that the nervous system prevents us from being calmly present and observant of our experience. This is why starting with cold or cool showers can be a more appropriate option than jumping into an ice bath straight away.

Too little hormetic stress and no benefits are derived. Too much exposure to it, however, might trigger an adverse reaction from the body and mind. The space between the two, the *window of tolerance*, is where we want to spend most of our time practicing conscious discomfort. When we practice within our experiential window of tolerance, titration with conscious discomfort can enable the body to process and integrate emotional wounds and slowly teaches us how to create space for settling, regulating and resolving triggering experiences.

Sometimes with conscious discomfort, we might assume that *more is always better* and try to cram more benefits into a single session by disregarding what the body is feeling and blindly following the prompts of the mind for more-more-more. *I have to spend an extra minute in the ice bath today. I can't miss a single day of breathwork.* But our body processes, learns and integrates differently than the mind (as we'll read in the next chapter, *Radical Self-Acceptance*). It's wise to attune to the body instead of abiding by a specific program created by the mind.

Listening to the body will tell us if it is opening or closing in relation to our conscious discomfort practice. Openness is an important quality for developing self-awareness and compassion. When the body is open, we are more willing to have full emotional, visceral and social experiences. We can be curious observers of our experience – both internally and externally – because our mind perceives safety. Indeed, when we are open, we feel the vitality of life.

Closing is the natural counterpoint to opening. Closing itself off to the stress allows the body to integrate, process and assimilate the conscious discomfort experience. Sometimes closing can result from overwhelm, which is often more sudden, drastic and uncomfortable.

This kind of closing is when we drastically and suddenly overshoot our window of tolerance. We have moved past our window of tolerance and our body quickly reminds us it's no longer experiencing safety as tension floods the body and our fight-flight-freeze reaction grabs the steering wheel. This automatic process leads to shutting down, numbing out, dissociating or freezing, especially when we don't notice the body signals telling us we need to close for processing and integrating. Opening ourselves to future experiences requires rest and recalibration, which occurs during periods of closing.

It might be helpful to liken conscious discomfort practices to settling into a hot bath. If we just jump into the hot water, we'll scream in pain, jump out and possibly burn ourselves. Better to enter the tub slowly, one body part at a time, giving each part of the body time to acclimate to the temperature of the water before submerging completely. If we approach our bath slowly and mindfully, it can be a soothing and relaxing experience, as opposed to potentially damaging or traumatizing.

No set regimen or protocol universally accounts for everyone's window of tolerance. Each person, and moment, is unique, meaning every time a person engages with conscious discomfort, it should be treated as a new experience. It's wise to connect and listen to the body rather than follow a rigid, strict protocol. *What is my body telling me today? How does my body feel about this?* Only the individual knows when an experience has become overwhelming and the body has closed off. Listen to the body and it will tell us.

Only we can determine the degree to which we are open or closed to the unfolding experience. Conscious discomfort can help us develop this intuitive capacity. Respect the body in the moment rather than some preset schedule imposed by the mind. It's through connection with the body that our window of tolerance grows.

If we aren't well-versed in the language of the human body, we can get confused by what the body is signaling and what it needs in that moment for support. When we can name it, acknowledge it and validate what it is telling us, we come to see this part of our inner knowing as a compass and teacher. *I'm closed right now.* Expressing it verbally helps us normalize and pass through the experience rather than resisting and avoiding it.

Conscious discomfort builds the capacity of the nervous system to be with uncomfortable sensations, pain and emotions sustainably and therapeutically. Titration allows this process to happen with a reduced risk of overwhelming the body and putting the system into shutdown.

Through conscious discomfort, we learn more about when and how our body becomes triggered and begins closing. There's incredible value and utility in understanding and identifying when we are open and when we are closed and, more importantly, being able to feel the difference in the body. Only we can determine if an experience is safe; our body is where we'll get the message.

***

That said, it's hard for me to say that titration is the *only way* to practice conscious discomfort. It's not. It certainly wasn't for me. Or rather that I titrate in ways that I feel safe and comfortable. *Safety and comfort are not synonymous.* We can perceive safety while experiencing discomfort, one of the many benefits and lessons taught by conscious discomfort practices. I've shared the limits I've pushed my body through throughout this book, so it's only natural that I perceive safety within more intense experiences of discomfort than others who may not have had the same experiences. What's important to note here is that every person is responsible for exploring what *safety* means and feels like for them.

Safety cannot be guaranteed by external circumstances or variables. Yes, safety can be *supported* by external contexts, but safety is an inside job. We perceive ourselves to feel safe or unsafe based on physiological phenomena or experiential evidence happening at the physical level. When we say we *don't feel safe*, we are saying that there is some tension, restriction or constriction in the body that the mind interprets as uncomfortable.

This means that titration looks very different for every person. Proper titration is based on *feeling*, not something that can be created or manufactured externally. And feeling is inherently an individual, subjective experience, not something based on pre-developed programs, no matter which expert created it.

We determine what's safe and effective for us in the moment. The more we trust our body, the safer we feel exposing it to external stimuli. The more connected and comfortable we are in our own skin, the more likely we are to calmly explore the edges of our comfort zone.

People often think I am crazy or masochistic for my regular repertoire of practices. Masochism, self-flagellation and craziness have nothing to do with it. I have complete faith in my body. *I trust my body.* It's earned my trust. I've built a resilient body capable of facing, managing and processing the most challenging experiences. And because I know my body feels safe in the face of immense discomfort, I listen attentively when I do feel my body's twinges of fear and apprehension in everyday life. In these moments, my body is trying to tell me something. I listen and pay attention.

To develop trust in the body's capacity to pass through stress and discomfort, sometimes we must push our perceived boundaries of the body's incredible abilities to see for ourselves. As such, it's helpful to jump into the deep end from time to time.

Life and its many triggers don't always provide us with the setting that allows us to comfortably adjust our experience to fit neatly within our window of tolerance and sense of safety. Life – as we have all experienced - can be wildly unpredictable, unexpected, intense and overwhelmingly triggering. We don't get to choose the intensity of triggers when they get activated.

Life isn't always *safe*. Life gives us unexpected shocks or jolts. Trying to manufacture safety externally and constantly thinking about safety is a trap because safety is not an external circumstance or setting. *Our perceived level of safety is equal to the amount of trust we have in our body's capacity to face, handle and process a situation.*

Conscious discomfort can teach us that we can feel safe regardless of circumstances. This is why there is merit to pushing our boundaries, jumping into the deep end of discomfort, and practicing being calm, present and open to whatever experience arises. It's when we soften, surrender and open to the discomfort of conscious discomfort practices that we learn that safety is a perception and that all discomfort eventually passes.

With conscious discomfort, our inner experience is examined under a microscope within the laboratory of the body. We act as observers within that laboratory, interested in what is happening rather than assuming a particular outcome. We learn to gently turn toward discomfort instead of avoiding it and running from it. We become interested in the qualities of, and changes in, the sensations we feel from moment to moment. We settle in and notice. Everything.

***

Consciously and compassionately embracing our discomfort represents the path to freedom. When internal experiences have been the driving force of reactive behaviors for a long time, settling into a sense of stillness to face those experiences should be done patiently, carefully and safely. Eventually, and always, the body processes the internal triggers and relaxes. The experience passes. All experience passes.

Pain isn't synonymous with suffering. Avoided pain and discomfort lingers, subconsciously impacting us in ways we are unaware of, no matter how distant the memory or pain is. This is what we call *suffering*: pain that we hold on to.

Pain can, however, be a source of growth and a calling to get curious about the depths of the unknown. Practicing conscious discomfort can show us that. After each brave dip into the seas of discomfort, we emerge with more spaciousness, openness and freedom. Confrontation with discomfort is an unavoidable part of the healing journey.

We utilize discomfort to assist us in shedding unnecessary layers of reactivity, desensitizing overactive and conditioned 'fight-flight-freeze' responses, removing the weight of past trauma, and integrating unprocessed emotions that keep the body tense and constricted. The cherries on top are the many health benefits experienced by the body. Even though it may be uncomfortable, these practices are not intended to be a form of punishment. Conscious discomfort is not torture. It's healthy, nourishing and healing.

Compassionately practicing conscious discomfort is a gift to the body. When we engage in conscious discomfort, only we can look in the mirror and honestly assess the intention and posture we bring to each session. *Am I curiously exploring my inner world and gifting my body with a stimulus that supports and nurtures it? Or am I beating myself up because I perceive myself as 'not good enough' in some way?* Intention matters. How we relate to our experience before, during and after conscious discomfort practices is as important as the practice itself. Even while experiencing pain and discomfort, we can be kind, loving and compassionate with ourselves.

The Encounter with Resurfacing Trauma

This final section provides an important subtlety related to conscious discomfort that will likely be relevant for certain readers, especially those in the helping profession. Additional caveats and nuances should be considered for those experiencing chronic pain, those who have experienced significant trauma in the past, and for therapists working with clients who experience distress or challenges connecting to their bodies.

Unbeknownst to many, meditation and conscious discomfort practices can exacerbate traumatic stress symptoms. When instructed to pay close, sustained attention to the body's inner world, people struggling with past trauma might experience flashbacks, dysregulation, immense pain, numbness or dissociation[180]. This is one of the unavoidable possibilities when we engage with any practice that invites us to become still and introspective. We meet what was previously unconscious and below the surface of our awareness. We may not always like or enjoy what we find. This is not a new trauma or re-traumatization, but rather contact with something previously ignored, avoided and already there, likely for a very long time.

We set ourselves up for the mental perception of disappointment when we assume, expect or desire some specific experience or state as we engage with a meditative stillness or conscious discomfort practice. We face the authentic experience of ourselves and our bodies when we practice. That is often not pleasant when first starting on the journey of healing. As a therapist and practitioner, I want to share my personal philosophy and how I work with clients in practice.

I believe that leaning into pain and discomfort represents the pathway toward healing. *The only way out is through.* My lived experience, studies and spiritual teachers have all pointed in the same direction: toward pain.

Pain has been a teacher for me. It has revealed a capacity of resilience within myself that I lean on in everyday life. At times, the experience of pain kept my attention wholly and entirely in the body. Otherwise, my mind would have wandered off. By befriending pain, I've welcomed the experiences of joy, peace, happiness and harmony. I appreciate them all and no longer take them for granted. Pain keeps me humble and grounded. Above all else, I believe pain is necessary for living a life of meaning and purpose. These are, however, only my beliefs and experiences with pain. What I don't do in professional practice is assume, expect or force my beliefs about and experiences with pain onto those I work with.

As a therapist, I meet my client where they are at. I intend to be the objective mirror through which they can see themselves more clearly. This means that my interpretations of and experiences with pain must be held in check so that I can see my client clearly, and they, in turn, see themselves more clearly. I've come to acknowledge and appreciate that my comfort level with and acceptance of *their* pain will impact my client's experience of pain.

When clients come into contact with pain and discomfort within our sessions or in stillness practice, I don't react as if something terrible has happened. If I did react by trying to help or fix it, I'd be sending the unspoken message that there is something *wrong* with their experience. I instead trust my client's process and don't impulsively act to save my client from their experience of discomfort. I ask questions and get curious about how they are relating to their experience of pain in the present moment. I meet my client where they are and help them explore their experience.

I've already mentioned that I see my client in their potential, not their present circumstances, but while I don't overreact, get worried or concerned, I also don't force them to stay with their pain or try to convince them they should. This is vitally important. This is their journey, not mine. They guide the direction of any session, not me.

My intention is to help my clients meet their present moment experience, whether that's pain, pleasure or anything in between. When pain is present, I come alongside them and help them navigate their discomfort, resource them if they've let me know they need it, and have given me permission to assist them. I ask questions like: *are you okay that the pain is here with us? How would you like to respond to your experience of pain in this moment? Do you need anything right now? What is your understanding of why the pain is here right now? What is the story you are telling yourself about the pain you feel? Would you like to explore your beliefs around the pain you're feeling right now?* There is more to gain with this exploration than simply pulling the parachute as soon as the client encounters pain. When we impulsively disengage from our client's experience of pain as therapists and helpers, it reveals more about our beliefs about pain than the client's.

For both therapists and individuals, it's essential to ask ourselves questions that help us reflect on our beliefs regarding pain. *What do I believe about the experience of the person in front of me presently feeling pain and discomfort? How are my beliefs about pain shaping how they relate to pain? How do I respond when someone around me –family, friend or client – is experiencing pain?*

Confrontation with pain is inevitable on the path toward healing. Our role as therapists, teachers and healers is to empower our clients and trust each client's unique healing process. If pain is present, then it might be precisely *what's necessary for healing*. If we react from our own fear and avoidance, this will be the reaction we model for our clients, which serves to further reinforce their avoidance strategies. If we respond with curiosity, gentleness and compassion, we offer our clients a different approach to understanding their pain so that they can move through it and beyond their trauma.

Whether it's stillness through meditation, stillness in conscious discomfort or stillness being practiced in the relational container created by a skilled therapist, we must go into our pain. The more comfortable we become with our pain, the easier it will be to be present with others when they are in contact with theirs, thus empowering them to learn a different way of relating to it. When working with others, however, the key is to let the person feeling pain dictate if, when, how much, how intense, and how often that exposure to pain occurs. The client – not the protocol – is the master. When we navigate these challenging experiential waters with our clients, we begin to help them foster autonomy, empowerment, intuition, and reconnection with their bodies.

Chapter Summary Points and Key Takeaways

- If we want to change our lives in the direction of meaning, purpose and fulfillment, it will require confronting and embracing pain and discomfort.

- Reconnecting with the body is uncomfortable because we have been disconnected for so long. The body will feel foreign, strange and uncomfortable at first.

- Conscious discomfort practices may be uncomfortable for the mind, but they are healthy for the body.

- When it comes to conscious discomfort, intention matters. Our intention is the difference between a practice being a gift for the body or a form of self-punishment.

- When beginning the journey with conscious discomfort practices, stay connected to the body and start with intensity levels that don't overwhelm the mind and body. Stay within the experiential window of tolerance.

Three Ways to Get Started with Practice

1. **Explore your relationship with pain**. Reflect on your understanding of pain and discomfort. How have your perceptions about pain shaped how you relate to discomfort in everyday life? Where did you learn these beliefs?

2. **Get Funcomfortable!** Choose one of the conscious discomfort practices in this chapter. If you're new to conscious discomfort, find a teacher to guide your first experience(s). Most importantly, stay connected to your body as you experience discomfort.

3. **Step outside of your comfort zone.** After practicing conscious discomfort, see if you can apply the same embodied resilience as you face an uncomfortable experience in everyday life, whether it be a challenging emotion, stressful situation or difficult circumstance.

Chapter 6
Radical Self-Acceptance

"We cannot change anything until we accept it. Condemnation does not liberate, it oppresses." - Carl Jung

"The curious paradox is that when I accept myself just as I am, then I can change." - Carl Rogers

"I bask in the glory of my most magnificent self." - Debbie Ford

Though I had 'quit' porn a handful of times during my 20s, I hadn't addressed the core issues beneath the surface of that coping behavior. For this reason, porn always found a way back into my life whenever I attempted to walk away. Whenever I'd set the intention to quit, a little voice in my head always screamed '*bullshit!*' in response to my declaration of abstinence. That voice knew it could call my bluff because I still *needed* porn. Porn was fulfilling emotional needs that I didn't know existed, needs that I didn't know how to fulfill without it.

For a long time, I believed I was not good enough; something was wrong with me. I don't think I'm the only person who has acknowledged, held, or worked through similar beliefs. From time to time, that belief still resurfaces.

I eventually realized that through porn, I was seeking externally what I didn't know how to give myself internally. In a way, the women on the screen gave me validation, acceptance and a sense of self-worth. I suppose it was because an actress on a screen couldn't ever reject me. These experiences may have been fleeting and illusory, but the lack of genuine validation I experienced growing up meant I had nothing reliable to measure it against. How could I have expected to know what validation and acceptance *felt* like if I hadn't ever experienced them myself?

My dependence on porn was, therefore, a symptom of a deeper yearning to feel connection, intimacy and to be seen. The pain of disconnect and loneliness could be temporarily numbed with porn. During my bouts of abstinence, however, my mind would find a new source of validation: real women. Getting attention from and ultimately sleeping with women artificially propped up my sense of self-worth.

Supporting a non-existent sense of self-worth requires constant attention and external validation. Whenever I intermittently stopped using porn, I immediately turned to use women as emotional Band-Aids. I would increase my dating and pursue more casual sexual encounters. While my mind may have been satisfied with itself that porn was no longer around, I was instead using women to fill the same emotional void. My drip feed of fleeting validation could never be allowed to stop. I wasn't wise to the reality of this cyclical pattern.

Subconsciously using women as a crutch for my ego came with unintended consequences. It seemed that I had an internal radar that could detect a woman's presence no matter how far into the horizon they might have been. My attention would, seemingly at random, be drawn in a certain direction, only to find my eyes gazing upon the outline of a woman. It happened at any moment and regardless of who I was with at the time. The reader might see how this subconscious habit got me in trouble if I was with another woman at the time.

As I became aware of these patterns, I experienced shame when I realized my mind wouldn't engage, speak with or talk to women who weren't potential sexual conquests. I didn't know and had never learned how to be friends with a woman without the relationship being related to sex.

My mind immediately sexualized every woman that crossed my periphery as a potential sexual encounter and thus another hit of validation. It was an all-consuming impulse. I couldn't control the sexualized thoughts that filled my mental landscape when in the presence of a woman. As a result, women's role in my life was as objects of sexual gratification and ego validation. And it was a program so deeply ingrained that it was completely unconscious. I had no idea it was there. I thought this was normal. This way of relating to women was painful to acknowledge, humbling to own, and challenging to write about here. I know that many men have, or do, struggle with a similar way of relating to women. I hope that these words can serve as a catalyst for reflection.

Becoming aware of my thought processes and facing the fact that I didn't have any genuine friendships with women provided a much-needed wake-up call. I wanted to be in relationship with women without the tension and agitation of sexual impulses dictating my thoughts, words and actions. I wanted to feel comfortable and at ease with women without this automatic reaction taking hold.

I knew these reactions were also preventing me from connecting with others, in general, because even when I was with my friends, I was preoccupied with thoughts of women. And if a woman was physically present, I'd subconsciously begin peacocking and trying to impress her. After sincere reflection, I arrived at a clear conclusion: if I learned how to authentically accept myself, I wouldn't need a woman's approval and the need for porn would evaporate.

That is exactly what happened.

On my final voyage away from the solitary and lonely island of porn use, I knew I wouldn't return to this isolated and isolating place. Not only did I fully understand the fundamental needs porn was meeting, I also noticed that the voice in my head didn't interject. No protest, no sarcastic laugh and no voice screaming *bullshit*. This time there was no bluff to call.

The part of me that had previously proclaimed I was full of crap *knew* I had finally figured out what was holding me back; I had to attend to my own emotional needs by going inward instead of reaching outward for temporary self-soothing and relief. That part finally trusted that my intention had his best interests in mind. I knew or would learn how to attend to his needs so I didn't lean on porn or women to do it for me.

***

My previous attempts to quit porn had failed and were destined to fail from the start. When I didn't have porn actresses to validate me, I could use a real-life woman's attention and interest instead. If I didn't accept myself unconditionally, I'd continue seeking to fill an internal void of self-loathing through external means, whether through porn or sexual conquests.

It was time to pull out the root of my seeking validation from the out-side world, specifically from women. The path forward then spontaneously presented itself without much thought, effort or planning: celibacy. No porn, masturbation, sex orgasms or physical intimacy of any kind. Nothing. This felt right. My body was calm.

I didn't want to be controlled and governed by sexual urges for the rest of my life, so I set the ground rules for myself and started with my intention. Firstly, I didn't tell anyone what I was doing. This was a gift, journey and exploration solely for me. I also didn't intend to remain celibate for the rest of my life, though I intentionally didn't set a specific time frame. I left open the possibility of meeting someone with whom I was truly aligned, not just a casual sexual encounter. I'd remain celibate until I met someone with whom I was emotionally and physically connected. I was scared and curious about how long my vow of celibacy would last.

Additionally, I maintained an intention to learn how to hold my own emo-tions and accept myself, to stay connected to myself so I wouldn't unconsciously seek superficial connection with others. I committed to staying connected with myself, my body and its feelings. This was possible through the consistent and patient application of stillness.

Remaining embodied and attentive to myself in the presence of women required earnest effort. I checked in often and stayed connected with my body. This required extra effort and attention at first. I had to be ruthlessly honest about my intentions and bodily impulses from moment to moment. And, not surprisingly, my body never lied.

I became acutely aware of the urges, compulsions and drives previously below the surface of my conscious awareness. When I felt the characteristic rush of sexual energy, I returned to my senses and stayed present with myself. I even found myself walking away from interactions when I noticed the flirtatious part of my personality emerging within the conversation.

By being present and attentive to my body, I learned to give myself the connection I would have otherwise sought from the woman in front of me. I quietly gave myself caring and compassionate words when I felt the presence of a strong sexual urge. If or when I broke celibacy, I knew that these sexual impulses wouldn't be the driving force behind the connection. I had been down that road many times and knew exactly where it led.

While I knew perfectly well the trap that I was avoiding, what I didn't know, however, was what I was on the lookout for. *What experience would let me know it was time to break my vow?* I honestly didn't know. This was uncharted territory. I trusted that my body would let me know when I met it. I knew my body would *feel* it.

Celibacy offered some unexpected lessons and insights. I realized and begrudgingly came to terms with the fact that I couldn't stop my mind's sexualized thoughts and reactions. The more I tried, the more my mind ruminated and judged myself. On and on the cycle of self-judgment continued.

Eventually, the subtleties of this cycle of self-judgment became apparent to me, at which point I was able to reflect on it with some objectivity and compassion. *Why am I judging myself for a reaction I have no control over?* The habitual thought pattern of my mind resulted from having been exposed to mainstream porn since childhood and being conditioned to believe that every woman is ready and willing for sex at a moment's notice. I didn't intentionally embed that reaction into my nervous system. I hadn't put the reaction there, yet I was beating myself up as if I had. There had to be a different way of relating to my thoughts that wouldn't result in the self-judgment that invariably fueled the next cycle of reactivity.

Instead of fighting, I tried a different approach that aligned with the qualities I had developed and cultivated through my personal practices. I began practicing surrendering to the possibility that this conditioned mental reaction might be with me for the rest of my life. This seemed like a real possibility I'd have to learn to accept. That's what happens after nearly 25 years of watching porn.

Instead of judging the reaction, I began noticing it when it arose and stopped giving it self-critical attention. I learned to notice and acknowledge the thoughts without judging them and subsequently practiced shifting my attention back to the person or context in front of me.

Judgment only serves to maintain and perpetuate any and all reactions. Judging our reactions is one factor that keeps the cycle of reactivity going, something that will be further explored later in this chapter. It was only when I stopped judging porn as bad that I was able to stop. Similarly, when I accepted my thought patterns, my mind's reaction of sexually objectifying women began to lessen, shorten and unravel.

Not only did the thoughts become less frequent, their impact on my physiology became less pronounced. Without the regular input and programming provided by porn, as well as the regular input and programming provided by my self-judgment, the automatic reaction slowly faded as a result of living my life in a different way. Rarely does my mind automatically sexualize women anymore. When it does, that sexualization doesn't control my actions and behaviors.

Relating to the world and the people within it differently changed my default ways of thinking. *Acceptance, not willpower, determination or force, cultivated authentic change.* Celibacy, at least for me, had provided the introductory lessons in radical self-acceptance.

It's worth noting that I didn't want my experience of celibacy to be synonymous with renunciation or closing myself off from life. That's a path I don't prescribe to or personally recommend. To me, renunciation is a variation of avoidance, but I can also admit that this is just my interpretation of that path.

I could have locked myself in my room or gone off to live in a cave to ensure my celibacy, but I don't think I would have been able to learn what I did if I had. My intention was self-inquiry and self-knowledge, not simply celibacy for the sake of being celibate.

I consciously chose to continue living life as usual. I went salsa dancing, spent plenty of time with friends and enthusiastically went to social gatherings. It was comforting and entertaining being the wingman in case one was needed. I found it strangely empowering to go out knowing with absolute certainty that no sexual experience would come of it. There was no internal pressure to perform. A huge weight was lifted from my shoulders and I could relax and be myself instead of some version of myself I thought would be sexually desirable.

Ironically, by being myself, it seemed that I had instantly become more attractive to women. And then came the real tests. I knew I had authentically committed to my intentions when I started saying 'no' to women who expressed their sexual interest in me. My body's intuitive sense made it evident that the encounter would have been nothing more than a rendezvous. I felt comfortable and confident that celibacy was building a sturdy foundation of self-acceptance that would benefit my next relationship, whenever that would be.

In the end, I maintained my vow of celibacy for nine months, during which time I learned how to accept myself and honor my emotional needs. What became apparent was that the label and construct of 'celibacy' was less important than the intention of not seeking out validation through sexual encounters. My mind needed the structure that celibacy provided as I learned how to validate, appreciate and celebrate myself during the process. After my vow ended, my mental landscape was no longer dominated by thoughts of women or sex. The impulse to impress or flirt had waned. It was a liberating experience.

My mind and body could now attune to and broadcast the frequency for mental, physical and emotional connection that wasn't solely focused on sexual validation. When the meeting finally happened, I knew there was a more profound connection. Markedly absent were the primal urges to chase and pounce, the elevated heart rate, or the impulse to perform and peacock. Instead, when our eyes met, they didn't break their connection for nearly 30 minutes. There was a calmness throughout my body. I felt completely safe to be myself in her presence.

It was self-acceptance that made it easy to show my authentic self and, in turn, meet someone who embodied the same qualities. I had serendipitously found myself in the beginning moments of my life's first real, connected and vulnerable relationship. A story that lasted nearly three years, finally ended my repetitive 2-year curse and came to a natural, conscious, and beautiful conclusion after life decided we had learned and experienced what we were supposed to from each other. We continue to be friends.

Practicing Self-Acceptance

When we practice self-acceptance, our hearts open and we become less defensive. When we soothe our painful feelings with the healing balm of self-compassion, not only are we changing our mental and emotional experience, we also change our body chemistry and physiology. We shift our body from the threat system to a sense of safety, activating our mammalian immune-boosting, health-promoting and care-giving attachment system[181]. This awakens our ability to 'self-soothe', which triggers the release of opiates and oxytocin, generating feelings of safety and peace. The safer the body feels, the more open and flexible we are in response to our external environment.

We can choose a more compassionate way of relating to ourselves. We practice radical self-acceptance when we forgive ourselves for our perceived imperfections or for not getting it quite right the first, hundredth or thousandth time. We practice when we notice and change the harsh words we use to describe ourselves and our experience. In these moments, we can offer compassion toward the part of us that is only seeking to protect us from pain, as we'll soon explore in an upcoming section. If we want to heal the wounds we've been carrying throughout our lives, nothing short of radical self-acceptance will suffice.

Radical self-acceptance firstly requires honesty. This initial step of objective observation of our behavior requires a ruthless, relentless, unapologetic type of honesty. On my journey, I had to be radically honest, look in the mirror and admit to what I saw. I had to own the knowledge that porn no longer served me or the intentions I had for my life. I had to own my anger and quick-temperedness. I had to admit that I didn't know how to relate to women as human beings. But in accepting the shadow, the possibility of these parts coming into the light was made possible. I don't watch porn anymore. I don't consider myself an angry person anymore. And I have many platonic relationships with women.

As long as we deny our dark parts, shadows and supposed imperfections, they will influence and govern our behavior. We can embrace them, spend time with them and inquire into their nature. *What are they hiding? What are they protecting? What are they trying to say? What do these parts need?* The deeper I dove into my triggers and reactivity, the more I learned about myself and what drove these reactions. With more awareness came a change in the words I used toward myself.

During my early years as a helping professional, I had never given much credence or attention to specific words as I believed actions spoke louder than words. My journey into radical self-acceptance has shown me that even a single word can increase my understanding of myself and how my body responds to my diction. Even the pace, tone and intentionality of my words provide a clearer awareness of myself.

My professional training in Compassionate Inquiry, the psychotherapeutic approach created by Gabor Maté and Sat Dharam Kaur, taught me to listen intently to how clients speak about themselves. I do this because their words reveal their beliefs, as well as how they are presently relating to themselves, their behavior and the world around them. Our subconscious and core beliefs are hidden beneath the surface of our verbal expressions.

I listen intently because no matter what the context, authentic change only begins when we stop judging, criticizing and punishing ourselves. If I don't help the client to see these subtle self-judgments, they will unknowingly continue to fuel reactivity.

When we accept ourselves, we allow ourselves to move through the world with a more profound sense of compassion for ourselves and others. We have greater resilience to withstand challenge and adversity because we are empowered to stand by our own side, regardless of whether the mind labels our experience as a failure or an accomplishment. When we can shamelessly admit faults, be vulnerable with our flaws and own our words, thoughts and actions, everything around us changes. Including us.

The Physiology of Self-Criticism

Self-criticism and judgment are habitual reactions of the mind. For most, self-criticism is the default way they relate to themselves. So much so that even the thought of saying something kind, loving or compassionate about ourselves is a challenge. The fact that we are so unkind, judgmental and critical of ourselves is yet another reflection of being disconnected from our bodies.

We would stop if we could see and feel the impacts of our self-criticism. One way to imagine the effects of our self-critical words is to imagine those same words being spoken to a small child. If we watched as the child's eyes watered, head dropped, shoulders slouched and body tensed in response to our words of self-judgment, how quickly would we pause, stop and reflect? Disconnected, however, we don't see the inner child within us having the same reaction. The inner child within us is tense and cowering in response to our self-inflicted harshness.

Self-criticism stresses the body. Self-judgment triggers the brain's danger system, causing feelings of threat and distress, marked by a faster heart rate, secreting a nervous sweat and activating the *sympathetic nervous system* (see *The*

Wise Body, Who's in Control?). When the body's threat system gets triggered, the brain releases cortisol, which activates the body's fight-flight-freeze response. This is why when our harsh inner critic becomes active, it's as if we are attacking ourselves.

When we criticize, judge or condemn ourselves, it immediately impacts the body. To illustrate this effect, I'll invite you to try another experiment. First, you can read the instructions that follow and then you can close your eyes and try it for yourself.

With your eyes closed, take your attention inward and allow it to rest in the body. Spend a few moments being present with whatever happens to be alive and active within you in the here and now. After a few moments of stillness and silence, say the word *yes* out loud. Then pause and pay attention to how the body responds. Following the pause, say *no* out loud and repeat the same process of pausing and attuning the body's response to the word. Repeat the process once more for each word.

Then, as the next step, say *yes, yes, yes* out loud while staying connected with the body. After a pause, do the same with *no, no, no*. Finally, take a deep breath and scream *YES* as loud as you comfortably can or to the degree warranted by your surrounding environment. You can then open your eyes. Thank you for joining me on such an experiment.

What did you notice? What was your body's response to *yes*? My guess is that there was a softening, release or relaxation somewhere in the body. The body opens in response to a *yes*. What was your body's response to *no*? It was likely characterized by tension or constriction somewhere in the body. The body tends to close in response to a *no*. And if there was a different response – such as numbness to both or a constriction in response to 'yes' – this, too, can be an invitation for curious exploration and reflection in the name of self-awareness.

The connection here is that when we are self-critical and judgmental toward ourselves, we essentially say *no* to ourselves. Denying, rejecting or suppressing emotions is like saying *no, you don't belong here, no, you shouldn't be here*, or *no, go away* to the emotional state we are experiencing at the time. The effect on our body will be palpable and immediate. Whether we are presently consciously aware of it or not, the body will tense and close. The self-judgment will reverberate through the body as a *no*, adversely impacting every system within it. We can, however, learn to say *yes* and experience a contrasting physiological response.

The Power of Saying Yes

To say yes to our emotions represents not only the soothing balm of welcoming acceptance but also acknowledges that every emotion carries a gift. When we deny the gift of the emotion, we get stuck in the emotion precisely because we reject or judge its existence and presence in the body. Avoidance of a feeling doesn't make our experience go away. Instead, avoiding an emotion temporarily places it outside of our conscious awareness. At some point, that emotion will return – likely with greater intensity – since the need to express that emotion grows in response to the stress of our everyday life experience. It is often better to feel our emotions in the moment they are being experienced so that we don't fall into the pattern of carrying and intensifying our emotional experience. Indeed, when we do allow ourselves to feel an emotion as it arises, we bear witness to the gifts that it brings.

Pain, already discussed extensively in the previous chapter, brings the gifts of healing and growth. When its expression is denied or suppressed, immobility can result. Sadness carries the gift of reflection. When sadness is denied, it can cause depression, isolation and hopelessness. Anger brings strength, energy and motivation. When denied, anger can become rage that irresponsibly and unintentionally explodes outward toward another. Fear comes bearing the gifts of wisdom and protection. Deny or avoid those gifts and fear can turn into panic, anxiety and paranoia. Shame and guilt can teach the value of humility or provide the gift of making amends. Or it can produce worthlessness if rejected. Even joy, the bringer of hope, healing and connection, can turn into hysteria if it is denied or repressed. No matter the emotion, a gift, lesson or insight is always available to us.

The power of saying yes is equally relevant to the beliefs we hold about ourselves. We don't control when our automatic, conditioned and self-limiting beliefs pop up in the mind. When we say no to them, we engage in a fight with ourselves that adds tension and stress to the body. As difficult as that may sound, it's in understanding the origins and functions of our beliefs that we pave the way for accepting beliefs that the mind labels as destructive, detrimental or debilitating. The following paragraphs demonstrate this process of saying yes to a belief.

There is a single belief from which all our perceived suffering emerges. I call this belief the *seed of suffering*. Everything in our life that brings us unnecessary pain and suffering stems from this fundamental belief. That seed, idea or belief can be stated as either *I am not good* enough or *there's something wrong with me*. Both point to the perception of a fundamental lack within ourselves.

All the seemingly different iterations and variations of *I am not good enough* or *I am wrong* are merely branches that have grown from a tree that started as this single seed. This tree is fully matured because the seed of suffering has been watered by our environment and then by us throughout life. But the only thing wrong with us is the *belief* that something is wrong with us.

That something within us needs fixing, healing, changing, altering, removing, augmenting, transforming, shifting or destroying is only a thought. And what we've learned throughout this book is that thoughts aren't always true or a great representation of reality. *Thoughts give us a story.*

We judge ourselves as imperfect beings because we've been conditioned to do so. The world told us we are imperfect, flawed and incomplete. We believe we are not enough because our parents taught us so, albeit this was most likely unintentional on their part. We desire to change our bodies because of the influences of media and advertising. Christianity talks of original sin. Buddhism and Hinduism call it a karmic debt carried over from past lives. At every turn, we are taught that something is fundamentally wrong with us at our very core, that we are not inherently good enough as we are. It is only the mind – *our mind* – that judges and labels something or someone as inadequate.

It was in anchoring my awareness to the body and the present moment that led me to question, challenge and, eventually, discard any belief system built atop a central premise of lack or inadequacy. Compassionate Inquiry is one of those systems and approaches that honors our innate wholeness.

I believe everyone will face some iteration of this belief on the path to growth and healing. In that moment of recognizing such a belief, we can say 'no' to it, confronting the belief as if facing an adversary. When we meet our beliefs with a *no*, the body will respond in kind.

Alternatively, we can say *yes* to it as if meeting an old friend because even the belief of not being good enough has brought gifts. If we reflect on our own life, we may find that many, maybe all, of the goals we've reached, skills we've acquired and challenges we've pursued were born out of the seed of *not good enough*.

I wouldn't have played professional football, traveled the world making documentaries or played a meaningful role in my son's life had it not been for my fully mature tree of not believing myself good enough. We only require some time for reflection to identify the qualities within ourselves that have been cultivated – as well as accomplishments that have been achieved – as a reaction to our limiting beliefs. To condemn and reject the belief is akin to firing the worker who's been working their hardest for us. Instead of meeting our beliefs with judgment, it would be more appropriate to say *thank you*, which has an equally, if not more profound, opening effect on the body as a *yes*. When we meet our belief in this way, we are saying *yes* to it.

Saying *yes* to a limiting belief we hold of ourselves isn't synonymous with saying it's true. In this context, saying yes is acknowledging that it's happening, without resistance or judgment, and thanking it for the gifts it has provided. In addition to reflecting on the qualities and events that could be attributed to our limiting beliefs, what makes the process of thanking easier is the recognition that the belief of not being good enough was arguably essential for learning how to survive in the material world.

It's within this context that Maté provides an explanation that invites radical self-acceptance for our limiting beliefs. For a child dependent on their external environment for physical survival, what's safer for the child to believe: that their environment is incapable of supporting their physical, mental and emotional needs? Or that there is something wrong with them? If the child believed the former, it would risk their survival. Believing the latter may have long-term consequences, but at least survival is ensured in the short-term, which takes precedence during these vulnerable stages of early childhood.

And so, the belief that something is wrong with us becomes our protector, through thick and thin, for better or worse. We continue leaning on this protection, consciously or subconsciously, until we consciously begin choosing a new belief. Choosing new beliefs isn't easy and requires time and patience. When we notice the presence of a limiting belief, we can ask ourselves questions: *do I want to relate to myself and this moment in this limiting way? Do I want my limiting belief to be the only way of relating to these moments of my life? How would I respond in this moment if I believed myself to be whole and enough? How would I perceive and respond to this situation if my healing was complete? What does that part of me believing itself not to be enough need in this moment?*

As we reflect and make different choices, we automatically feed a different belief and way of being. The precious little moments of change that feed a different belief could be walking away from an argument or potential relationship we know won't serve us, enforcing a boundary or taking the first step toward a goal or intention we've been hesitant to take.

Even when the hard work of feeding a belief of ourselves that aligns with our life's meanings, values and intentions is done, does that mean we cut down the fully matured tree that grew from the seed of *not good enough*? Trying to do so would be a mistake and couldn't be done even if attempted. That tree represents a significant part of us and has contributed to shaping who we are today. Instead, we can honor and memorialize the tree with a sign acknowledging it for all the gifts it has given us. We can thank the old way of being for bringing us this far and let it serve as a reminder that we've learned a new and different way of moving forward.

***

When we say 'yes' to our sensations, emotions and beliefs, we invite the soothing experiences of acceptance and gratitude to soften our physiology. Our nervous system responds by settling into a relaxed, parasympathetic state. When we say 'no' to our uncomfortable or unwanted experiences, our body and its nervous system responds as it would to a threat; our posture closes, our mind becomes defensive, tension grips our connective tissue and cortisol floods through our body.

We can say 'yes' to all our emotions even though the emotions might be challenging to experience. Before we can manage an emotion, it must be accepted.

Before an emotion can be accepted, it needs to be identified and acknowledged. Acknowledging an emotion starts when we say *yes* and *thank you*.

To judge ourselves, no matter how subtly, only feeds and perpetuates the belief that we are not good enough. These judgments, whether toward our emotions or beliefs, are directed toward us. It's when we start saying *yes* and *thank you* to the parts of ourselves we've tried hiding from the world that we're practicing radical self-acceptance.

The Cycle of Reactivity

Reactivity is at the core of our challenges and our suffering. Every time we set an intention for change, regardless of context, the cycle of reactivity keeps us seemingly stuck and asking ourselves: *why does this keep happening to me?* While a reaction may seem like a singular phenomenon, experienced as a single moment, when we unpack the moment of reaction under the microscope of stillness, we find separate and distinct experiences within it. An understanding of each of the components of reactivity can help us consciously and intentionally pause the habitual cycle of reactivity and break it at any one of the points.

The cycle of reactivity can be broken down into four parts. The first is the external or environmental stimulus coming into contact with one of the body's senses. This could be a particular smell, a visual cue like seeing a familiar person's face, or a part of the body being exposed to touch.

When the external stimulus comes into contact with the body, this produces a sensation that is experienced and then processed by the body. The second part of the cycle of reactivity is the sensation that arises due to contact with our external environment. Whether or not we consciously *feel* the sensation is influenced by many factors, such as the intensity of the sensation (stubbing our toe against a rock versus the feeling of a shirt sleeve rubbing against our arm as we walk) or the degree to which our attention is within the body rather than lost in thought.

The sensations then trigger our learned, automated and conditioned reactions. This *conditioned, reactive impulse* is the third part of the cycle of reactivity. It can be experienced as a thought – *a glass of wine sounds good about now* – or a behavior that seems to be outside of conscious awareness, such as finding oneself in front of an open pantry or opening a web browser to visit a porn site.

Whether or not we react – as well as how and to what degree – is also determined by the story that the mind superimposes onto our raw experience. *I'm experiencing pain. Pain is bad. Pain must be avoided at all costs.* When we experience what the mind perceives as pain, our impulse to react is based on our past experiences of pain and our understanding of it.

The first three parts of the cycle of reactivity – the stimulus, sensation in the body, and the impulse to react – happen very quickly. It can seem as if all three are happening simultaneously. Indeed, these three experiences can happen so fast that *we are our reaction.* Identifying with, and as, our reaction is natural when that reaction is entirely unconscious, seemingly happening within a single moment.

The fourth and final component of the cycle of reactivity is the mind's self-judgment and criticism that follows reactive behaviors. The mind tries to explain and justify what has occurred, but it does so with inaccurate assessments, such as *I can't sit still, I'm depressed, this is impossible, I can't focus, I can't stop drinking, I can't control myself,* or *this is just who I am.* These statements are inaccurate because they assume that what has happened in a single moment is universally true and will always remain true.

With the assistance of the mind, a single experience becomes solidified as a permanent state. It is the mind's extrapolating that contributes to making the reaction permanent. As a result, we set ourselves up for the repetitive reaction to occur over and over again, unimpeded. When we naïvely declare we will stop our reaction without appreciating the individual parts involved in our reactive cycle, it can seem like a Sisyphean task as we try to change.

If we dissect a moment of reactivity, identifying its constituent parts, we can better intervene with and manage the individual components of our unique cycle of reactivity. For example, many men try and fail to quit habitual porn use simply by trying to stop watching it. This method fails 99.99% of the time because it doesn't consider all the parts of the cycle of reactivity. Instead, by exploring the components contributing to the reaction, we see several available points of entry for creating change.

The Cycle of Reactivity

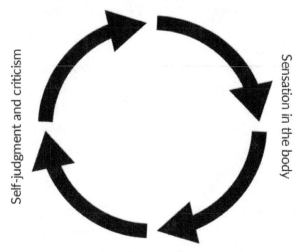

Suppose we realize that one of the external stimuli – the first part of the cycle of reactivity – contributing to our impulse toward watching porn is browsing YouTube and coming across suggestive thumbnail photos. In that case, we can intentionally avoid that website. Or, we might notice that our impulse toward porn use is at its highest when we are stressed out at work. In this case, we might become aware that the particular sensations and emotions – the second part of the cycle of reactivity – that come with work stress are at the core of our reactivity. We then can create a strategy to help us have a better work/life balance so that we experience less of this particular sensation or emotion.

Another possibility is that we find it immensely challenging to experience uncomfortable emotions like fear, anger or sadness. The reactive impulse to reach for porn – the third part of the cycle of reactivity – serves as the buffer against these unwanted experiences. In this case, we've already explored the utility of stillness as an intervention for helping us objectively experience a reactive impulse within the body.

Finally, we might recognize that we judge and shame ourselves for succumbing to our reactivity and watching porn. In this scenario, our continued use is reinforced by our self-criticism and judgment – the fourth part of the cycle of reactivity – because porn is, in fact, the only present strategy we have for managing uncomfortable emotions like guilt and shame. With such insight, we consciously practice radical self-acceptance to see how it impacts and influences our reaction to reach for porn.

The point is that the cycle of reactivity can be broken down into parts and addressed in different ways. Through stillness, we reveal the series of interconnected moments that make up those reactions that seem to happen as fast as the snap of two fingers. And when we can see the reality of those interconnected moments as their separate parts, we then have the power to engage with and influence them.

When stillness shines the light of awareness on our reactivity, we are empowered to pause, disrupt and break the cycle of reactivity at any point. We become equipped to avoid situations and environments that make it easy to fall back into reactivity. We can reduce the intensity and frequency of uncomfortable sensations arising in the body by applying lifestyle choices that support the body's health and healing. We can also cultivate a greater capacity to be present with uncomfortable experiences with conscious discomfort practices. A different way of relating is accessible and available to us if only we consciously choose to practice.

Finally, we can even break the cycle of reactivity *after* the reaction has happened. The judgment and criticism that solidifies our reactions in the body can be replaced with radical self-acceptance. It's possible to *accept ourselves exactly as we are now.* Rather than judging ourselves and labeling our experience as a permanent state or quality, we can be more compassionate toward ourselves by choosing different ways of speaking to ourselves: *I can't do this* can be transformed into *presently I am having difficulty doing this*, while *I always mess things up* is more accurate when stated as *things didn't go the way I wanted them to this time around.*

The way we talk with and describe ourselves impacts our direct experience. We've already explored the contrasting ways the body responds to *yes* and *no*. As yet another experiment, close your eyes and repeat the contrasting phrases from the previous paragraph aloud and see how the body responds to the different ways of expressing the same experience.

Despite the consistent and patient application of stillness, our best efforts and intentions may not be enough to disrupt and stop the reactive behaviors that no longer serve us. In those moments, the opportunity to meet our reaction with kindness and compassion is always there and can be realized in the way we speak to ourselves. While the mind may not label an experience as *change* because the behavior has still expressed itself (such as when we lapse, relapse or react in some way, shape or form), when we pause the judgment and criticism toward ourselves and practice radical self-acceptance, we stop throwing additional fuel onto the fires of reactivity. The mind may not think so, but we are creating change by disrupting the cycle of reactivity at its most crucial point.

Real Change Happens in the Body

The journey of change is never a straight line. The mind, of course, hates when things aren't perfectly logical, rational or linear. With change, there are ups, downs and twists-and-turns in-between. The mind may have intentions, strategies and plans for what the finish line might look like, but change doesn't move in accordance with the mind's rapid-fire desires and shifts in expectations. If we let the mind decide what is or isn't acceptable for change, we're setting ourselves up for perpetual self-criticism. When we misstep or don't meet our lofty expectations (which is always), it's easy for the mind to label the experience, or ourselves, as a failure.

It is helpful to understand the difference between the illusory rate at which the mind changes versus the natural rate of change that occurs in the body. The cyclical nature of change highlights the difference between these two referential viewpoints.

The mind can change in the blink of an eye. Just pause to listen in on your internal dialogue and you'll notice how quickly and often the mind jumps back and forth between seemingly opposing viewpoints as it engages in debates with itself. The mind has no trouble with changing because the change it represents isn't real. *It's imaginary*. Indeed, the mind *thinks* it's creating change all the time. Since the mind can quickly shift, move and solve, it will always judge and criticize outcomes and the speed with which we get there. Results achieved in the real world and in real-time can be minimized, dissected and scrutinized by the judgmental mind.

Real change, which is the kind of change that is palpable, tangible and evidenced by our direct experience in the real world, can only happen in the body. Real change moves at the rate the body's systems can cope with and process. In other words, *the body changes when it's ready*, in accordance and alignment with its natural, intrinsic and innate processes that move it toward healing, health and thriving (see *The Environment of Healing and Healing*).

This means that the body changes at its own pace, influenced by internal metabolic factors, genetic variation and our external environment. The mind will only play a *role* in this process and not the conductor's role. This means the mind must understand that the process of change requires patience, trust and time. The mind hates it when things take time, which is one reason why the mind judges so harshly even when we are making progress.

Depending on where we align our viewpoint, either with the mind or the body, the cyclical nature of change will result in drastically different interpretations. From the mind's point of view, we miss the mark or target every time because the goals it sets are often out of sync with what's possible. As a result, the mind continues to judge our progress negatively. And what do self-judgment and criticism regarding our intentions for change do to the body?

From the body's perspective, however, not quite getting to the intended outcome simply means that the body wasn't ready for such a significant shift. The body doesn't even set targets, so from the perspective of the body, failure isn't even an option. *There is no failure when assessing change from the body's perspective*. If the body doesn't move at the expected pace of the mind, it would be more accurate to say that the body needs more time to process the change occurring before it can manage more the next time the cycle repeats itself.

The body is always moving toward healing and growth. It will continuously recreate the conditions and contexts necessary for the cycles of change to repeat so it can have another opportunity to process, integrate, and heal a little more. The subconscious drivers within the body seek the settings, situations and relationships that will allow it to process the previously-suppressed or repressed experiences or memories.

That is why we consistently find ourselves in similar relationships, situations and life contexts over and over again, no matter how much we *think* we don't want them in our life. With each re-enactment and experiential cycle, we give the body a chance to process the emotional residue while simultaneously allowing ourselves to choose a new behavioral pathway, belief, and new way of being that – little by little – begins to deviate starkly from our programmed and conditioned reactions. I've already discussed how precious little moments of change accumulate to create authentic change.

The mind may hate these repetitive cycles, but the body requires these cycles to feel, release and heal what it wasn't able to in the moment when the original event occurred. It's not easy processing all that pain all at once. The external circumstances, contexts and relationships may look slightly different on the surface during points of our life, but the body is only recreating and re-enacting similar internal experiences so that it can process, integrate and heal itself[182]. Cycles help the body slowly and incrementally process and integrate the underlying pain at a manageable pace, rate and intensity.

Each time we cycle through a feeling, behavior, habit, substance, belief or relationship, we learn more about ourselves and the contexts that perpetuate our cycles of reactivity. When we engage with the process of change in this conscious and reflective way, we transform the cycle of reactivity into the *cycle of responsiveness*.

These cycles may seem self-sabotaging, but in reality, they are cycles of potential, possibility and change, offering the opportunity to practice a different way of relating to ourselves and the present moment each time they come back around. In these moments, we get to practice a different way of being.

This is why radical self-acceptance is so crucial for the process of change. Whereas the judgmental mind continues to chastise us for not meeting its unrealistic goals, the inherent growth processes of the body continuously offer opportunities for change for as long as we live. Every moment is rich with new potential and possibility. The more the mind understands and accepts this, the easier it is to step out of the way and let the body change. Despite its best intentions, the mind's intrusions are often counter-productive and can even slow down the change process.

Life gives us the same lesson over and over again until we've learned it, until the body has processed what it needs to process. The mind doesn't get to control when or if that happens. But knowing that the body will not stop setting up the conditions for an important life lesson until it is finally learned allows us to trust the process rather than trying to control, and thus inadvertently thwart, the process. Along the way to thoroughly learning and integrating whichever lesson is being learned, we acquire wisdom about ourselves that serves us moving forward, such as gaining a deeper awareness of our bad habits, understanding and fulfilling our unmet needs and discovering both the internal and external resources that we can lean on during times of distress.

The repetition of painful cycles contains opportunities to observe, learn and change. And the key to taking advantage of those opportunities lies in the body because the body does not lie. The body wants to shed its deeply embedded reactivity and heal. That's what it's programmed to do. The best thing the mind can do is to continue exploring and understanding the body so it can learn to trust the body during this process.

***

Throughout this book, I've explored the most profound understandings and insights related to the many contexts that contributed to forming my porn habit. I've shared the emotions and experiences that made me impulsively reach for porn, the interpersonal skills that made porn an easy option to turn toward, and the deeper emotional needs that porn was attempting to fulfill. In an upcoming chapter, *The Miracle of Healing Trauma*, I'll share more relevant contexts around my porn use, specifically its origins and potential root causes. I've provided the reader access to all of this information to illustrate the nuances, subtleties and interconnected complexities of what maintains our habitual re-actions.

The same process is relevant and required for any behavior or reaction if we wish to move into a space of possibility and potential rather than staying trapped in the repetitive cycle of reactivity. When we ask ourselves *why* and sincerely seek answers, we begin unpacking all of the contexts that led to our reactive behaviors and understanding why we continue perpetuating them. The more we learn about the realities of how our behaviors came into existence, the less harshly we judge ourselves for our reactivity. Understanding paves the way for radical self-acceptance.

No matter how many times we mess up or *think* we've messed up, we can hold the intention to practice radical self-acceptance. When we begin to see that our reactions, regardless of how unhelpful they seem on the surface, have always been our protectors, then we relate to them with acceptance rather than with judgment. We can break the cycle of reactivity by giving ourselves the kindness and compassion that naturally emerges from our increased understanding of ourselves.

Before we can accept any aspect or part of ourselves, we must fully understand that part. We must understand the *why* beneath the reactivity. That understanding includes reflections on why that part exists, the roots and origins of that part, why that part came to be in the first place, what that part is still doing for us, what otherwise unmet needs that part is fulfilling, and which beliefs are connected with that part. When we truly understand why a part of us came to be, radical self-acceptance, rather than judgment, reveals itself as the *only way* of relating to it that makes sense.

When we reflect and understand to this depth and degree, we see that thankfulness might be more appropriate than judgment. We begin turning toward our impulsive thoughts and saying *thank you. I can hold myself in this experience;* the tension in body disappears, leaving the warm and opening experience of gratitude in its place. From this place, we can consciously move toward new possibilities, beliefs and a new way of being.

Chapter Summary Points and Key Takeaways
- Self-judgment and criticism have detrimental physiological impacts on the body.

- Every emotion – whether we like it or not and whether it is pleasant or not – has something it can teach or gift us.

- The belief that we are not good enough or that something is wrong with us is the seed of suffering – the core belief – from which all of our suffering emerges.

- The mind can change its opinions, positions and stories quickly. The body changes at a far slower rate. It is challenging for the mind to accept the body's rate of change.

- We can pause and disrupt the cycle of reactivity by being kinder and more compassionate with ourselves when we don't quite meet our expectations, intentions or goals.

Three Ways to Get Started with Practice
1. **Practice radical self-acceptance**. When you catch yourself in a moment of self-judgment and criticism, pause and take a breath. See if you can try a different response with yourself. Also, try speaking your response out loud since expressing it aloud involves the body's senses. The expression makes it real.

2. **Keep a self-gratitude journal.** Try a different kind of gratitude and write down the qualities, behaviors and things you are grateful for within yourself. This might be more challenging than expected. Notice how your body reacts to expressions of self-gratitude.

3. **Practice saying *yes*.** When facing challenging moments, sensations or emotions, rest your attention in the body and say *yes*. Practice accepting the moment as it is before consciously responding.

Chapter 7
Relationship

"We are born in relationship, we are wounded in relationship, and we can be healed in relationship." - Harville Hendrix

"Self-Mastery is born in solitude, nurtured through experience, and made useful through connection." - Jesse Elder

"Everyone – and everything around you – is your teacher."
- Ken Keyes Jr.

For many people who have made drastic transformations in their life, it's often a specific moment, event or circumstance that provides the spark that made the shift possible. The death of a loved one, a divorce or affair, hitting rock bottom after addiction took hold of their life or a near-death experience are some common contexts that can cause a 180-degree turn on someone's life path. Identifying the specific catalyst for my journey of transformation is easy: Jack, my son. When he was just over a year old, I was separated from him for three months while working on *A Million Ways to Live*, my documentary project. The pain of separation was amplified as I didn't know when, if or how I would see him again.

Jack was born in March 2014. I didn't know then that my greatest teacher was taking his first breaths as he lay on my chest. The most unfortunate wake-up call was splitting from his mother as I finished my work project. During those months of separation, every time I sat down on a plane, train or bus to travel, seeing another infant, or hearing a child cry, sent tears streaming down my face.

My son was the meaning in life I had been searching for while circumnavigating the globe in a subconscious attempt to run away from myself. The immense pain and subsequent reflective process helped me see with perfect clarity that my new life would be in New Zealand. No matter the cost or sacrifice, I would be in my son's life. My son was worth whatever challenge awaited. There were many.

Becoming a dad is one thing, but embracing and committing to the role of being Jack's father changed me forever. Fatherhood represented a seismic shift in my way of being. Fatherhood softened me. I learned that being a man isn't what had been ingrained into my psyche during childhood. I didn't have to hide emotions out of shame, fear of rejection, or because my feelings weren't valid or important. Through the intentional practices already discussed and explored in previous chapters, I learned how to flow through emotions and allow my body to feel sensations without reacting. I practiced openly communicating my vulnerabilities. I've had to learn about safety and boundaries, concepts that didn't make any rational sense to someone who had no previous experience of self. I joined men's circles and groups to connect with other men passing through similar challenges. Fatherhood showed me that it is possible to discard the hardened shell passed down to me from my father and his Polish ancestors.

It wasn't until I became a father that I accepted and embraced my Polish identity. I had previously rejected my culture because of my deep-rooted disdain toward my dad. Ironically, the relationship with my father healed when I was able to see myself through Jack's eyes and my father through my own. I experienced love and appreciation for my father as I recognized firsthand how challenging fatherhood truly is. It was through Jack that I realized how much my father loved me and how his pain, trauma and conditioning prevented him from showing me love in a way that I could understand or receive.

Seeing the relationship between my father and myself at a distance, separated from the tightly-wound knot of constrictive trauma, allowed empathy, forgiveness and love to sprout from the mud of resentment. I eventually confronted my dad and spoke my truth to him at my brother's wedding. I told him that he had never told me he was proud of me, never once that he loved me. He stood there, shocked to hear my words. He never realized it was something important to say or hear. He hadn't even considered it. Since then, no conversation goes by that we don't say *I love you* to each other.

Jack continues to show me my blind spots. His presence shows me when anxiety, sadness or frustration arise. My love for my son gives me the motivation necessary to sit with my inner experience so that it doesn't leak out and create relational tension. I can still feel the residual impulses to work and *get shit done* from time to time. I still notice the presence of the limiting belief that bases my worthiness on productivity and utility. It's empowering to know that I now have a choice in how to respond to those beliefs. I've learned to accept old patterns and conditioning manifesting as somatic discomfort and not identify with them or let them grab hold of the steering wheel. *Which belief do I want to feed? Which response do I want to nurture?*

Embracing the vital role of being a father demanded my growth and maturity. I had to allow my old ways of being to shed and fall away. It was my life's greatest challenge and calling to break the generational cycle that had pervaded my family. The dominoes had to stop falling at some point, so why not with me?

Judgment transformed into understanding, rejection to acceptance, shame to compassion. I vowed to be for my son the person I needed when I was hurting, not the person who hurt me. I vowed to heal myself, so my son wouldn't be left broken. I will pass down wisdom, not wounds.

***

Love for his children is often the most powerful thing that liberates a man from self-obsession, addictions, defeat and depression. His love for his child makes a man willing to take the necessary steps for personal growth and be thankful for doing so. As a result, I'm a better man, partner, friend, son, brother, helper and human. My son showed me that relationships matter in this life, not material success and fulfilled ambitions.

The quality and state of my life's relationships have become the litmus test for whether I am living a fulfilled life. When I take care of my body, listen to what it's saying and attend to its needs, my relationships are infused with more calmness, compassion and harmony. I can be present with another without my mind being distracted or agitated. When I notice myself getting triggered or over-reacting, I see it as a sign that my body likely has needs unmet.

Previously, I had utilized income and productivity as markers of life success. This old way of being had burnt many bridges and resulted in many broken relationships. It couldn't continue. A new way of being meant focusing instead on the state of my interpersonal relationships, which provided a more meaningful purpose for my practices that would have otherwise been lost on *self-mastery*, *personal optimization* and *bio-hacking*. The gifts I cultivated through healthy living, stillness, conscious discomfort and radical self-acceptance could now be shared with others.

I learned to be with stress so that I wouldn't get easily triggered by others. I sat with my pain so I could be the empathic container needed by others as they bravely faced their pain. I took care of my body so that it would be relaxed and at ease when I was with my son. Giving my body the nourishment it needs allows me to be in service to those that I love and care for.

My life's practices became more meaningful when I began bringing their lessons into everyday life. The practices, when integrated in this way, cultivated a way of being that allowed my relationships to break away from cycles of conditioned patterns of internalization, suppression and repression.

Everyone in our life benefits from our practice. When the dominos of reactivity start falling around us, they can stop at us because we've grown and know how to calmly step aside without being too bothered. We can choose a conscious response that is aligned with our authenticity.

***

Relationships are a practice of self-discovery in and of themselves. In the moment of trigger and activation, we can ask ourselves: *who do I want to be in this moment? What belief do I want to feed? What lesson do I want to practice or learn within this relationship? Is this an opportunity to practice acceptance? Boundaries? Authenticity? Vulnerable communication? Assertiveness?* Indeed, triggers in relationship represent opportunities to connect with the body and heal. We begin to notice the situations, circumstances and events that create tension in the body. *Why do I panic when I step into the middle of a circle and everyone sees me? Why does my body tense when someone hugs me? Why do I avert my gaze when someone looks me in my eyes?* The nuggets of insights, reflections and lessons that emerge from inquiring into these types of questions are only possible through relationship because they are inaccessible through personal practice alone.

Lastly, just as we can't control the things that happen to us, we also can't control or change the people in our lives (as much as we'd like to sometimes). What we can control, however, is how we *respond*. When triggered in relationship, we can apply the lessons of radical self-acceptance to consider the different possibilities available to us when the mind labels a specific moment in a relationship as a *failure*. There is always an opportunity to see ourselves more clearly, break the cycle of reactivity, or consciously create a precious little moment of change.

What use were all the gifts of personal growth and self-awareness I had learned if not to share them with the relationships that constituted *my* world? The more I work on myself, the more I'm able to show up for others. I can be present with the person in front of me instead of ensuring my 10-year plan is perfectly executed. I regularly enjoy cooking and sharing an evening meal with friends instead of working long hours into the night. The concentrated grimace on my face has been replaced with a soft and subtle smile because I can see everything and everyone around me more clearly. It's through relationship that I celebrate being a human being.

The journey inwards of self-inquiry and self-understanding might be the most selfless thing I've done. I've welcomed checking in on the status of my life's relationships as a barometer of progress. When the energy in certain relationships is tense and heavy, I tune into my body to begin understanding what is unfolding. Being in relationship has made me appreciate the often-lonely journey of personal growth from a more meaningful perspective.

Bringing the Body into Relationship

Bringing the body into relationship isn't just another way of practicing staying connected with the body, it's also the graduation ceremony of *Somawise*. All the individual work involved in becoming *Somawise* develops the qualities and self-awareness that infuse relationships with presence, peace and connection.

When the body lives in an environment that supports its healing and thriving, we have enough energy to engage with and be present with another. The healthy lifestyle choices we gift ourselves become gifts shared with others. It's easier to be calm, focused and compassionate when the body isn't full of stress and tension.

Stillness allows us to focus fully and completely without being distracted by thoughts or other uncomfortable experiences. We can listen attentively to others without being swept away by the stories playing in our minds. As a result, we *see* the person in front of us instead of engaging with snow.

When we meet moments of trigger in relationship with others, conscious discomfort practices provide the training grounds for facing such challenges. In relationship, we reap the rewards of the investments made in ice baths, cold showers, yin yoga classes and breathwork sessions. Conscious discomfort has empowered us to face relationship tension with more clarity, calm and ease. It's easier to manage conflicts because we are stable and grounded within ourselves.

All the reflective inquiry and self-awareness work that comes with radical self-acceptance makes it possible to be more accepting and non-judgmental of the person in front of us. When we have acknowledged and worked with our own self-limiting beliefs and harsh inner criticism, it's easier to have empathy for others as they learn to navigate the relationship with their beliefs and self-criticism.

When we stay embodied while related to another person, we can be present with the other because we better understand what's ours and what's *theirs*. When we notice something coming up for us, we see it as an opportunity to attend and respond instead of blaming or judging. We've learned how to stay connected to the body rather than get whisked away by the drama playing out in the mind. Any outwardly projected label of negativity offered by the mind often reflects our blind spots, not what's playing out in front of us.

When we bring the body into relationship with another person, our embodied presence will make it easier for us to choose a response rather than fall into the same reactive traps. Moving away from knee-jerk reactions and toward conscious responses can significantly impact our relationships because we are empowered to take ownership and accountability for our part and role in the relational dynamic.

Staying in the body invites curiosity and leaning in, rather than tension and disconnect. For example, before mental stories of jealousy lead to a quick-tempered eruption of anger, it's possible to stay with the body's experience instead. When choosing to respond, we must acknowledge the story, feel the sensations of tension and constriction that correspond with the mental stories, and allow the emotion to arise, peak and pass away. It's then that we can choose an appropriate response. This stillness-infused curiosity leads to connection rather than the relational discord that typically follows anger-laden reactivity.

In turn, when we see something come up for the person we are in relationship with – whether a trigger, an emotion or a sly self-judgment – we can hold more empathy for the other because we know how challenging it is, first, to become aware of the subconscious reaction and, second, to work through it. It's easier to take things less personally when we see beneath the surface of the external expression of the person in front of us. There are always emotions, sensations, thoughts and beliefs that influence the *what, how* and *why* of someone's communication and expression. When we've explored these contributing factors within ourselves, they become more apparent – and sometimes blatantly obvious – in another. But because we know there is a way out, we can relate to this person while holding their potential and possibility, rather than solely relating to their subconscious reactivity. What has been described in this section are the many gifts that we can bring into relationship with others.

***

Practicing embodied presence in relationship requires keeping a portion of our attention within the body. Staying embodied keeps the mind focused on what's happening in the present moment. Through practice, we learn to hold and manage our own experience, focus on the body of the person in front of us, and pay attention to their story. All three focal points provide information that can help us understand the person and situation. When we become capable of giving this kind of attentiveness to another, we can notice the same qualities in others and are better able to attract and choose relationships with those who have the awareness, capacity and skill to reciprocate such gifts.

As we might imagine, bringing this type of attentiveness into intimate partnership is a special gift. When embodied in relationship with a partner, friend or family member, we can receive and process multiple sensory reference points that help us understand the situation more clearly. We can hear what the person is saying, not just the words they're using, but also the tone and pace of their voice. The rhythm of the voice might give us information beyond mere word choice.

We can also watch their body language for signals and cues indicating the presence of emotions or sensations they may be experiencing. How someone breathes, their posture, where and for how long they rest their gaze, or even the color of their skin can alert us to whether we should dig deeper with a question or let them continue.

How our body receives and responds to their words further improves our capacity to understand the true meaning of what is being said. The sensations that arise within the body might indicate an empathic response, a conditioned reactivity resurfacing or a combination of the two. When we hold that experience in stillness, we can differentiate between what is ours and what is theirs. Knowing the difference helps determine what we are responsible for (our experience) and what is out of our control (the experience of the other).

Learning how to listen deeply to others in this way directly stems from having learned how to do it with our own bodies. The number of subtleties we notice and detect in another is directly related to our capacity to do the same with ourselves. Anyone can improve their ability to attend to the present moment in this way. We don't have to get bitten by a radioactive therapist to gain empathic superpowers. This level of attentiveness is available to those who wish to work at it. As with all things in life, *practice is required*. The secret to deep listening is simple: stay connected to *your* body. I can confidently state that I wasn't born with this ability. It was something I cultivated through practice.

If nurtured through consistent practice, this level and depth of connectedness to ourselves and others compounds and increases over time. As we spend time with people – whether friends, family or clients – in a state of complete attunement and presence, our understanding of their beingness correspondingly deepens.

We'll be able to sense when something isn't quite right long before the other intends to share it. We notice the slightest deviations from behavioral norms, which piques our gut instinct's curiosity. Fortunately, and sometimes unfortunately for them, the ability to sense the subtle pauses, changes in posture, or atypical shifts in eye contact turns our body into a highly accurate lie detector. Those closest to us may find this quality particularly annoying!

Bringing presence into relationship with the world can be considered the epitome of what it means to be mindful because life happens in relationship. *We are always in relationship.* Some relationships are interpersonal, whether a parent with a child, two lovers, a teacher with a student, or a manager with an employee. We are also in constant relationship with ourselves. Our inner relationship influences how we relate to others, hence why the most important relationship is the one we have with ourselves. Finally, we are also in relationship with every external object in our life, such as work projects, meals or material possessions.

We cannot escape being in relationship because we cannot exist in isolation. Just as we depend on the food, air and water of our physical environment for survival, we cannot see our traits, qualities, skills and other aspects until they are mirrored and reflected back toward us by another person. We require relationship to *know* ourselves. As Martin Buber said: *all real living is meeting*.

How to be Present with Others

One of the ways we can practice being with another person is by *listening attentively*. If we want to give someone a gift today, listen. Like, *really* listen. It only took about 30 years, but when I finally learned how to listen, it transformed how I work with clients, how I connect with loved ones, and the depth of my relationship with my son. Whether we're a parent seeking connection with our children, a couple trying to understand each other's respective worlds, or a helping professional seeking to infuse our professional practice with more empathy, listening is a fundamental skill for cultivating presence in relationships.

Listening sounds easy, and maybe it is for some, but it wasn't for me. I can say with absolute certainty that my ability to listen grew as I learned how to authentically listen to my own needs. When my body is agitated, tense or triggered, staying present with another is challenging. When my body is relaxed, I quickly drop in and deeply experience the world of the other.

When we listen, we focus our full attention on the person in front of us and consciously settle into our bodies. We must use our ears, eyes and all the body's senses to listen deeply. Each sense provides a layer of depth regarding the words being verbally expressed and what the person in front of us is experiencing. Our ears hear the narrative, the story and the content. Our body might twitch, adjust or move as it picks up on words and phrases entangled with strong emotions, perceptions and beliefs. Our eyes notice facial expressions, physical tension, postural changes, shifts in breathing patterns, and flushes or paleness in the skin. We can use these somatic cues of the other person to notice when they are experiencing a physiological reaction to their spoken words. We can listen with all our faculties to hear the real message, to what's happening beneath the words.

Our body will mirror and *feel* what the other person is feeling, which is one of the crucial aspects of developing connection[183]. In these moments, we can choose to hold the intention of not running from or avoiding their emotions. We often don't do that because *we* don't like how those emotions feel in our bodies. Often the soothing things we say to another person are subconscious attempts to relieve *us* of our discomfort, not to relieve them of theirs.

It's helpful to turn off the advice-giving voice in our head that wants to fix, save or teach. The person in front of us is not broken, so there's nothing to fix. Even if we think we're experts and our words can help, now is not the time for that. They don't need us to solve their problems. If they did, they'd ask. We can be there to meet them where they're at because, most often, what they need is the space to be heard, understood, and where they can feel the emotions and physical sensations beneath their story.

Most of the time, someone needs a sounding board, a space to offload some heavy content from their mind so their body can express and process it. As such, it might be helpful to learn and practice mirroring skills, an effective technique for establishing safety, rapport and comfort with the person we're communicating with[184]. Through effective mirroring, we reflect what the other is yearning for. When we mirror another, they can see themselves more clearly. There's no space for the other's authentic expression if we expect, assume or interrupt from the referential point of our world. If we're not listening deeply, we only consider our experience and perception, substantively defending ourselves.

Remember that the information shared is the tiniest tip of the iceberg. We have no idea what other life experiences are contributing to this moment. Notice the thought *I know* and relate to the person in this moment as if meeting them for the first time. This invites curiosity into the shared space. Remember that whatever advice we want to give is from our autobiography, based on our lived experience – our fears, judgments, expectations and values. All of which is *our stuff*. But this isn't about us, so put that aside and spend some time in their world.

The listening process reaches its completion when we thank the person for sharing. Being the recipient of someone's authentic expression is a gift we aren't automatically entitled to. This is their inner world and they've felt safe and comfortable enough to let us in. Sincerely thanking the other sets up the conditions for sharing in the future. If we don't thank- or worse, if we criticize or reject –it's like placing a sharp blade into an already-bleeding heart. If someone has vulnerably taken their bleeding heart from their chest and risked it by putting it on the chopping board in front of us, we should choose our response wisely. A vast responsibility has been thrust upon us.

Just as vulnerability is a skill, so, too, is listening. A skill that takes time to refine. Through listening, we get to know the other and their world. This isn't about knowing their favorite color or meal, but rather their more profound and meaningful aspects that may not be shared with anyone else. Through listening, we understand a person's trauma, behavioral patterns, coping mechanisms, attachment style, and how they regulate their emotions. With this understanding, we can better respond when we notice the presence of a trigger.

The more we listen and learn, the more aware we'll be of the state of their nervous system, which part of them is speaking, and empathically empower them to navigate themselves back to a state of safety. In this sense, listening to each other fosters mutual respect for uniqueness and autonomy. Relationships naturally and effortlessly become more at ease when we practice listening in this way. Not only are we attuned to and connected with the entire beingness of the other, we're also aware of and able to take responsibility and ownership of our stuff as and when it comes to the surface within the exchange.

When I started paying attention to my body in relationship with others, it was shocking to experience how often my internal triggers were activated during conversation. I noticed how often reactions arose to interrupt, give advice or share my perspective. Without interoceptive awareness, communication with another is like navigating a minefield where the potential for reactivity exists with each step. Inevitably, there will be an explosion. Indeed, one of the ways that relationships have been a barometer of progress for me is noticing when I can pass through conversations and experiences as if they are nothing more than a notable event.

Not only are we empowered to communicate more authentically, peacefully and accurately when we listen from this level of presence and awareness, our somatic reactions also help us gain insight into our triggers. While it may be challenging to accept in the moment, the person in front of us is the messenger, not the message. When we feel an emotion come up in the body or watch upsetting stories play out in the mind, these are opportunities and signals to look inward and examine what may be happening on the inside that is attempting to dictate how we react on the outside.

Our inner experience is our responsibility, so before we react inappropriately or based on an inaccurate assessment of what is happening, we can tune in and stay connected with our experience. *What am I feeling right now? Is this about what is happening right now, or does it remind me of something that's happened before? Is this a habitual pattern for me? Do I have any evidence for the story playing out in my mind? Is this mental story true?* What others stir up in us is *our* stuff, *our* story and *our* conditioning. If not wholly, then at least partly.

The same is true for the other. The triggers, interpretations and reactions of the other are *their* stuff. When tension inevitably arises in relationship, it can quickly become a tennis ball match of defensiveness if each person reacts to their triggers instead of staying connected to their bodies. This is when we get activated, entangled by emotions, and swept away by thoughts, memories and interpretations. When we become aware of this and lean into these tensions skillfully rather than fight them, everything that happens in relationship can become an opportunity for personal growth and a deeper understanding of ourselves and the other.

Four Guidelines for Managing Conflict

My experiences with dysfunctional relational dynamics have given me four guidelines for managing conflict. While they are all easy to accept, they are sometimes difficult to practice. I offer them here because they have served me in following my intention to navigate relationships with grace and ease. I am sharing them as valuable tools when triggers, tension or disconnect arise.

Don't Take Anything Personally

Firstly, the most challenging – yet most beneficial – guideline for our personal growth and connection in relationship is *don't take anything personally*. Our body might squirm in discomfort as somatic triggers arise and defenses get activated (especially by those who know how to push our buttons). Still, any reaction in self-defense leads to a tennis ball match of back-and-forth defensiveness, with each retaliatory reaction stronger than the previous one. This can escalate out of control quickly to the point that *you didn't take the trash out* turns into *get the hell out*. Or worse.

Not taking things personally is far easier when we've traversed the uncomfortable terrain from reactivity back to our senses and learned to take responsibility for our explosiveness. When we can see and appreciate the extent of our own immensely powerful reactions, we can see the reactivity in others with more empathy and understanding.

The antidote to 'taking things personally' is *curiosity*. I've learned the tough lesson that defending myself and proving my point isn't as important or helpful as bringing a sense of peace back into the relationship. *Do I want to be correct, or do I want to understand the other? Do I want to win, or do I want to mend this relationship?*

Genuine curiosity on our part disarms the defenses of the other because they no longer perceive a threat. If we're not attacking or reacting, they have no one to defend themselves against. That's because people defend when they consciously or subconsciously perceive an attack.

When the other gets defensive, and we can authentically say we held no intention of harm, these moments become an opportunity to unpack and explore the world of the other. Asking rather than assuming (i.e., believing the stories of our mind) takes us out of the mind and builds a bridge that connects directly to the world of the other.

When my mind starts conjuring up stories, I've learned to disengage and seek clarity from the other as to what's really happening for them. I ask questions like *what's happening for you? What's the story in your head? What are you feeling right now? What do you need right now?* Ironically, when we seek to understand the other, their body relaxes into a physiological state that is more open and receptive to us sharing our understanding of the situation when the time comes for us to do so.

Arguments don't happen when one person attacks. To play tennis, we have to keep hitting the ball back and forth. In the same way, both people in an argument have to react for the argument to happen at all. This means the second reaction, not the person who started it, creates the argument. The second instance of taking it personally, not the first, signals the beginning of arguing.

I'm not perfect, but I've become better at not hitting the ball back to the other person's side of the court. If I react, I know I'll be sucked into an argument. At my best, I can hear a criticism, a passive-aggressive jab, or a harsh judgment and notice the trigger before it grabs the steering wheel and dictates my decision-making. I can defuse situations with humor or say something like *you must be feeling angry to be trying to hurt me right now*. Infusing empathy, compassion and ease into relationships takes priority over winning and being right.

Own Your Stuff

The second guideline to dissolving relationship tension is to *own your stuff*. Owning our stuff means being vulnerable and taking responsibility for our emotions, thoughts and reactions. We often project those emotions, thoughts, and reactions onto the other instead of seeing them as our own. Suppose we are finding ourselves constantly on edge, always on the brink of saying something hurtful, lashing out at our partner, or shutting down and stonewalling. In that case, it could be a sign that we need to own our stuff and strengthen our capacity for emotional regulation. When we vulnerably identify and openly communicate our emotional states and take accountability for our words and actions without blame, projection or attack, we effectively put down our defenses and vulnerably reveal our authentic experience.

It doesn't matter who started it, who finished it, who apologized first, or what was said or done. We can own our stuff. Fully and completely. Until we own our part in a conflict, argument or situation (yes, we played a part), the defenses of the other will stay on high alert.

One small admission of ownership often leads to an avalanche of reconciliation from both sides. This is because relationships are a mirror. When we're tense, the relationship is tense. When we soften, the relationship tends to soften. When we get defensive, so does the other. One person has to put down their walls so connection and communication can be re-established.

I've been both the recipient of my partner owning her stuff and also owned my stuff plenty of times when in tension and conflict. As challenging as it may be – and no matter how convincing the story of the mind – when I resist the impulse to defend and instead admit an overreaction, an intention to punish, or an uncomfortable emotion attempting to dictate my behavior, I feel the soothing impact on my nervous system. My partner's nervous system soon follows.

It doesn't matter who starts the process; the outcome of owning our stuff tends to be the same: intimacy, understanding and connection. As a man who subconsciously believed in toughing it out and being brave and strong, I now know that communicating vulnerably is often the bravest demonstration of strength.

Punishing is Not Our Responsibility

There is a difference between assertive communication when our boundaries are encroached upon and punishment. Punishment is focused outward and perpetuates conditioned reactions of internalizing, suppressing and avoiding authentic emotional states. Assertive communication stems from authenticity and helps us maintain an empowered sense of self.

The third guideline is to *refrain from punishing the other*. When another person hurts us or makes us suffer, whether intentionally or unintentionally, it is because they are suffering and that suffering is spilling over. They don't need to be punished. They don't need us to continue recreating and re-enacting their childhood environment.

What they need is help, support and understanding. Their body is in pain. That's the real message being sent when anyone is acting out. When we punish our partners, we teach them that we are not a safe place for them.

My body taught me that I only attacked, defended, or hurt others because I was hurting. *Only hurt people hurt people.* We would never initially want to hurt or harm the ones we care for, so when we say and do things we don't mean or intend, they come from a place of self-protection and defense. The reaction to a trigger is intended to protect us, but it unintentionally erodes relational connection in the process.

When we punish our partners, whether consciously or unconsciously, we unintentionally solidify their conditioned belief that something is wrong with them or that they should be shamed and made to feel guilty. I don't want that role in their life. The guilt, shame and resentment that arise from punishing the person we care for make it harder for the other to feel safe, secure and understood.

We won't show our authentic selves if we fear being punished for our authenticity and vulnerability. Many do not show their true selves because they're so terrified of rejection. We desperately want to be seen, heard, understood and accepted but choose to hide because we fear being punished further for our expression of vulnerability. Punishing those closest to us perpetuates this hiding.

Why would someone reveal their bleeding heart only to have it cut further? Of course, we are not perfect, and when we are triggered, we might say and do things out of self-protection and defensiveness that we later regret. If or when this happens, see step #2 (own your stuff), and own it immediately. It may sound something like this: *regardless of how I feel and who started this, I want to apologize for my part,* or *I shouldn't have said or done that, no matter what had transpired before,* or *I want to own my contribution to this conflict.*

Ignoring the Noise

The final guideline may help with the first three. We take things personally, react from a place of defensiveness, or punish the other because of the narratives playing out in the mind. Our mind creates the justification that makes it easier to remain disconnected from the body and react instead from a place of self-protection and defensiveness. I now use a term to describe the unhelpful stories that emerge from my own mind: noise.

Listening to the noise of my mind prevents me from seeking connection, asking for help, asserting my needs and communicating vulnerably. The content of my noise almost always points the finger of blame toward the other and prevents me from seeing my role and part in the challenging relational context. I've learned not to believe my noise because – for the most part – it's not true.

I've learned to distance myself from the noise of my head by attaching a separate identity to it. In fact, *The Noise* is exactly what I refer to it as when I am in relationship with my partner and don't want to keep ruminating on the content being offered by *The Noise*. And my mind can come up with some of the most absurd, paranoid, scary stories. My mind sometimes conjures stories of fatal accidents when my partner is late from work. When we go out dancing, every male in the room can quickly become a competitor or threat. When I don't get what I want, my thoughts explore how to best rebel, pout or punish. When I verbally express what *The Noise* is saying, projecting or wanting me to do, it has consistently proven itself as an effective way of soothing this part of myself. The noise stops. These thoughts don't control me anymore. My partner and I now often share a laugh about what *The Noise* has to say.

When the noise of my mind is at its peak – just as it is for many others – it is projecting fear-based stories and worst-case scenarios. When we invite the other into our world by saying things such as *guess what my voice in my head is saying now,* or *it's really hard for me to connect right now because I have a lot of noise in my mind,* it serves as a way of uniting us with our partners in a common objective that carries with it a smaller chance of getting triggered, activated or taking it personally.

By externalizing our unwanted mental activity as if it's an unwelcome third party attempting to intrude on the relationship, we can speak about what's happening *impersonally*. It makes it easier to infuse the qualities of humor and playfulness into a potential conflict. *The Noise*, which can potentially dominate mental landscapes to the point that it ends relationships, can be related to as if nothing more than a pesky voice that we acknowledge and share with each other from time to time.

***

It's helpful to understand and accept that conflict within relationship is *supposed* to happen. We can think of it as a cyclical pattern that provides learning and healing opportunities. Conflict, and the body's expression of it, signals that something needs attending to within ourselves, the other, and the context of the relationship. Rather than avoiding confrontation, we can begin to treat tension arising in relationship as a gift.

Tension is an opportunity to grow both personally and in relationship. We can deepen our connection and understanding of each other and help soothe old wounds that otherwise would not have been possible to touch. This is why I get curious when I get triggered or sense a reaction in my loved ones. I lean in, listen and learn more. As most problems are rooted in misunderstanding or avoidance, tension can be the catalyst for helping us communicate and heal.

Tension has taught me what matters most in relationships: being able to sit with the other in times of sadness and pain, not just in happiness and joy. Nothing has created more trust, safety, intimacy and connection in my relationships than holding my partner's pain and being held in my own. I've learned to accept and embrace all of the other, even during times of tension and discord.

When we begin infusing our relationships with this kind of consciousness and reflection, we face and accept the reality that relationships aren't a fairy tale. They take work and a sincere commitment to ourselves. Relationships provide the perfect space for mutual growth and evolution. While it's not possible to perfectly navigate the other's trauma, never fall into an old reactive pattern, or to always be supportive, we can learn how to invite the other into the sacred space of our inner world and how to treat the other person when we are invited into their sacred space. We were born in relationship, we learned to disconnect in relationship, and we can, with consistent practice, heal in relationship.

***

A final note on managing conflict within relationship is about the unavoidable truth that a relationship between two people is a relationship between two completely different and conditioned universes. Each person represents a unique combination of memories, values, genetics, goals, culture and life experience. This means that everyone is showing up in a different – yet perfectly appropriate for them – space and place in their life.

While the strategies, tools and reflections provided in this section can be helpful when both people in the relationship are committed to and invested in the process, it's a different story when one, or both, of the people in the relationship lack self-awareness or a willingness to look at themselves deeply.

One of the most beautiful aspects of a conscious relationship between two individuals who engage in their inner work – side by side and simultaneously – is the reciprocal nature with which the interpersonal gifts of listening, attunement and attending to are freely exchanged. When a relationship becomes one-sided, it can leave one side of the relationship experiencing resentment or being taken for granted. This isn't a formula for a sustainable relationship.

Sometimes we may practice the four guidelines of managing relational conflict only to find that the other doesn't return the favor. This can be a disappointing experience. Additionally, not only does reconciliation not always pan out, some relationships simply don't work. It may be perfectly appropriate and precisely aligned with our intention to be more authentic with, kind to, and compassionate toward ourselves to ask ourselves *why is it always me that's doing the work?*

Indeed, one of the most challenging decisions we might make in relationship is choosing what is authentically aligned for us, knowing that our decision will simultaneously mean we are choosing to move away from our present connection with another. Closing one door may open several others more aligned with our authentic selves, but closing that door is still difficult and painful.

Expression Heals the Body

The long-standing mainstream culture and narrative around masculinity calls for emotional stoicism. What it means to *be a man* hasn't left the space necessary for boys and young men to express and open up about their emotionality or psychological distress. Growing up, boys are given clear messages to be strong, tough, and never cry or show emotion. Hence, speaking up or reaching out for help goes against the ingrained cultural expectations of masculinity.

As a result, men generally don't get help for problems, especially related to mental health. Instead, they make their symptoms worse by isolating themselves from the connections that could help them work through their emotional distress. This is what makes porn the perfect coping strategy for men. Porn is viewed alone and anonymously, making it the perfect coping strategy for someone indoctrinated under traditional western masculine norms.

Given that all the participants in my doctoral research were volunteers, it's not surprising that they unanimously reported feelings of shame and guilt after viewing porn. Indeed, experiencing shame and guilt was one of the contributing factors they mentioned as the reason for reaching out for help. They wouldn't have volunteered if they hadn't had negative experiences watching porn.

These participants typically viewed porn to cope with and manage stress and discomfort, such as unwanted thoughts, distressing memories or negative feelings. When life became too challenging, instead of seeking professional help or talking to someone, they reached for porn.

The temporary relief from the discomfort that porn provided was quickly followed by shame and guilt. The downward spiral can be fast when we can't talk about the pain triggering porn use. Nor do we talk about the porn problem itself since it's shame-ridden and stigmatized. And this is precisely how and why porn use eroded these men's lives.

Most would have guessed, and this certainly didn't constitute groundbreaking research findings, that my participants didn't openly share or talk about their porn use and masturbation habits with others. Men, in general, don't talk about their porn use. They keep it private and hidden from the world. I knew this from personal experience but neglected to consider it during my doctoral research. For nearly every participant, our interviews together represented the first instance these men could openly and vulnerably talk about their porn use.

Porn, as it turns out, is an incredibly effective topic to open men up about other issues in their lives. These men were given a safe space to be vulnerable and communicate without being judged, told to stop complaining and grow up, or *toughen up* and take a *concrete pill*. The walls of their self- and culturally-imposed isolation began breaking down when they emailed me to participate in my study.

The men could break their silence and shed the shame and guilt that was just as hidden as their porn use. Hearing themselves speak their stories out loud helped them see more clearly why and how porn use had originated in their life, why they considered their porn use a problem, and the contexts that explained their continued viewing.

While it wasn't my intention for these interviews to be therapeutic, nearly every man shook my hand after their interview and expressed gratitude for being provided a safe place to share. Some men said they felt they were taking tangible steps away from porn simply as a result of the interview. For the first time, these men could express themselves openly and *feel* their bodies relax and soften in response to their vulnerable expressions.

This is what expression does for the body. It releases tension and stress. These men also felt connected to another person, a connection that every human being needs and yearns for. When we do not, cannot, or don't know how to connect to another person in a deep and meaningful way, we find fake connections through substances and behaviors. I could relate because this is what porn provided me before I knew how to connect authentically to another person.

I came across a quote that has been used for recovering alcoholics: *you're only as sick as your secrets*. There was a period, a long period, during my journey that I thought I could meditate my problems away. I thought if I sat in solitude for long enough, my external circumstances would somehow fall into place. I was wrong. And it's obvious why it was a mistake from the beginning.

If loneliness and disconnect were the key contributors to my problems and challenges, why did I think the solution would be found through continued isolation? While personal and individual practices are imperative, there is healing work that can *only be done in relationship*. If I wanted to learn to communicate and express vulnerably, I had to practice those skills with another person, not in a dark cave sitting cross-legged.

Keeping things bottled up inside creates tension, constriction and agitation. The tension that accumulates is related to expression, or rather the lack thereof. When we can express ourselves, especially the things we've hidden from the world in shame, the body breathes an immediate sigh of relief. A heavy burden is lifted from our shoulders because the body is freed from carrying the load of that secret.

Self-awareness deepens when we learn how to express ourselves. My first counselor, teacher, and now colleague and close friend, Graham Mead, was the first person I shared my inner world with. While Graham also introduced me to meditation and stillness practices, the way he unconditionally and nonjudgmentally received and responded to my expressions was most transformative for me. Indeed, Graham was the motivation and reason for pivoting away from a health and wellness career focused primarily on physical challenges to one that prioritizes mental and emotional wellbeing.

The key ingredient that makes expression such a cathartic experience is that it is done *through the body*, either vocal or physical, and not merely as a thought. Thinking, reflecting and analyzing won't suffice because those mental activities haven't been made *real* yet. As explored in the previous chapter, real change happens in the body. It's only imaginary until the body and its senses get involved.

Expression is what invites the body into the process and what makes the thoughts of, and intentions for, expression *real*. We express when we speak, dance, paint, write or involve the senses of our body to participate in some way. The mind thinks. The body expresses.

My study participants reminded me never to underestimate the power of expression. Sitting and being present with someone in a non-judgmental and unconditionally accepting way is therapeutic precisely because it invites authentic expression. Stress, angst and tension wash away when someone feels safe within a relational container. The parts of us experiencing shame, rejection or guilt don't have to run away when they are seen, heard, welcomed and held in relationship.

Whether someone is a professional helper or not, know that helping to facilitate change in others has less to do with the strategies, tools, techniques or interventions chosen and more to do with the presence, attunement and attentiveness of the listener[185]. If listening skills were taught in school and we knew how to be present and unconditionally accepting, there'd be fewer therapists. When we enter relationship in an embodied way, every encounter carries the potential to be therapeutic.

The Dance of Relationship

Dancing. I had to write about it at some point. I met the love of my life dancing. Dancing helped rehabilitate the surgically repaired ankle that doctors told me I wouldn't be able to run on by 40. Through dancing, I could face, process and move through limiting beliefs about myself that routinely caused embarrassment and shame. I learned how to express myself without caring what others thought about me. Dancing finally invited an activity into my life that was based primarily on fun rather than achievement, success or productivity. Since my first uncoordinated and clumsy introductory lessons, Latin dancing has become a passion that continues to reward me around every corner.

I could have included dancing in the chapter on health and healing. Dancing is a beautiful synergy of many of the Healthy Lifestyle Principles. The health benefits of dancing – from physical exercise and social connection to coordination and having fun – make it a health-promoting activity that can be added to any lifestyle[186]. I particularly enjoy dancing because of the diversity of movement that it provides for the joints of the body and the continued coordination challenges as I learn new moves and patterns.

I once had a nagging groin injury that wouldn't heal no matter how much time, rest and rehab I gave it. Then I went out dancing with a group of my friends. I woke the following day, and any sign of pain or injury was gone. I chalked up the miracle cure to how dancing creates micro-movements in many different angles and directions, rather than the fixed and linear ranges of motion of everyday life or traditional physical therapy. Dancing facilitates therapeutic stretching and circulation by manipulating fascia in various directions.

Dancing can also be a conscious discomfort practice. Dancing in front of people, at social events or even by ourselves can be one of the most fear-inducing experiences a person faces. I couldn't get out of my head when I started social dancing. Instead of hearing music and paying attention to the partner in front of me, I heard the limiting beliefs, self-judgments and harsh self-criticisms playing on repeat over the loudspeaker in my mind. If the discomfort of ice baths prepared me for anything, it was how to face the paralyzing tension and fear that seized my body as it stepped onto a dance floor.

Instead, I've chosen to use dancing as a beautiful and shockingly accurate metaphor for being in relationship with another human being. Though I've written this comparison with a lean toward the context of being in intimate relationship with another, the comparisons translate across other relational contexts.

I like the comparison between dancing and relationships because I don't think being in relationship can be navigated like a definitive science. Relationships, like dancing, are an art. If we rely solely on scripts, dialogues and tools for understanding and relating to our partners, then we are not understanding and responding to *them*.

Just like we get to improvise and have fun after learning a few basic dance steps, we ultimately connect with and spontaneously respond to the person we are in relationship with. If we stick to the same scripted questions, responses and rules, eventually, the other will know what's coming next. When the mind knows what's coming next, it will either perceive it as contrived, forced or fake, or react defensively as the mind anticipates the scripted response.

From the first encounter, dancing, like being in relationship, is an art form to be practiced and mastered. When we first ask a new partner to dance, our body tells us quickly if there's a connection. Sometimes the first dance, just like a first impression, is enough to let us know there will be more dances or that one dance was plenty.

When we first start learning how to dance with someone, it takes time to learn how the other person moves and to coordinate moves together. We won't dissolve into the other, understand each other's movements or flow to the music immediately. Instead, we'll likely step on the other's toes a few times, miss cues for movements, and shy away from the awkwardness of sustained eye contact or a close embrace.

With each song and dance, we learn more about our partner. We learn how to communicate with our partner so that we can flow with more ease. On the dance floor, we initiate cues, hand placements and weight transfers to let our partner know what to expect and see how they respond. In relationship, similarly, we learn how to ask questions, use our tone and pace, draw boundaries and respond in ways we know our partner can understand. The relationship is a playground for seeing how our words, tone and actions land for the other and the kinds of responses they elicit. The result is more ease within the relationship.

Like relationships, dancing requires us to practice the basics, learn new moves, and address our weaknesses or blind spots. I was blessed – and cursed – to find love with someone who had been dancing since the age of 4. My tall, uncoordinated, inexperienced body had a lot of upskilling to do to catch up to her natural ability.

In the beginning, my partner would get bored as she knew my next steps and quickly learned to anticipate combinations. She could predict what was coming next, which naturally led to some boredom. I wanted to continue making the experience spontaneous, fun and exciting. Just as we have to listen to the music, improvise when dancing, and learn new moves to keep things fresh, fun and alive, so too do we have to mix things up in relationship to maintain a sense of spontaneity.

When only one partner is committed to being a better dancer while the other is not, this limits the potential improvement that can be made as the skills of the uninvested partner create a bottleneck in the process. When both partners do the work and are committed to practicing technique, the result will be a beautiful, synchronized, flowing expression of attuned connection.

The same is true in relationship. Both people must develop the skills necessary to make a relationship infused with ease, love, compassion and harmony. Both have to practice skills like listening, vulnerable expression and compassionate communication. One person doing the work might help, but if we want the dance to keep going, both have to do their part and bring what they learn into the relationship.

Dancing requires us to be present, attentive and available during the dance. When we're dancing, we must get out of our heads and into our bodies to hear and *feel* the music. We have to feel to stay connected to our partner. When we are fully embodied in our relationship, our partners sense we are connected and attuned to them. They relax, knowing we are showing up fully present.

Finally, the unpredictable experience of dancing reflects the constantly changing experience of being in a relationship. Sometimes we'll like the music we're dancing to, and sometimes we'll have to dance to our partner's favorite song. Other times, we'll clumsily trip over ourselves. But there will also be profound moments when we get lost in the flow, together with the other, just two imperfect humans, moving, swaying, and learning to dance together as they listen to the music of life.

Chapter Summary Points and Key Takeaways

- When we remain connected to our own body in relationship with others, we are empowered to differentiate what is our 'stuff' and what is theirs.

- When we are triggered in relationships, it's an opportunity for curiosity, exploration and growth—both for the individual and the couple.

- We can learn to be present with others by learning how to listen with our whole body, and with all of our senses.

- Regarding conflict in a relationship, the four guidelines to follow are 1) don't take it personally, 2) own your shit, 3) never punish your partner, and 4) ignore *The Noise*.

- We can stop the mind's ruminating thoughts from interfering in relationship by expressing them out loud.

Three Ways to Get Started with Practice

1. **Practice listening with your whole body**. Choose a conversation that you will intend to listen to fully and completely. After the conversation, see if you can write down all the things you noticed while listening. What were the other person's emotions? Body movements? Breathing patterns? What was happening in your mind and body?

2. **Unpack a trigger in relationship.** You can unpack and explore triggers in relationship by asking self-reflective questions such as: *what am I feeling right now? What is the story I'm telling myself about this person and situation? Is this a similar relationship pattern I've experienced before? Do I know, and have I explored, what is happening for the other person?*

3. **Start upskilling**. Watch videos, read articles and take courses that focus on cultivating and developing interpersonal communication skills, such as listening, mirroring, emotional awareness and vulnerability.

Chapter 8
The Miracle of Healing Trauma

"Such wounds to the heart will probably never heal. But we cannot simply sit and stare at our wounds forever."
- Haruki Murakami

"All change is a miracle to contemplate; but it is a miracle which is taking place every second." - Henry David Thoreau

"Your transformation will be the miracle." - Holly Lynn Payne

A cknowledgment wasn't something handed out to me in droves growing up. Without pats on the back from my parents to show they were proud of me, I subconsciously took on the belief that no amount of achievement would ever be good enough. It wasn't until many years later that I realized my external world had grown from the seed of *I'm not good enough*. It required many more to realize it wasn't my parent's fault. They simply didn't know any other way of relating to me. They did their best. Today, I love them both.

I was born in California because of my father's involvement in *Solidarność*, The March for Solidarity, an anti-bureaucratic movement in Poland that used methods of civil resistance to advance the causes of workers' rights and social change. After my father was imprisoned for his actions against the government, he was given a choice between life in prison or political asylum in the United States. He chose the latter.

My family – mother, father and brother – were required to sacrifice their passports, symbolically handing over their Polish souls before departing for a new life in a foreign country. They arrived in Sacramento, California, without speaking a word of English.

To her surprise, my mother's medical exam in February of 1984 revealed that she was pregnant. My Catholic parents didn't need a basic comprehension of English to understand what the word 'abortion' meant when a nurse carelessly offered advice to the newly arrived immigrant family. The ensuing drama, culminating with America being introduced to my father's fiery Polish tongue, made the local paper.

I was born on July 7th later that year, eight weeks premature. I was so small and fragile that I was put in an incubator, disconnected from all human touch, for two weeks; the perfect amount of time for a mother's breast milk to dry up because she wasn't breastfeeding. I've read studies that premature babies are more likely to develop attention disorders[187], struggle with social difficulties and feel more shyness, anxiety and depression as adults[188]. Reading such studies made me curious about my ADHD tendencies and discomfort in large groups of people.

I've also read about children who weren't breastfed. I wonder if the anxiety and attachment propensities, fear of abandonment and trust issues I've struggled with are connected to these early developmental traumas. I also wonder if these were the origin points, or at least contributing factors, of my porn use.

I've accepted these explanations as possibilities but refrain from using them as an excuse or justification for my behaviors. *Whose responsibility is it but my own to address such psychological issues?* We don't always – some would say ever – get to control the things that happen to us, but we can, with patience, determination and a sprinkle of grace and surrender, choose how we respond. At least, that's the hope I hold for myself and those that come to me for help.

Polish people are already hardened due to a history of bad luck and poor geographic location. I traveled through Europe after finishing my undergraduate degree with James Michener's *Poland*, a historical novel written in 1983, in hand. It was a fascinating read which told the story of three interconnected Polish families across eight centuries, ending in 1981.

I cried through several parts of the book – certainly after reading the appalling accounts of the Holocaust – as I learned the history of Polish culture, heritage and struggles I hadn't previously been aware of, let alone identified with. How fitting that the book ended with the socio-political events that led to my own family's move to America.

I learned more about my father and his political actions from Michener than I did from the man who lived through the events himself. Such was the relationship between my father and me. Michener's book helped me appreciate the trauma my parents and all Polish people carried with them when they left Poland. The body stores everything. It does not forget.

When my parents had to give up their passports, they were essentially stripped of their identity, and without that, they were soul-less. I can only assume that having their Polish soul ripped from them took an additional toll on my parents when they arrived. As a result, my father drank a lot. The realities of being in a lower-income family also meant that both of my parents busied themselves with work so they could provide a better life for my brother and me. My home environment was, therefore, perfect for the survival instincts of the lone wolf within me to begin expressing themselves.

Lone wolves eat only what they kill, and they kill often. This is how I operated. The survival instincts of self-sufficiency and survival are, however, a double-edged sword. On the one hand, I cultivated that inner sense of resilience and resolve that is only possible when the surrounding stresses demand such an adaptation. On the other hand, those same survival instincts led me into my addictions.

My ability to focus, work hard and prove critics wrong brought me several achievements, adventures and modest material successes, which starkly contrasted with the humble beginnings of my childhood. This is the side of the wolf that people saw and celebrated. More to the point, it was the side that the lone wolf *chose* to show the world because it provided the admiration and validation that could temporarily hide the deeper experiences of loneliness, fear, anger and sadness. The world didn't see that the wolf was running fast and hard in an unceasing effort to avoid unprocessed pain: my own, my family's and the deepest wounds woven into the fabric of my Polish DNA.

When we are utterly self-sufficient and rely solely on ourselves, we also begin believing our emotions aren't important. I didn't think I needed or deserved help. I didn't even know how to ask for it, had the need dawned on me. The limiting beliefs of myself manifested and expressed themselves externally as workaholism and addiction to productivity and busyness. Productivity gave my life meaning. Being busy meant I didn't have to *feel* the accumulated pain boiling beneath the surface of my conscious awareness. The lone wolf hunting to survive has little time to tend to deep wounds.

The Timeline of Porn Use

The first time I watched porn was between the ages of 5 and 7. I grew up, rather fittingly, in what was considered the world's porn capital: The San Fernando Valley of Los Angeles, California. Better known as Porn Valley, Silicone Valley, and San Pornando.

The San Fernando Valley's proximity to Hollywood created an endless pipeline of eager, ambitious and fame-seeking talent, which included aspiring directors, production crews and actors. When they needed a little side income, porn was the answer to their respective needs.

Growing up in Van Nuys, California, I remember gatherings at my house where my parents and their fellow Polish immigrant friends would spend hours playing cards, smoking cigarettes, drinking beer and vodka (I am Polish, after all), and... soldering electronic chips and boards into cable boxes. You know, the regular things 1st generation immigrant families did to make a few extra bucks.

While the altered and definitely illegal cable boxes picked up free channels like HBO and Pay-Per-View, they also provided my initial access to porn. At some point early on, too early on, I discovered that there was a little switch on the back of the cable box that, when toggled, gave immediate access to Playboy and Spice, the two prominent adult content providers of the time.

Being left home alone, which happened often, was instantly transformed from a terrifying prospect to one that was welcomed. An empty house represented opportunities to sneak into my parents' bedroom to flip the switch on the cable box.

What else should a child do when left home alone for several hours during the day when there is no meaningful connection to caregivers? I may have only been a small child, but it was easy to realize that the sexual stimulation porn provided felt better than anything else life offered. Porn was the only relief from an external environment characterized by neglect and abuse and an inner world filled with the expected counterparts of such an environment.

No one had ever talked to me about porn or sex, so I'm not sure why I shamefully hid my viewing from the world. Why I didn't speak to my parents about it was obvious. I didn't talk to them about *anything*. Advice was something I never considered or wanted from them, and I instinctively knew that anything I shared would be met with a reprimand, punishment and Eastern European harshness. *It wasn't safe to share.*

I also couldn't speak with my older brother. We rarely spoke to one another, though we shared the same bedroom. There was a seven-year age gap between us and it wasn't until I was fourteen that my brother and I truly connected. This was when the common interest in football catalyzed the forging of a deep bond that all brothers should have; one that we continue to share. My brother was my biggest fan and supporter during my years of playing football. Before football, however, silence about something as personal as watching porn was assuredly the best option.

Silence. Porn. Silence. Porn. On and on this pattern went, until one day, the pattern stopped. My son arrived. I had contributed more than my fair share to the collapsed relationship with his mother. Still, with a child linking us together forevermore, I knew the self-destructive pattern had run its final 2-year lap. I couldn't run away or avoid myself any longer. Not if I wanted to be present in my son's life.

Destroying and rebuilding my life all over again wasn't an option as it had been so many times before. I had proven with great clarity that work, money, pornography and women weren't effective in calming my inner turmoil. My life did crumble once again, but for one, magnificently epic, final time.

I had finally exhausted the belief that accumulating money, material possessions, experiences, and sexual conquests would bring me happiness. Materially, I lacked for nothing, yet spiritually I was empty. It was time to stop running, repressing and avoiding the reality of my inner pain. I began looking inward for answers. I curiously examined my behaviors and began asking *why*.

The compass pointed inwards, and I was inevitably forced to scrutinize the world of my thoughts, emotions, assumptions, and beliefs I held of myself and the world. The practices I've highlighted and shared throughout *Somawise* served as the preparatory work for facing pain I had avoided for so long. Every chapter written in this book has touched on one of the crucial and interconnected aspects of how it became possible for me to sit with the pain that would allow my body, and thus my mind, to heal.

Healing requires a lot of hard work. That is a fact. The work spotlighted in each chapter so far has collectively and cumulatively contributed to allowing me to create authentic and permanent shifts in my life. Taking care of my body with regular movement, real food and adequate rest gave it vigor and vitality. These expressions of physical wellbeing gave me the initial strength I needed to face my pain. Indeed, we can lean on our physical strength and endurance as we learn how to lean into our emotional pain.

Stillness taught me a new way of relating to my body and living in the world. Carrying my stillness practice off the meditation cushion and into the world helped me understand what it means to sit with and observe my body as it passes through challenging sensations and emotions.

Nothing replaces or can substitute for feeling the underlying pain of our deep emotional wounds. Conscious discomfort practices, however, provide the preparation needed for experiencing the real thing. I learned to stop judging and criticizing myself when I realized that even my worst habits had started as solutions to the emotional pain I had never been taught to manage.

The greatest challenge with healing trauma is that it has to occur within the safety of a trusted relationship. When life conditions reactions into our body that make it unsafe to trust others, this process of trust is nearly impossible at first because the very thing we are most frightened of, most likely to avoid, and have no example from our own lives to follow – *relationship* – is precisely what facilitates the process of healing. Learning to trust in relationship is one of the most painful experiences many will live through.

When healing our trauma requires trusting in a new experience of relation-ship – one that contradicts our previous experience– the stamina developed through healthy living, stillness and conscious discomfort can carry us through. The gifts cultivated through personal practice helped me to pass through the emotional discomfort I felt on my way to being more loving, vulnerable and compassionate in relationship with myself and others.

Gabor Maté's teachings showed me that trauma isn't the external event that, sometimes tragically and horrifically, happens to us. Trauma is what happens to us *on the inside*. Potentially traumatic events don't become trauma until our external environment's lack of support and nurture leads to a disconnect from the body. According to Maté, the real trauma is disconnecting from ourselves and the reactivity that emerges as a result.

Every step of my journey back into my body contributed to healing my trauma. The amount of grief, fear and pain my body processed during my healing is difficult to articulate with words. Tears were involved—many of them. Crying is one of the most therapeutic experiences for the body as it releases stuck emotions and trapped energy.

Early in my healing journey, I believed I had consciously created my life circumstances myself and that I deserved to be punished for my wrongdoings. I believed the negative experiences and emotions were *my fault*. The voice in my head was repeating and reinforcing old, no-longer-useful beliefs that I wasn't good enough and that something was wrong with me. But the truth was that my coping mechanisms – porn, productivity, money and women – were utterly unconscious, and the structure of my reactivity was set up when I was a scared, lonely kid yearning for the love and connection that every child needs to survive.

The more I considered the experience of my younger self – my inner child – the more compassionate I became with myself. I stopped judging myself through the insights and work made possible as a result of my personal and professional involvement with Maté and Compassionate Inquiry. I've already shared how porn impacted my life, as well as my journey away from it. Yes, I cried and faced immense amounts of pain, but the more tension my body released through those tears and the more I surrendered to what was being expressed by my body, the more connected I became with myself and others.

At many times during the healing journey my mind thought I was done. *Surely, this is enough. Surely, there is no more pain to feel.* But my body would always remind me of who gets to decide when the healing is done. There is always more healing to do, more to uncover. I don't know if the work ever really stops. I'm okay with that because I've learned how to welcome these healing experiences into my life by replacing self-judgment with curiosity.

I can say definitively that I reached a point where I was okay with myself and my life. There might always be work and healing to attend to, but I don't chase or force it anymore. I'm fine. I'm content.

My body lets me know when that sacred time for healing and those precious little moments of change arrive. In between, I am free to enjoy the details of my life, unburdened, or at least significantly less burdened, by the reactivity of my mind. Being fully healed (whatever that means) doesn't really matter anymore. That's just an idea the mind likes to obsess about. My body is content. That's what matters. The chronic states of tension and constriction are no longer my dominant experience. When those states arise, I've learned how to listen and respond to my body's needs. I love my life *as it is*. I wouldn't change anything.

The Source of My Trauma

If porn was initially a solution to my pain, what was the original wound that used porn as a subconscious Band-Aid for so long? What was the *source* of my trauma? Why did I have to go through such an incredibly uncomfortable and challenging journey to begin with? Why did the disconnect with my body happen in the first place? That's what my mind, and probably every mind, wants to know. *The mind always wants the answer.*

The mind will never stop obsessing about getting a quick answer. The mind thinks that knowing the definitive answer to the question leads to spontaneous healing. That with an answer, the work is done. *It was childhood trauma. Mystery solved. All done. Healed.* Not quite.

Of course, my mind had plenty of options and possibilities to choose from. Did my original trauma stem from my development in the womb of a mother experiencing massive upheaval and overwhelming stress in her body at the time[189]? Or did it originate with my premature birth and the resulting isolation during my incubation period[190]. Not being breastfed certainly carries some evidence-based weight[191]. Maybe my time in the incubator and not being breastfed caused my trust issues with women, my anxious attachment style when I'm triggered, and the insatiable need for female validation. Growing up in a lower socioeconomic bracket provides another possible explanation for my reactivity[192]. And there's always the fact I grew up with an alcoholic and abusive father[193]. Not to mention the many adolescent experiences of social ostracization and bullying I passed through[194].

The list of potential suspects continues with my fear-laden Catholic up-bringing, mainstream media and the intergenerational trauma[195] that had worked through my Polish lineage. An unlikely addition to the lineup could be past life trauma that I'm not fully aware of[196], yet might somehow hold the answer my mind is looking for. A final possibility could be that none of these ever happened at all. Maybe I have memories that never happened because overactive minds can conjure false memories[197]. *Which one is it?* The mind always has stories to choose from when searching for answers.

The truth, however, is that it doesn't matter which experience triggered the trauma that embedded the reactive conditioning into my body. It's the result of that experience that matters. Without an environment that supported processing, integrating and passing through pain, I disconnected from my body. My unique manifestation of subconscious reactivity was born.

What happened to us is only a piece of the puzzle to be solved when deter-mining the presence and extent of trauma. It's a small piece when compared to the rest of the puzzle. As Maté emphasizes, just because something terrible happens to us doesn't automatically mean that trauma will result.

The more crucial question is whether and how a person was *supported through* what happened to them. Did their environment provide a safe relational container to feel, process and move through their traumatic experience? *For me, no.* Did they have someone to talk to? *I didn't talk to anyone.* Was someone present with them as they felt and passed through challenging emotions? *Ha!* Were their feelings validated, normalized and held? *Again, and sadly, no.* Or did their environment teach them to survive by burying their feelings, internalizing their experience, and learning that speaking about their emotions wasn't safe? *Bingo!* What happens after a potentially traumatic experience determines whether that experience leads to a disconnect from the body, resulting in trauma, or whether it builds emotional awareness and resilience.

***

The real trauma, therefore, is not what happens *to us*, but rather what happens *within us* because of not being supported through the things that happened to us. This is likely the most important of Maté's gems. We disconnect from the body. We disconnect from ourselves.

This is why it's not helpful to compare what happened to us with others. *I didn't have it so bad. Compared to others, I shouldn't even be talking. It doesn't feel right to complain about what I went through.* This is precisely the kind of rationalization, minimization and intellectualization that perpetuates the disconnect from the body because it prevents us from looking inward and acknowledging our own pain. The mind deploys self-protective defenses that prevent us from feeling the reality of the pain present within the body.

What happens after traumatic experiences, whether big 'T' trauma or an accumulation of little traumas[198], is The Great Disconnect (see *Introduction: The Wise Body – The Great Disconnect*). With no one to talk to, we take on the belief that it's not safe to talk about our emotions or that our emotions aren't important. These beliefs are reinforced with only a few well-chosen words repeated once too often: *stop crying... Quit being a baby... Calm down... Stop being so scared... Don't be sad... Smile and be more positive.* When a child hears, over and over again, that their emotions aren't valid, this is precisely what they internalize. It's safer for them, in that case, to stay silent about what the body is experiencing to avoid receiving a reprimand.

The learned conditioned reaction is nothing more than a survival mechanism. We disconnect from the body to survive, to avoid pain and discomfort that no one ever showed us how to manage. We subconsciously learn that feelings are *bad, wrong or weak.* More than any of the previously described circumstances, this was likely responsible for the conditioned reactivity embedded in my body.

***

To *heal,* we must *feel* what we've previously been taught to suppress, numb and avoid. There is no *healing* without *feeling.* And guess where we must go to feel? *The body.*

To break free of the ball and chain of our conditioned pain-avoidant reactivity, every one of us must take a journey back into the body. The real trauma, regardless of the story or narrative, is the accumulation of conditioned reactions stored within the body.

My story is not an isolated instance. Who isn't running away from an internal state? Who isn't caught up in some variation of external *doing*, all in an attempt to fix their inner turmoil? No one taught us how to manage emotions, so when, as children or at some point in the past, we found something that helped us quickly and effectively avoid them, we kept doing it right into adulthood.

Is it any wonder that we self-soothe any experience that begins to touch our edge of discomfort? Though my story involves porn use, the reflections, insights and lessons gained from my experience can be applied to any substance or behavior, whether it's smoking, shopping, money, work, alcohol or success. We're all doing the same dance of avoidance.

We've all adopted ritualized compulsive pain avoidance behaviors, whether consciously aware of them or not. We do anything and everything to avoid the dark void that becomes all too palpable and obvious when we stop being busy doing stuff and notice the state of our chaotic mind and tension-riddled body.

Which behavior we engage in doesn't matter if continuing to constantly seek something outside of ourselves to quell an insatiable yearning for internal relief. Furthermore, judgment isn't the appropriate antidote to apply to those behaviors. Behaviors, such as my porn use, are merely an individual's unique way of scratching an internal itch; it's the makeshift way their developing nervous system learned to survive in their world at the time. We're all doing the same dance around the void of pain.

That is why the source of trauma anyone should go with, is whichever story provides the mind with the evidence convincing enough for it to put down its defenses, step aside, and let the body do its healing work of feeling. Just as the mind has to be convinced that dipping into an ice bath will be healthy and beneficial, it similarly has to understand why it should let the pain it is avoiding come to the surface and be felt in the present moment. It's in the present moment that the pain can be held in a way that it wasn't when it first originated.

The mind needs to be convinced why feeling the pain associated with past experiences is not only helpful, but necessary. Otherwise, the mind will always revert to automatic protection. When the mind changes how it relates to the events that happened to us in the direction of healing, traumatic memories and emotions become more like everyday life events and no longer hijack our physiology and psychology[199]. When faced with the inevitable pain and discomfort of healing, the mind must let the process unfold and unravel without interfering.

If the mind doesn't have buy-in for the process, it will defend itself. When the mind understands and accepts a story as a possible explanation for the experience of pain it perceives, it is more likely to step aside and allow the experience to unfold. Strange, foreign and unknown pain is transformed into an experience that the mind understands. That understanding enables it open to what was previously impossible to face. Just as the mind settles into the pain of an ice bath when it understands the benefits, so too will the mind settle into emotional pain when provided with a valid explanation for its present state of pain and discomfort.

The Inevitability of Trauma

The moment of our conception likely represents the single moment that we are indeed a blank canvas of pure and unlimited potential. From that moment onwards, that canvas is painted onto by our immediate and surrounding environment. Our programming begins then, though it's arguable that the cumulative conditioning from our ancestors, going back as far as our ancestral bloodline, is embedded in the fabric of our DNA.

In the womb, the physiological experiences of our mother's body influence our development[200]. Her experiences and perceptions of the world leave imprints and conditioned reactions on our nervous system. After birth, parents, peers, siblings, teachers, media, religion and, indeed, the world builds the imaginary perceptual walls that confine our limitless potential into a restrictive box that dictates what our socially acceptable way of being should be. We learn how to live in the mind to survive in a world that prioritizes mental engagement above all else. The trauma of disconnecting from the body is inevitable because it is *required* for surviving in our mental world.

The journey of trauma – into discovering its presence in our body, its imprint on our nervous system, processing, integrating and eventually moving beyond it – is thus a universal human experience. What was once an epic adaptation to an environment we had to survive within, eventually became the very thing holding us back from experiencing and expressing our authenticity. Healing from trauma, in this sense, can thus be considered a rite of passage to a life of meaning and fulfillment. One that we can have only by first experiencing some form of trauma.

We cannot be free and fully ourselves until we've shed all the layers that aren't actually *us*. Our upbringing, religion, culture, socioeconomic status and early childhood experiences each add a layer of paint to the canvas that is us. Over time, those layers harden like walls. Even though they are walls built by others, it is up to us to break them down so that we can see the world through our own eyes. Going back to the state of a blank canvas is impossible and unnecessary. Indeed, radical self-acceptance reveals to us that the version of who we are is exactly who we are meant to be in this moment. What we are empowered to do, however, is dictate how we paint our canvas moving forward.

We can challenge the beliefs of our minds by remaining anchored in our bodies. What is true will prevail; what is false will fade away. So many parts of us are yearning to be unraveled so we can truly live as our authentic selves rather than as a collection of programmed and conditioned inherited reactions.

Life is a traumatic experience we all pass through. Everyone is traumatized. If we sit with someone long enough and listen to their story, we soon realize that we've all had things happen to us. We all carry trauma to some extent because of how modern society operates. We may all exist at different positions along the spectrum of trauma, but none are free of its burden and impact on the body. We were all conditioned and programmed by our childhood experiences. We've all disconnected, to some degree, from the body.

How we pass through the processing of healing trauma is up to us. This mindset, posture and way of relating to life's inevitable traumas will shape how and when we move through. For some time, I embodied the role of victim and the 'poor me, pity me' mentality, which kept me stuck in finger-pointing and blaming. But no matter how much fault I placed on my parents' shoulders, it didn't help me move any closer to healing my core wounds. As long as the victim stays stuck in their story of victimhood, they remain stuck in the story.

We are a blank canvas onto which our surrounding world paints its beliefs, perceptions and projections. Any belief system, regardless of how seemingly supportive, productive, helpful or loving, is a box that invariably imposes limits on the developing child. It is thus inevitable, to some degree or another, that we will 'mess up' and traumatize our children. We can, and should, do our best to foster qualities of authenticity, openness, integrity and creativity, exploration and autonomy with our children, but the practical realities of the world in which we live require specific rules, guidelines and regulations we all must play by to some degree. We are not, after all, wild animals in Nature, left to govern our life leaning solely on our animal instincts.

These mental limitations, however, impose perceptual walls on our children which, even with the best of cases and conscious parenting, leave trauma and reactive conditioning embedded within the child that they must eventually work through when they are ready to break down the walls of the boxes they've been indoctrinated with. When they are ready and when they choose to do so, this is precisely how the child will grow and mature into their own sense of authenticity.

I've already accepted that I will, in some way, shape or form and with no ill will or intent, contribute to some degree of traumatization of my son. I'll mess it up somehow. All parents do. I will do a better job than my father teaching and supporting my son as he passes through these inevitable experiences. I hope that I can instill a secure attachment style that allows him to lean on his own inherent and cultivated resilience while at the same time knowing that he can vulnerably ask for help, support and love when he needs it.

Most importantly, I want to teach him that he is deserving of help and love no matter what. But no matter what I do or how hard I try, it's inevitable and necessary for him to pass through his accumulated *stuff* when he is called to do so and when the time comes. It is his life journey to demolish the perceptual walls that I've contributed to building around him so that he, in turn, can find his meaning and purpose in life. It should be stated here that our role is not to intentionally create trauma for others. Rather, it's unavoidable, no matter how hard we try. Indeed, maybe the only way we can begin to reduce the trauma we contribute to others – especially our children – is by attending to our own healing.

It's easy to point fingers at some person, parent, institution, class, culture, sex or race as the cause of our trauma. Indeed, if we give the mind enough time, there will be countless potential sources of trauma. But blaming external sources for our suffering is a trap. Victimhood is a self-imposed prison. It's a story that keeps us stuck and prevents us from moving forward.

All of the above-mentioned external sources played some part in developing our internal trauma. That doesn't mean fault can or should be assigned to any single source. Even those who performed abusive acts likely didn't intend to create long-term consequences for their victims. They were reacting and self-soothing their own pain and trauma in the only way they knew how at that moment. Unfortunately, as Maté explains, victims found themselves within someone else's traumatic cycle through no fault of their own.

It's imperative to note here that this is not intended to dismiss or minimize the heinous acts and atrocities committed through our individual lives and collective histories. For those victims, the seemingly-impossible part of the healing journey is taking responsibility for our perceived victimhood and forgiving both the perpetrator and oneself for carrying the physiological burden all these years. Maté's teachings talk about how externalizing fault and blame only perpetuates the disconnect from the body. Indeed, refraining from blame and finger-pointing is an act of empowerment. This may be a big ask for some readers, and understandably so. For now, the seed of possibility has been planted.

Whose Fault? Whose Responsibility?

While the external world played a part in how our inner world formed, the process of reconnecting to our inner world and healing our bodies is an inside job. Only we can take the journey inwards to reconnect with our bodies. While we can have people *talk* for us, *do* things for us, or even *think* for us, it is impossible for someone else to *feel* for us. We can't outsource the work of connecting with the body.

If healing trauma means going back into the body, then, ultimately, we are the ones responsible for our salvation. Trauma may not be anyone's *fault*, but it is our *personal responsibility*.

Without personal responsibility, we have forsaken a future of possibility and potential before it ever comes. We have to do the work, every one of us. The work that's involved requires feeling. Talk therapy alone brings intellectual understanding, but that's not enough. Through talk therapy, our mind may gain some respite after it finds a potential source of suffering, but the mental relief doesn't last. The body will humble the mind, eventually showing us the Truth.

Even if our parents, culture or distant ancestors are the root cause of our conditioning and trauma, healing trauma and deconditioning reactivity need to be dealt with on a personal and individual level. The cycle of reactivity gets passed down through the generations until someone says: *why not me?* That's what I had to ask myself and come to terms with. No one was going to fix my problems and heal my soul other than me. But what most don't realize is that our work on ourselves ripples outward, impacting those closest to us. We undo, or at least activate and bring to the surface, the knots of reactivity of our immediate family members and loved ones.

***

A light may bring a dark room into visible awareness, but the mess still has to be cleaned up. The lightbulb of understanding may turn on, and there might even be a therapeutic cathartic release. The entrenched nervous system and physiological reactions, however, will remain. It's like turning off a fan. It takes time for the fan to eventually come to a halt after it's been turned off. It takes time and patience to decondition the human body of its reactivity. It takes work. We do the work by getting out of the head and into the body.

The automatic reflex of the mind is to figure out the cause, memory or reason why this tension and agitation is present, but that is the trap. Staying with the body is what is required for healing. Diving into our body's experience begins to loosen the straitjacket of our subconscious conditioning as we allow ourselves to feel the trigger. From this space, we can choose a different response than the reflex output provided by the mind. This is what personal responsibility is all about: being able to respond.

I've heard it said that people don't change. I don't think that's true. Admittedly, change is hard. But people don't change because they don't know how, because they don't realize what's keeping them stuck or, if they do, they're not willing to do the inner work required to get there. Noticing, feeling, processing and releasing the body's stored and accumulated tension, aka trauma, is what *Somawise* is preparation for.

The path of authentic change that is presently calling us requires work never anticipated, yet a transformation never thought possible can be the result. The mind will be dropped to its knees in humility. It will be worth it.

I'm thankful for the challenges, adversities and difficulties of my childhood. I learned that alcohol and cigarettes don't interest me after I saw how they impacted my parents. I learned the importance of hard work, determination and self-efficacy when my peers told me I was too skinny, slow and unathletic to play sports. I eventually played professional football in Italy.

Humble beginnings taught me to see and appreciate the little things in life as gifts. I don't know if it's a personality characteristic, genetic variant or environmental cue responsible for instilling an unwavering and intentional way of living. It's just as likely to be an act of grace, and I played no part in the choice. Regardless, I am thankful that I answered the calling to move beyond my initial circumstances and childhood conditioning.

It is amazing how the passage of time changes the interpretations and meanings of our personal history and the lessons garnered from it. On my journey of healing, I thought I had unearthed rotted skeletons buried deep in the closet of my subconscious mind. But when my body was given the space to process and integrate, it became apparent that what I had found was gold. When the body speaks its truth, the stories of the mind change.

It is our journey and mission in life to mature and grow beyond our limited beliefs given to us by our parents, media and popular culture, to break down the walls of our indoctrination and to challenge and suspend our long-held beliefs. We do all this to journey into the unknown to find our true, authentic self.

Healing Trauma is a Miracle

I've realized that healing trauma by coming out of the conditioning that disconnects us from our bodies is truly a miracle. When something transformational happens that cannot be explained, understood or known by the mind, it's called a *miracle*.

Healing trauma is a miracle because the mind doesn't get to dictate when, how or even if this sacred act happens. Through practice and patience, we immerse our body in the practices that support the process of, and create the necessary conditions for, healing. The mind, however, must cease its reactivity for trauma to heal. We have to get out of our heads and into our bodies.

What we can influence is the preparatory work that sets the stage for such shifts within ourselves, which is precisely what is offered throughout *Somawise*. Through *healthy lifestyle choices,* we help to cultivate the physical strength, vitality and resilience that makes it easier to face the uncomfortable experience of integration and healing. Through the practice of *stillness*, we develop a way of relating to our present moment experiences that invites acceptance. *Conscious discomfort practices* reveal that we can face discomfort and that our body can process experiences the mind labels as painful. Through *relationship*, we stay connected to our body as we practice new ways of relating to ourselves and others, thereby softening and extinguishing conditioned reactions embedded in our nervous system. However, even with all these committed, consistent and intentional practices, healing trauma requires a sprinkle of the magic ingredients of faith, surrender and trust.

We miss opportunities for connection, integration and healing when the mind intrudes with its endless suggestions of *doings. The feeling is healing.* When the mind rushes to control the process, it instead stops it. When the mind begins to believe that all its work is done, it prevents further trauma processing from occurring. The mind must surrender to and trust the will of the body. Healing is work only the body can do.

The body heals at its own pace and accord when it's ready. The body is wise. It can heal itself. When we tap into the body's innate wisdom, trust in its inherent healing processes and have faith in these natural processes, the body can unravel the constricting knots of conditioning and integrate layer after layer of embedded tension. We then experience the world with a sense of calm and inner peace. A miracle is exactly what happens.

Chapter 9
A New Way of Being

"Nothing, in all of the Universe, is more delicious than to be in this physical body allowing the fullness that is you to be present in the moment." - Abraham-Hicks

"We do not think ourselves into new ways of living, we live ourselves into new ways of thinking." - Hillary McBride

"Everything you need to know is within you. Listen. Feel. Trust the body's wisdom." - Dan Millman

I had a dirty little habit of buying books. I bought and collected them exponentially faster than I could read them. And I read *a lot*. Each book would give me a bit of a high as I would get intellectually stimulated by the intriguing concepts, theories, methods and philosophies. Often, I'd read a true gem whose words resonated so deeply that it would send shivers of ecstatic euphoria down my spine. With my mind satisfied by its brain candy, I'd think, *yup, I get it now.*

I thought the learnings I acquired from words would transform my life simply because I had read them and deemed them true. But this satisfaction was always short-lived. I eventually reverted to old ways and thought patterns. Another hit from another book, article or expert was around the corner. No amount of knowledge, however, will ever be enough for the mind to be truly content. I stopped compulsively buying books for two reasons.

First, the reconnection to my body that I experienced caused me to reflect on my purchasing. When the impulse to buy a book arose, I paused and began tuning into my body. When I paused, I noticed a distinct, palpable agitated state of tension within my body.

When I inquired about that tension, I noticed a sense and a perception of lack in that moment. Upon further investigation and reflection, I realized I was buying books because of my belief that the knowledge they contained, the knowledge I would acquire (if I read it), would somehow make me good enough, smart enough or competent enough. In the presence of that impulse, I realized that buying the book while in that specific moment would only serve to maintain and solidify the belief that I wasn't good enough.

With this clarity, I paid attention to the moments that I felt the impulse to buy books and, instead, paused for a moment of stillness and tuned into my body. Without fail, an uncomfortable sensation triggering reactive self-soothing was beneath the surface of my mind's desire to purchase books, courses and certifications.

Becoming *Somawise* taught me to be present with the agitation without reacting and to relate to my subtle activation of pain gently and compassionately. I didn't want to buy or collect credentials while in this state of lack because I knew it would only fuel and perpetuate the belief that I wasn't fundamentally *good enough*.

Since then, I've only purchased books and completed courses that I was genuinely curious about rather than ones that originated as an impulse of craving or pain avoidance within the body. My body lets me know the difference. I've purchased *a lot* fewer books and courses since.

The second reason I stopped compulsively buying books is that living an embodied life provides wisdom unattainable from books. When I started paying attention to the details of my daily life experience – my relationships, work contexts, lifestyle choices and how I related to my mind, body and emotional states – I realized I was tapping into a source of wisdom that no book could come close to touching. I was learning unique and enormously valuable lessons from my lived experience. Suddenly, every moment contained the potential to be a powerful teaching. Everything I was seeking externally with intellectual knowledge was available to me *right now*, if only I paid attention to my internal environment.

Becoming *Somawise* taught me to live my life from the inside out. I had spent much of my life focused externally, on everything *out there*, confused and frustrated about what was happening internally. I turned the microscope of my attention and awareness around and focused instead on the body, paying attention, first and foremost, to how the present moment impacted my body.

From the moment I wake in the morning until the moments that my body drifts off to rest for the night, I try to maintain a portion of my awareness in the body, keeping one ear open toward my inner experience so that I am present to hear anything my body might have to say. This is what all the practices within this book have supported me in doing. My life, my moment-to-moment experience as it unfolds, has become my practice. Everything, everyone, and all moments of life are infused with rich learnings. I continue to be awe-struck, humbled and amazed at how much wisdom is packed into every moment.

I've learned more about the world, and the people within it, by staying connected to my inner experience than by obsessively accumulating knowledge from the world outside myself. I've explored the mysteries of the universe by observing that which is made of the same substance: my body. The answers to the unanswerable questions of the mind reveal themselves when we begin understanding the frames, lenses and filters through which we interpret reality.

When we start living life anchored with our attention in our body and staying in close connection with the guiding wisdom of the body, we invariably begin living life from the inside out. We experience the world through the lenses and filters of the senses of our body. The better we understand our body, the better we understand the filters shaping how we perceive the world around us. Therefore, the more we understand our body, the more we understand the world. I stopped blaming the external factors in my life and always, and I do mean always, focus on how the moment feels within my body. My body is the starting point for navigating my life.

Life is constantly happening through us. The body's senses constant contact with the external environment, collecting, processing and interpreting the information. Everything we see, hear, feel, touch and experience results from this contact between the body and its environment. Everything we ever need to learn about life, ourselves and the world is happening *right now*. This is when the practices outlined in this book, of *health, wellbeing, stillness, conscious discomfort, radical self-acceptance* and *relationship*, begin to permeate and infuse everyday life. There is always some nugget, morsel or gem of insight available to us if we stop and pay attention. Through the body, I've learned many lessons unique to my life, yet outside this book's general scope. I will, however, share a few here to demonstrate the myriad of lessons that can emerge from the well of wisdom within the body.

The Power of I Don't Know

Reconnecting with the body requires us to embrace the only certainty in life: uncertainty. The unknown is a universal part of the human condition and an existential given. The mind's discomfort with the unknown and near-constant compulsion toward control creates a correspondingly constricting effect on the experience of life itself. When we are uncomfortable with uncertainty, aka being a control freak, we create structures, routines and lifestyles that keep our experiences within a limited frame of reference.

When we leave some space for *I don't know*, we make space for something new. And it's precisely in embracing the uncomfortable space of not knowing that we begin to discover and explore our authenticity.

By living in the body and surrendering control, every moment becomes alive with richness, wholeness and fresh perspective. New possibility emerges when we stay connected to the discomfort of not knowing and curiously explore what's on the other side. The courageous souls that can smilingly say *I don't know* are the very same ones who paradoxically try to understand and befriend the unknown, a quest for meaning that is equally exhilarating as it is fulfilling.

Getting Shit Done

Living in the body showed me that my greatest fear of detaching from the busyness of the mind was unfounded and categorically incorrect. As I transitioned to a life guided by my body's intuition rather than my mind's ambition, I feared I wouldn't get anything done if I wasn't chasing, pursuing, or prioritizing material pursuits and productivity. This success-based equation has been etched so deeply into the fabric of our collective psyche that our sense of identity and worth is often tightly-coupled with external measures of success.

What put my final doubts to rest was seeing that disconnecting from the thoughts and beliefs of endless productivity made me *more* productive. It's not that surprising when we reflect on it.

What happens when we show up entirely in the present moment and focus fully on the task in front of us? What happens when we detach from the outcome and give all of ourselves to the task of the present moment? What happens when we remove the ruminating, worrying and distracted mind from the equation of our workday? Finally, what happens when we do that on a consistent basis?

Today, I get more done (much more) in less time. And, most importantly, with a lot less stress. I had to experience this to believe it. I wave this evidence enthusiastically in the face of my old limiting beliefs when they get activated and triggered. I have to do this from time to time to remind some of my parts that it's safe and okay to be still, rest and savor the moments of life.

The goal of being in the present moment is, after all, precisely that: to be in the present moment. The purpose of being in the present moment cannot be productivity. Otherwise, the mind succeeds in inventing a different version of the same old habit and pattern. As has been the case throughout this book and the practices explored within it, intention matters. Only we can truthfully reflect on our present moment experience and the goals and motivations beneath the surface of our actions.

Don't Take Serious Work So Seriously

Another gem from the well of my body's wisdom was not to take serious work so seriously. I can think of no worthier challenge or greater calling in life than the adventure inward to explore the potential, possibilities, capabilities, nuances, subtleties, complexities and simplicities of the body and our lived experience. *Why else are we here but to understand ourselves?* When we habitually chase the momentary highs of happiness and success, we miss everything else.

The journey inward has given my life meaning and represents the only way of being that makes sense to me. There's a lot more to a fulfilling life than success and happiness. And yet, despite the serious nature of the path that I've chosen to walk, I've learned that even the most serious work shouldn't be taken so seriously.

We are the path. Everything is happening now. There's nowhere to go, nowhere to be. When we realize that the present moment is all there is, we step out of the crazy rat race, sit down and enjoy the beauty of everything and everyone around us. We don't have to sprint toward the finish line or reach the final goal because there is no goal. There is no path. We *are the path* because life is constantly flowing through us. The path flows through our bodies. We don't have to wait until the work is done to curiously play, explore, laugh, smile and express ourselves. If we wait until we get *there* – an imaginary destination created by the mind – that will never happen because we are always *here*.

Being Offended is a Personal Responsibility

My body showed me that being offended is *my* responsibility. Being offended by music, language, clothing, behavior or anything for that matter, is a learned response. At some point in life, we are conditioned by our external environment. Whatever is offending us in the present is a reflection or a reminder of that past conditioning. We've run these automatic reactions so often that we don't even realize they're optional. We think they are part of us, that they *are* us.

When we get offended, it's difficult to recognize the reaction for what it truly is: a conditioned response. For example, think back to how your mind and body reacted when they read the word 'fuck' earlier in the book. The specific reaction to that four-letter word is automatic and conditioned. Someone or some experience put it there. We weren't born with it, and it's certainly not part of our inherent being. Our conditioned reactions to the world were taught to us, even if they feel so 'strong' and 'right' in the moment we feel them.

When we are offended by someone or something else, our reactive response creates more harm in us than that external trigger does. In effect, when we are offended, we are being offended by ourselves and not by that outside thing or person. The *feeling* of being offended is conditioned and learned. When we get offended, nothing really changes. Nothing apart from our own triggered reaction, which is personal to us. Suppose we attack the other person as a reaction to their offense. Then things do change, and usually for the worse. Changing the other's attitude or behavior that 'caused' the offense will not happen.

On the other hand, when we take responsibility for our triggered state of being offended, we are more responsive, conscious and intentional with important matters. This is especially important when it comes to contexts such as social issues and movements we feel called to engage with and support. How much of our engagement is rooted in reaction, and how much is in intentional, conscious, meaningful action? This is an important distinction because we will be in service to a far greater degree and with more potency if we have attended to and managed our internal states.

Being triggered leaves us temporarily blind. With each perceived offense, we can learn more about our behaviors and conditioning and how to manage uncomfortable emotional states rather than having the emotional state control us. It's possible to be emotionally available enough to be passionate about our work and projects while still being able to self-regulate and access our higher cognition. When we cultivate an ability to respond, we are truly empowered to create significant change in the world.

Life: It's Not About Me

I firmly believe that we're here to serve others. This will undoubtedly differ from person to person, but I know that my life intention is based on giving to and helping others. When my body is free of tension, constriction, agitation and pain, it's easy to focus on what's in front of me rather than on what's happening within me. When I lose sight of caring for my body, I notice how quickly I withdraw into myself and generally become unconscious to what's happening around me. Self-care has revealed itself to be quite a selfless act and practice.

What proves itself to be true over and over again is that the more I give, the more I receive. Firstly, my body receives all the wellbeing benefits that go hand-in-hand with altruism, including increased levels of happiness, lowered levels of depression, and positive results for those suffering from chronic disease[201]. It even improves health and slows the aging process[202]. In this sense, my body reaffirms my life intention because it responds when I am focused on giving and helping rather than constantly chasing after and trying to satisfy my mind's desires.

Because I am paying attention to my present moment experience, I've also noticed how the universe returns the favor in droves. The more love I give my partner, the more that seems to be given in return. I try to always be there for my friends when they need me. I am not surprised anymore, but indeed supremely thankful, that they are always there for me in return. This is not to say that giving and helping are 'tit-for-tat' acts, because giving *simply to receive* would tarnish the intention behind the giving with expectation and self-interest.

This requires 'in-the-moment' ruthless honesty with oneself. When reflecting on and distinguishing the difference between authentic giving and using the act of giving as a coping mechanism for control, manipulation and attachment, intention – as always – matters. If we listen, the body can help us know the difference.

When I tune into my body, I can *feel* whether my intentions are clean or whether there's a hook related to my actions. When I've given for the sake of giving, my body responds with lightness, calm and peace. These acts of kindness are gifts to my soul, only for me to know, that don't have to be shared with everyone. Feeling the health-promoting pleasure of helping is enough of a reward. My body responds to altruism, not selfishness masked as giving. When I give, I practice staying connected to my experience to ensure it's an expression of authenticity.

Mindful Solitude

To understand how we relate to the world, we must turn away from it from time to time. After all, the caterpillar emerges from its cocoon with its wings during the season of complete loneliness and isolation. Mindful solitude gives us the space to reflect on ourselves. We can discern who we are, what works, what doesn't, and consciously move forward, allowing those parts of ourselves that no longer serve us to be understood, integrated and healed.

Being alone, certainly with the backdrop of stillness and silence, is one of the most uncomfortable states for the mind. Many of us feel discomfort as we are incapable of eating in silence without tv, going to the bathroom without a phone or driving without music. We aimlessly browse the internet or scroll through newsfeeds to fill the void. It's an endless quest for nothing, mindlessly consuming content to avoid the perceived state of aloneness.

And yet, being alone can remove the constant distractions that prevent us from going inward and doing inner work. My yearly silent meditations have provided the necessary time for pruning the weeds and branches of my soul. I periodically tend to my inner garden to nurture the parts of myself that require support.

Solitude and loneliness may seem similar on the outside, but the only characteristic both have in common is the state of physical aloneness. Inside, solitude and loneliness are tremendously different experiences. While solitude is chosen, loneliness is imposed by others or by the perceptions we hold of ourselves and the world. We can consciously choose solitude and embrace the lessons it offers beyond the initial experience of discomfort.

Sex and Intimacy

While porn might provide users with sexual variety, a myriad of sexual positions and actresses, it doesn't scratch the surface of portraying deep intimacy between partners, mental and emotional connection, tenderness or making love.

Porn is designed to appease the visual sense and nothing more. We get easily sucked in with the plethora of eye candy available at the click of a mouse. This is why watching porn too often is usually the road to more and more extreme scenes, as the brain requires increasingly more intense and extreme visuals to receive the same degree of dopamine stimulation and pleasure.

When I reconnected with my own body, I began feeling the fullness of the sexual experience, not just orgasm. Connected with the body, we can tune in to the subtle sensations of pleasure previously pulsing, tingling and vibrating outside of conscious awareness. Relatedly, our ability to face, process and communicate our emotional states also forges the connection necessary to spark a holistic sexual experience with another person. It's not surprising that when we increase our sensitivity to body sensations and emotions through the various processes and practices described in this book, sex is one of the experiences that is invariably impacted.

Sexual intimacy has revealed itself as a byproduct of the deep emotional connection I feel with my partner. The safer I feel and the more vulnerable I allow myself to be, the more euphoric, adventurous, and playful expressions of sex that emerge. Sex isn't something to do; it has become a barometer for how well the rest of the relationship is going. When two people are completely relaxed, open, transparent, vulnerable, honest and communicative with each other, sex can be pure bliss.

Sex can be more than just a race to the finish line and simply using another body to get off. Sexual expression is therapeutic when we engage in it with more authenticity, vulnerability, equality and communication. I don't think

I'm overstating it when I say that we can touch the Divine through a deeply intimate and connected sexual experience.

The End of People Pleasing

An entire lifetime can be wasted trying to change ourselves to 'be' someone acceptable to others. This becomes especially harmful when those others are highly critical and seem never to be satisfied with us, no matter what we do. How tedious, draining and all-consuming people pleasing can become if it goes unchecked.

There is, however, another option.

We can leave them be. We can let others think whatever they'd like and stop trying to please them to make them like us. We can even let them hold negative opinions because those negative opinions they have of us are really projections of themselves. Whatever negativity they choose to see in us is nothing more than a reflection of negativity they've not recognized or seen in themselves. They see us through the lens, whether positive or negative, of their past. What they see is not us; it's their own trauma, memories and conditioning, not us. We're just playing a role in their universe. And maybe in this moment on their path, our role, whether we like how we're being perceived or not, is *exactly what they need* to grow. Maybe they need us to be a negative projection so that it can act as a catalyst for their self-reflection and growth.

It takes some practice. Letting people, sometimes those who are close friends and family members, say things that trigger immense fear, angst and sadness is challenging at first. When we trust that the other person is exactly as and where they are meant to be, we encounter an incessantly catastrophizing and ruminating mind. We can face our experience without reacting to it and choose not to believe the fear-based content. This practice has been immensely rewarding.

I've learned to let people keep their negative opinions of me without attaching my identity to their projections, without trying to manipulate them into liking me or contorting my sense of self to be likable to them. I stopped being a dancing monkey and committed myself to standing as my authentic self, regardless of context. As Maté and Compassionate Inquiry taught me: *the choice to be authentic is always accompanied by risk to our relationship with and attachment to the other*. I may have fewer acquaintances in my life, but I have deeper and more meaningful connections with kindred souls.

The Integration of Mind and Body

Somawise overall presents the case for living a body-centered life. At times, it may even be an attack on the mind and its contents. While this book intends to provide a compilation of evidence that supports living a life anchored to the body, the connection between the mind and body cannot be ignored.

What *being Somawise* has taught me is that when my body is free of tension, my mind demonstrates and expresses its true potential. It's easy for me to be productive, creative and focused when I, firstly, tend to my body's needs. My mind can fully engage and be present with the personal and professional relationships that give my life meaning because my body is calm and relaxed.

The intimate connection between the mind and body has also provided a handy barometer to let me know when it's time to reconnect with my body and listen to what it has to say: the state of my mind. When my mind starts getting scattered, distracted, jumpy, or ruminates on negative situations, it's the first sign that something in my body requires attention. As soon as the mind starts overthinking, it's a sign that something is happening in the body. When I tune in, I meet the tension, constriction or stress it was reacting to.

The mind is not an enemy. I believe it's important to state that clearly. Once we provide the body with what it needs to heal and thrive, the mind becomes our powerful ally, friend and helper as we continue our journey through life.

BYOG - Be Your Own Guru

I hold the hope and possibility for authentic change and growth for everyone who crosses my path because I don't think there's anything incredibly exceptional about me. I simply got curious and started to question the world around me. That curiosity led me to challenge my inner world. Eventually – slowly and over time – my life completely changed.

When I work with clients, I honestly and sincerely *know* that I'm like a set of training wheels that must eventually be discarded so they can ride the bike of life themselves. That's what my teacher, Graham Mead, taught me. My intention for those that I help is that they, too, learn to trust their own inner experience as their guide, roadmap, and compass. We can learn to be our own teachers and gurus.

BYOG – Be Your Own Guru – is an acronym and invitation to start initiating, guiding and moving toward change while staying connected to and guided by the body and its present moment experience. Personal growth and transformation are personal responsibilities, and BYOG honors that.

Holistic wellbeing, authentic change and harmonious relationships are journeys, not static destinations. On these uniquely individual journeys, direct experience will be our best teacher. We can connect with our body and use it to experiment with our direct life experience. Listen to the body; it is the best teacher. Keep the strategies that work. Discard the rest. BYOG. This is a lifelong education in connecting with our body's innate wisdom and understanding what it needs to thrive.

The only thing we can be an expert in is our own life. The only things I know for sure are those lessons I've experienced directly. I know my path deeply and intimately. I speak from my path. I teach from my experience. I hope my journey and sharing will inspire you to do the inner work for yourself.

***

These were a few of the shifts, insights and learnings that have emerged from my commitment to living a body-oriented life. When we pay attention to the experience of our body, from moment to moment, we don't need to collect books, degrees and credentials to learn 'enough' and certainly not to *be enough*.

We can embody a way of being that is more natural, open, spontaneous and in harmony with ourselves, our relationships and the world. We can stay connected to the body to learn what it needs to thrive. In turn, the gifts we give the body will be exponentially reciprocated as we experience vitality, calmness, energy and focus that help us engage with and manage the unique contexts of our respective lives.

Staying connected to our body empowers us to process and integrate the deeply embedded sensations and emotions beneath our conscious awareness. Through our sense of feeling, we can break the cycle of reactivity and consciously move toward authentic change. When we embody our present moment experience, we are invited to infuse and transform the many relationships within our lives, both the relationship we have with ourselves as well as with those around us.

Becoming *Somawise* turns our everyday, moment-to-moment life experience into a profoundly fulfilling practice. I am thankful for being reconnected with my body. I know the same is possible for anyone seeking and starting on the path of becoming *Somawise*. So now, only one question remains: *what will your body teach you?*

Acknowledgments

"Collective strength is the force that makes the impossible happen." - Mohammed Zaid

"When we give cheerfully and accept gratefully, everyone is blessed." - Maya Angelou

"We are the superhero, none of us individually, but all of us together." - Hank Green

Writing this book was harder than I thought and more rewarding than I imagined. After completing *A Million Ways to Live* in 2014, I told myself I wouldn't write a book again. Completing that book – and documentary series - took too much of me; physically, mentally and emotionally. I made one exception: I'd write again if the world asked me to.

As I scribbled ideas over the following years, the structure for *Somawise* began to form and solidify slowly. Despite this, I continued to wait until I felt my book was needed. Then, as if the world was telling me it was ready to hear what I had to share, students and clients began asking if I had a book they could use as a reference guide to support their therapeutic journey. It was time. *Somawise* took seven years to complete and would not have reached this point without so many people's help, guidance and love.

I want to thank my soon-to-be wife for always believing in me, especially when I questioned myself and whether I should move forward with this book. At no point did your confidence in me and my message waiver. You are my rock.

To Jack, my incredible boy, I want you to know that none of this happens without you. You have made me the father, therapist and man I am today. You are wise beyond your years and have taught me more than you'll ever know. I am grateful to be your dad.

To my family members, who always accepted me as the black sheep of the crew. My mom, who didn't bat an eyelid when I told her I'd be sharing stories from my own life. My father, who continues to soften and explore his emotional vulnerability. My brother, my number 1 fan since I played football.

I want to thank the people who treated this book as if it were theirs. Tamara, thank you for enthusiastically engaging with *Somawise* with a fine-toothed comb. You made the process stressless and your contributions truly shaped the final product. Roland, thank you for guiding me through the terrains of authorship and always answering my questions about the writing process. Kimble, thank you for your keen eye and attention to detail.

Thank you to Compassionate Inquiry (CI), the organization, team members and curriculum that turned me into the therapist, helper and teacher I am today. I've been a lone wolf my whole life. CI is the first place I feel part of a team and community. Thank you for giving me the wings to fly, especially Sat Dharam, Rhonda, Pamela, Michelle, Stephen and Allison. I love being part of the CI team.

To my teachers, Graham, Gabor, Rupert and Phil. You are examples and leaders that I continuously look up to, attempt to model, and look to when I need to calibrate my internal compass.

Finally, thank you to all the readers who volunteered their time to review *Somawise* before it was ready for publishing. Thank you, Himanshu, Stuart, Samantha, Pam, Angela, Jeanelle, Dee, Warren, Joseph, Nina, Juliana, Mark, Steven and Luís. Your contributions and words brought this book over the finish line.

References

[1] Mirams, L., Poliakoff, E., Brown, R. J., & Lloyd, D. M. (2013). Brief body-scan meditation practice improves somatosensory perceptual decision making. *Consciousness and cognition*, *22*(1), 348–359.

[2] Price, C. J., & Hooven, C. (2018). Interoceptive Awareness Skills for Emotion Regulation: Theory and Approach of Mindful Awareness in Body-Oriented Therapy (MABT). *Frontiers in psychology*, *9*, 798.

[3] Young R. W. (2003). Evolution of the human hand: the role of throwing and clubbing. Journal of anatomy, 202(1), 165–174.

[4] Schmitt D. (2003). Insights into the evolution of human bipedalism from experimental studies of humans and other primates. The Journal of experimental biology, 206(Pt 9), 1437–1448.

[5] shCherbak, V. & Makukov, M. (2013). The "Wow! signal" of the terrestrial genetic code. Icarus, 224(1), 228-242.

[6] Winkelman M. J. (2017). The Mechanisms of Psychedelic Visionary Experiences: Hypotheses from Evolutionary Psychology. Frontiers in neuroscience, 11, 539.

[7] Zaltman, G. (2003). How customers think: Essential insights into the mind of the market. Boston, Mass: Harvard Business School Press.

[8] Smith, K. Brain makes decisions before you even know it. Nature (2008).

[9] Damasio A. R. (1996). The somatic marker hypothesis and the possible functions of the prefrontal cortex. Philosophical transactions of the

Royal Society of London. Series B, Biological sciences, 351(1346), 1413–1420.

[10] Correa, L. I., Cardenas, K., Casanova-Mollá, J., & Valls-Solé, J. (2019). Thermoalgesic stimuli induce prepulse inhibition of the blink reflex and affect conscious perception in healthy humans. Psychophysiology, 56(4), e13310.

[11] Xu, F., Xiang, P., & Huang, L. (2020). Bridging Ecological Rationality, Embodied Emotion, and Neuroeconomics: Insights From the Somatic Marker Hypothesis. Frontiers in psychology, 11, 1028.

[12] Zimecki M. (2006). The lunar cycle: effects on human and animal behavior and physiology. *Postepy higieny i medycyny doswiadczalnej (Online), 60*, 1–7.

[13] Wehr T. A. (2018). Bipolar mood cycles associated with lunar entrainment of a circadian rhythm. *Translational psychiatry, 8*(1), 151.

[14] JAMA and Archives Journals. (2010, May 7). Early childhood experiences have lasting emotional and psychological effects. *ScienceDaily.* Retrieved September 4, 2022 from www.sciencedaily.com/releases/2010/05/100503161332.htm

[15] Maté, D. G. (2018). *In the realm of hungry ghosts.* Vermilion.

[16] Rappaport, S. M., & Smith, M. T. (2010). Epidemiology. Environment and disease risks. Science (New York, N.Y.), 330(6003), 460–461.

[17] Katz, David. "The Case for Natural Foods." Prevention 62.3 (2010): 124-127.

[18] Barr, Sadie B., and Jonathan C. Wright. "Postprandial Energy Expenditure in Whole-Food and Processed-Food Meals: Implications for Daily Energy Expenditure." Food & Nutrition Research 54. (2010): 1-9.

[19] Lane, Kirstin, Dan Worsley, and Don McKenzie. "Exercise and the Lymphatic System: Implications for Breast-Cancer Survivors." Sports Medicine 35.6 (2005*): 461-471.*

[20] University of Washington. "Digestive Problems May Impede Overweight People from Exercising." ScienceDaily. ScienceDaily, 8 December 2005.

[21] Fonseca, Hélder, et al. "Bone Quality: The Determinants of Bone Strength and Fragility." Sports Medicine 44.1 (2014): 37-53.

[22] Jones, Simon. "Endurance Exercise, The Fountain of Youth, and the Mitochondrial Key." UBC Medical Journal 3.1 (2011): 26-27.

[23] Jackson M. Evaluating the Role of Hans Selye in the Modern History of Stress. In: Cantor D, Ramsden E, editors. Stress, Shock, and Adaptation in the Twentieth Century. Rochester (NY): University of Rochester Press; 2014 Feb. Chapter 1. Available from: https://www.ncbi.nlm.nih.gov/books/NBK349158/

[24] Delmonte M. M. (1984). Physiological responses during meditation and rest. Biofeedback and self-regulation, 9(2), 181–200.

[25] Taylor, W. C., King, K. E., Shegog, R., Paxton, R. J., Evans-Hudnall, G. L., Rempel, D. M., Chen, V., & Yancey, A. K. (2013). Booster Breaks in the workplace: participants' perspectives on health-promoting work breaks. Health education research, 28(3), 414–425.

[26] Murphy, M., & Mercer, J. G. (2013). Diet-regulated anxiety. International Journal of Endocrinology, 701967.

[27] Rao, T. S., Asha, M. R., Ramesh, B. N., & Rao, K. S. (2008). Understanding nutrition, depression and mental illnesses. Indian Journal of Psychiatry, 50(2), 77–82.

[28] Sender, R., Fuchs, S., & Milo, R. (2016). Revised Estimates for the Number of Human and Bacteria Cells in the Body. PLoS biology, 14(8), e1002533.

[29] Tillisch, K., Mayer, E. A., Gupta, A., Gill, Z., Brazeilles, R., Le Nevé, B., van Hylckama Vlieg, J., Guyonnet, D., Derrien, M., & Labus, J. S. (2017). Brain Structure and Response to Emotional Stimuli as Related to Gut Microbial Profiles in Healthy Women. Psychosomatic Medicine, 79(8), 905–913.

[30] Brown, K., DeCoffe, D., Molcan, E., & Gibson, D. L. (2012). Diet-induced dysbiosis of the intestinal microbiota and the effects on immunity and disease. Nutrients, 4(8), 1095–1119.

[31] Clapp, M., Aurora, N., Herrera, L., Bhatia, M., Wilen, E., & Wakefield, S. (2017). Gut microbiota's effect on mental health: The gut-brain axis. Clinics and Practice, 7(4), 987.

[32] Hilimire, M., Devylder, J., & Forestell, C. (2015). Fermented Foods, neuroticism, and social anxiety: An interaction model. Psychiatry Research, 228, 203-208.

[33] Heym, N., Heasman, B. C., Hunter, K., Blanco, S. R., Wang, G. Y., Siegert, R., Cleare, A., Gibson, G. R., Kumari, V., & Sumich, A. L. (2019). The role of microbiota and inflammation in self-judgement and empathy: implications for understanding the brain-gut-microbiome axis in depression. Psychopharmacology, 236(5), 1459–1470.

[34] Kiecolt-Glaser, J. K., Belury, M. A., Andridge, R., Malarkey, W. B., & Glaser, R. (2011). Omega-3 supplementation lowers inflammation and anxiety in medical students: a randomized controlled trial. Brain, Behavior, and Immunity, 25(8), 1725–1734.

[35] Francis, H., Stevenson, R., Chambers, J., Gupta D., Newey, B., & Lim, C. (2019). A brief diet intervention can reduce symptoms of depression in young adults – A randomised controlled trial. PLoS ONE 14(10): e0222768.

[36] Lai, J., Hiles, S., Bisquera, A., Hure, A., McEvoy, M., & Attia, J. (2014). A systematic review and meta-analysis of dietary patterns and depression in community-dwelling adults. The American Journal of Clinical Nutrition, 99(1), 181-197.

[37] Firth, J., Veronese, N., Cotter, J., Shivappa, N., Hebert, J. R., Ee, C., Smith, L., Stubbs, B., Jackson, S. E., & Sarris, J. (2019a). What Is the Role of Dietary Inflammation in Severe Mental Illness? A Review of Observational and Experimental Findings. Frontiers in Psychiatry, 10, 350.

[38] Firth, J., Gangwisch, J. E., Borisini, A., Wootton, R. E., & Mayer, E. A. (2020). Food and mood: how do diet and nutrition affect mental wellbeing?. BMJ (Clinical research ed.), 369, m2382.

[39] Stonerock, G. L., Hoffman, B. M., Smith, P. J., & Blumenthal, J. A. (2015). Exercise as Treatment for Anxiety: Systematic Review and Analysis. Annals of Behavioral Medicine: A Publication of the Society of Behavioral Medicine, 49(4), 542–556.

[40] Craft, L. L., & Perna, F. M. (2004). The Benefits of Exercise for the Clinically Depressed. Primary Care Companion to the Journal of Clinical Psychiatry, 6(3), 104–111.

[41] MacIntosh, Bradley J., et al. "Impact of a Single Bout of Aerobic Exercise on Regional Brain Perfusion and Activation Responses in Healthy Young Adults." Plos ONE 9.1 (2014): 1-7.

[42] T. J. Schoenfeld, P. Rada, P. R. Pieruzzini, B. Hsueh, E. Gould. "Physical Exercise Prevents Stress-Induced Activation of Granule Neurons and Enhances Local Inhibitory Mechanisms in the Dentate Gyrus." Journal of Neuroscience, 2013; 33 (18): 7770.

[43] Chekroud, S., Gueorguieva, R., Zheutlin, A., Paulus, M., Krumholz, H., Krystal, J., & Chekroud, A. (2018). Association between physical exercise and mental health in 1·2 million individuals in the USA between 2011 and 2015: a cross-sectional study. The Lancet Psychiatry, 5. 10.1016/S2215-0366(18)30227-X.

[44] Al-Khani, A.M., Sarhandi, M.I., Zaghloul, M.S. et al. (2019). A cross-sectional survey on sleep quality, mental health, and academic performance among medical students in Saudi Arabia. BMC Res Notes 12, 665.

[45] University of California - Berkeley. "Midday nap markedly boosts the brain's learning capacity." ScienceDaily. ScienceDaily, 22 February 2010.

[46] Freeman, D., Sheaves, B., Goodwin, G. M., Yu, L. M., Nickless, A., Harrison, P. J., Emsley, R., Luik, A. I., Foster, R. G., Wadekar, V., Hinds, C., Gumley, A., Jones, R., Lightman, S., Jones, S., Bentall, R., Kinderman, P., Rowse,

G., Brugha, T., Blagrove, M., ... Espie, C. A. (2017). The effects of improving sleep on mental health (OASIS): a randomised controlled trial with mediation analysis. The Lancet Psychiatry, 4(10), 749–758.

[47] Black, P. H. (2002). Stress and the inflammatory response: a review of neurogenic inflammation. Brain Behav. Immun. 16, 622–653.

[48] Cohen, Sheldon, et al. "Chronic Stress, Glucocorticoid Receptor Resistance, Inflammation, And Disease Risk." Proceedings Of The National Academy Of Sciences Of The United States Of America 109.16 (2012): 5995-5999.

[49] Hall, K. S., Kusunoki, Y., Gatny, H., & Barber, J. (2014). Stress symptoms and frequency of sexual intercourse among young women. The journal of sexual medicine, 11(8), 1982–1990.

[50] Hunter P. (2012). The inflammation theory of disease. The growing realization that chronic inflammation is crucial in many diseases opens new avenues for treatment. EMBO Reports, 13(11), 968–970.

[51] Slavich, G. M., and Irwin, M. R. (2014). From stress to inflammation and major depressive disorder: a social signal transduction theory of depression. Psychol. Bull. 140, 774–815.

[52] Strawbridge, R., Arnone, D., Danese, A., Papadopoulos, A., Herane, A., and Cleare, A. J. (2015). Inflammation and clinical response to treatment in depression: a meta-analysis. Eur. Neuropsychopharmacol. 25, 1532–1543.

[53] Furtado, M. and Katzman, M. (2015). Examining the role of neuroinflammation in major depression. Psychiatry Res. 229, 27–36.

[54] Jarvandi, S., Davidson, N. O., Jeffe, D. B., & Schootman, M. (2012). Influence of lifestyle factors on inflammation in men and women with type 2 diabetes: results from the National Health and Nutrition Examination Survey, 1999-2004. Annals of Behavioral Medicine: A Publication of the Society of Behavioral Medicine, 44(3), 399–407.

[55] Elenkov, I. J., Iezzoni, D. G., Daly, A., Harris, A. G., and Chrousos, G. P. (2005). Cytokine dysregulation, inflammation and wellbeing. Neuroimmunomodulation, 12, 255-269.

G., Brugha, T., Blagrove, M., ... Espie, C. A. (2017). The effects of improving sleep on mental health (OASIS): a randomised controlled trial with mediation analysis. The Lancet Psychiatry, 4(10), 749–758.

[47] Black, P. H. (2002). Stress and the inflammatory response: a review of neurogenic inflammation. Brain Behav. Immun. 16, 622–653.

[48] Cohen, Sheldon, et al. "Chronic Stress, Glucocorticoid Receptor Resistance, Inflammation, And Disease Risk." Proceedings Of The National Academy Of Sciences Of The United States Of America 109.16 (2012): 5995-5999.

[49] Hall, K. S., Kusunoki, Y., Gatny, H., & Barber, J. (2014). Stress symptoms and frequency of sexual intercourse among young women. The journal of sexual medicine, 11(8), 1982–1990.

[50] Hunter P. (2012). The inflammation theory of disease. The growing realization that chronic inflammation is crucial in many diseases opens new avenues for treatment. EMBO Reports, 13(11), 968–970.

[51] Slavich, G. M., and Irwin, M. R. (2014). From stress to inflammation and major depressive disorder: a social signal transduction theory of depression. Psychol. Bull. 140, 774–815.

[52] Strawbridge, R., Arnone, D., Danese, A., Papadopoulos, A., Herane, A., and Cleare, A. J. (2015). Inflammation and clinical response to treatment in depression: a meta-analysis. Eur. Neuropsychopharmacol. 25, 1532–1543.

[53] Furtado, M. and Katzman, M. (2015). Examining the role of neuroinflammation in major depression. Psychiatry Res. 229, 27–36.

[54] Jarvandi, S., Davidson, N. O., Jeffe, D. B., & Schootman, M. (2012). Influence of lifestyle factors on inflammation in men and women with type 2 diabetes: results from the National Health and Nutrition Examination Survey, 1999-2004. Annals of Behavioral Medicine: A Publication of the Society of Behavioral Medicine, 44(3), 399–407.

[55] Elenkov, I. J., Iezzoni, D. G., Daly, A., Harris, A. G., and Chrousos, G. P. (2005). Cytokine dysregulation, inflammation and wellbeing. Neuroimmunomodulation, 12, 255-269.

[56] Schwingshackl, L., Christoph, M., & Hoffmann, G. (2015). Effects of Olive Oil on Markers of Inflammation and Endothelial Function-A Systematic Review and Meta-Analysis. Nutrients, 7(9), 7651–7675.

[57] Lapuente, M., Estruch, R., Shahbaz, M., & Casas, R. (2019). Relation of Fruits and Vegetables with Major Cardiometabolic Risk Factors, Markers of Oxidation, and Inflammation. Nutrients, 11(10), 2381.

[58] Minihane, A. M., Vinoy, S., Russell, W. R., Baka, A., Roche, H. M., Tuohy, K. M., Teeling, J. L., Blaak, E. E., Fenech, M., Vauzour, D., McArdle, H. J., Kremer, B. H., Sterkman, L., Vafeiadou, K., Benedetti, M. M., Williams, C. M., & Calder, P. C. (2015). Low-grade inflammation, diet composition and health: current research evidence and its translation. The British Journal of Nutrition, 114(7), 999–1012.

[59] Mullington, J. M., Simpson, N. S., Meier-Ewert, H. K., & Haack, M. (2010). Sleep loss and inflammation. Best practice & research. Clinical Endocrinology & Metabolism, 24(5), 775–784.

[60] Woods, J. A., Wilund, K. R., Martin, S. A., & Kistler, B. M. (2012). Exercise, inflammation and aging. Aging and disease, 3(1), 130–140.

[61] Mushtaq, R., Shoib, S., Shah, T., & Mushtaq, S. (2014). Relationship between loneliness, psychiatric disorders and physical health? A review on the psychological aspects of loneliness. Journal of clinical and diagnostic research: JCDR, 8(9), WE01–WE4.

[62] Pearson, D. G., & Craig, T. (2014). The great outdoors? Exploring the mental health benefits of natural environments. Frontiers in Psychology, 5, 1178.

[63] Penckofer, S., Kouba, J., Byrn, M., & Estwing Ferrans, C. (2010). Vitamin D and depression: where is all the sunshine? Issues in Mental Health Nursing, 31(6), 385–393.

[64] Hoge, E. A., Bui, E., Marques, L., Metcalf, C. A., Morris, L. K., Robinaugh, D. J., Worthington, J. J., Pollack, M. H., & Simon, N. M. (2013). Randomized controlled trial of mindfulness meditation for generalized anxiety disorder: effects on anxiety and stress reactivity. The Journal of Clinical Psychiatry, 74(8), 786–792.

[65] Black, D. S., & Slavich, G. M. (2016). Mindfulness meditation and the immune system: a systematic review of randomized controlled trials. Annals of the New York Academy of Sciences, 1373(1), 13–24.

[66] Balter, L. J., Bosch, J. A., Aldred, S., Drayson, M. T., Veldhuijzen van Zanten, J. J., Higgs, S., Raymond, J. E., & Mazaheri, A. (2019). Selective effects of acute low-grade inflammation on human visual attention. NeuroImage, 202, 116098.

[67] Emmons, Robert A., and Michael E. McCullough. "Counting Blessings Versus Burdens: An Experimental Investigation of Gratitude and Subjective Well-Being In Daily Life." Journal of Personality & Social Psychology 84.2 (2003): 377-389.

[68] Tramullas, Mónica, Timothy G. Dinan, and John F. Cryan. Chronic Psychosocial Stress Induces Visceral Hyperalgesia. Stress: The International Journal on the Biology of Stress 15.3 (2012): 281-292.

[69] Mönnikes H., "Role of Stress in Functional Gastrointestinal Disorders. Evidence for Stress-Induced Alterations in Gastrointestinal Motility and Sensitivity." Digestive Diseases. Vol. 19, No. 3, 2001.

[70] Banno, M., Harada, Y., Taniguchi, M., Tobita, R., Tsujimoto, H., Tsujimoto, Y., Kataoka, Y., & Noda, A. (2018). Exercise can improve sleep quality: a systematic review and meta-analysis. PeerJ, 6, e5172.

[71] Black, D. S., O'Reilly, G. A., Olmstead, R., Breen, E. C., & Irwin, M. R. (2015). Mindfulness meditation and improvement in sleep quality and daytime impairment among older adults with sleep disturbances: a randomized clinical trial. JAMA Internal Medicine, 175(4), 494–501.

[72] St-Onge, M. P., Mikic, A., & Pietrolungo, C. E. (2016). Effects of Diet on Sleep Quality. Advances in nutrition (Bethesda, Md.), 7(5), 938–949.

[73] Kline CE. The bidirectional relationship between exercise and sleep: Implications for exercise adherence and sleep improvement. Am J Lifestyle Med. 2014 Nov-Dec;8(6):375-379.

[74] Spiegel, K., Leproult, R., & Van Cauter, E. (1999). Impact of sleep debt on metabolic and endocrine function. Lancet (London, England), 354(9188), 1435–1439.

[75] Khalsa, S. S., & Lapidus, R. C. (2016). Can Interoception Improve the Pragmatic Search for Biomarkers in Psychiatry?. *Frontiers in psychiatry, 7,* 121.

[76] Bahr, Megan N.; Chrisostom, Kandise M.; Chrisostom, Serena S.; Peters, Natalie K.; Thomas, Pheba M.; and Catts, APRN, PHD, Patricia A., "A COMPARATIVE ANALYSIS OF THE KETOGENIC, PALEOLITHIC, AND VEGAN DIETS" (2019). Nursing Undergraduate Work. 9.

[77] Mozaffarian, D., Hao, T., Rimm, E. B., Willett, W. C., & Hu, F. B. (2011). Changes in diet and lifestyle and long-term weight gain in women and men. The New England journal of medicine, 364(25), 2392–2404.

[78] Katz, D. L., & Meller, S. (2014). Can we say what diet is best for health?. Annual review of public health, 35, 83–103.

[79] Pacey, Verity, et al. "Generalized Joint Hypermobility and Risk of Lower Limb Joint Injury During Sport." American Journal of Sports Medicine 38.7 (2010): 1487-1497.

[80] McQuade, KJ. "A Case-Control Study of Running Injuries: Comparison of Patterns-of Runners with and Without Running Injuries." The Journal of Orthopaedic and Sports Physical Therapy. 1986;8(2):81-4.

[81] Shors, T.J., et al. "Use It or Lose It: How Neurogenesis Keeps the Brain Fit for Learning." Behavioural Brain Research 227.2 (2012): 450-458.

[82] Sparrow, William A., et al. "Aging Effects on The Metabolic and Cognitive Energy Cost of Interlimb Coordination." Journals of Gerontology Series A: Biological Sciences & Medical Sciences 60A.3 (2005): 312-319.

[83] Koike, M. K., & Cardoso, R. (2014). Meditation can produce beneficial effects to prevent cardiovascular disease. Hormone molecular biology and clinical investigation, 18(3), 137–143.

[84] MacLean, K. A., Ferrer, E., Aichele, S. R., Bridwell, D. A., Zanesco, A. P., Jacobs, T. L., & ... Saron, C. D. (2010). Intensive Meditation Training Improves Perceptual Discrimination and Sustained Attention. Psychological Science (0956-7976), 21(6), 829-839.

[85] Mrazek, M. D., Franklin, M. S., Phillips, D. T., Baird, B., & Schooler, J. W. (2013). Mindfulness Training Improves Working Memory Capacity and GRE Performance While Reducing Mind Wandering. Psychological Science (0956-7976), 24(5), 776-781.

[86] Hafenbrack, A. C., Kinias, Z., & Barsade, S. G. (2014). Debiasing the mind through meditation: mindfulness and the sunk-cost bias. Psychological Science, 25(2), 369-376.

[87] Rosenkranz, M. A., Davidson, R. J., Maccoon, D. G., Sheridan, J. F., Kalin, N. H., & Lutz, A. (2013). A comparison of mindfulness-based stress reduction and an active control in modulation of neurogenic inflammation. Brain, behavior, and immunity, 27(1), 174-184.

[88] Black, D. S., & Slavich, G. M. (2016). Mindfulness meditation and the immune system: a systematic review of randomized controlled trials. Annals of the New York Academy of Sciences, 1373(1), 13-24. https://doi.org/10.1111/nyas.12998

[89] Furman, D., Campisi, J., Verdin, E., Carrera-Bastos, P., Targ, S., Franceschi, C., Ferrucci, L., Gilroy, D. W., Fasano, A., Miller, G. W., Miller, A. H., Mantovani, A., Weyand, C. M., Barzilai, N., Goronzy, J. J., Rando, T. A., Effros, R. B., Lucia, A., Kleinstreuer, N., & Slavich, G. M. (2019). Chronic inflammation in the etiology of disease across the life span. Nature medicine, 25(12), 1822-1832.

[90] Felger J. C. (2018). Imaging the Role of Inflammation in Mood and Anxiety-related Disorders. Current neuropharmacology, 16(5), 533-558.

[91] Lee, C. H., & Giuliani, F. (2019). The Role of Inflammation in Depression and Fatigue. Frontiers in immunology, 10, 1696.

[92] Zeng, X., Chiu, C. P., Wang, R., Oei, T. P., & Leung, F. Y. (2015). The effect of loving-kindness meditation on positive emotions: a meta-analytic review. Frontiers in psychology, 6, 1693.

[93] Khoury, B., Lecomte, T., Fortin, G., Masse, M., Therien, P., Bouchard, V., Chapleau, M. A., Paquin, K., & Hofmann, S. G. (2013). Mindfulness-

based therapy: a comprehensive meta-analysis. Clinical psychology review, 33(6), 763–771.

[94] Sturgeon, J. A., & Zautra, A. J. (2016). Social pain and physical pain: shared paths to resilience. *Pain management, 6*(1), 63–74.

[95] Kross E, Berman MG, Mischel W, Smith EE, Wager TD. Social rejection shares somatosensory representations with physical pain. Proceedings of the National Academy of Sciences of the United States of America. 2011 Apr;108(15):6270-6275.

[96] Biro D. (2010). Is there such a thing as psychological pain? And why it matters. Culture, medicine and psychiatry, 34(4), 658–667.

[97] Zeidan, F., Emerson, N. M., Farris, S. R., Ray, J. N., Jung, Y., McHaffie, J. G., & Coghill, R. C. (2015). Mindfulness Meditation-Based Pain Relief Employs Different Neural Mechanisms Than Placebo and Sham Mindfulness Meditation-Induced Analgesia. The Journal of neuroscience : the official journal of the Society for Neuroscience, 35(46), 15307–15325.

[98] Zeidan, F., Grant, J. A., Brown, C. A., McHaffie, J. G., & Coghill, R. C. (2012). Mindfulness meditation-related pain relief: evidence for unique brain mechanisms in the regulation of pain. *Neuroscience letters, 520*(2), 165–173.

[99] Wallace, R. K., Benson, H., & Wilson, A. F. (1971). A wakeful hypometabolic physiologic state. *The American journal of physiology, 221*(3), 795–799.

[100] Hölzel, B. K., Lazar, S. W., Gard, T., Schuman-Olivier, Z., Vago, D. R., & Ott, U. (2011). How Does Mindfulness Meditation Work? Proposing Mechanisms of Action From a Conceptual and Neural Perspective. *Perspectives on psychological science: a journal of the Association for Psychological Science, 6*(6), 537–559.

[101] Marlatt, G. & Chawla, N. (2007). Meditation and alcohol use. Southern Medical Journal. 100(4), 451-453.

[102] Shafiei, E., Hoseini, A. F., Bibak, A., & Azmal, M. (2014). High risk situations predicting relapse in self-referred addicts to bushehr

province substance abuse treatment centers. International Journal Of High Risk Behaviors & Addiction, 3(2), e16381.

[103] Larimer, M. E., Palmer, R. S., & Marlatt, G. A. (1999). Relapse prevention. An overview of Marlatt's cognitive-behavioral model. Alcohol Research & Health: The Journal Of The National Institute On Alcohol Abuse And Alcoholism, 23(2), 151-160.

[104] Wetterneck, C., Burgess, A., Short, M., Smith, A., & Cervantes, M. (2012). The role of sexual compulsivity, impulsivity, and experiential avoidance in internet pornography use. Psychological Record, 62(1), 3-17.

[105] Berking, M., Margraf, M., Ebert, D., Wupperman, P., Hofmann, S., & Junghanns, K. (2011). Deficits in emotion-regulation skills predict alcohol use during and after cognitive behavioral therapy for alcohol dependence. Journal of Consulting and Clinical Psychology, 79(3), 307–318.

[106] Dvorak, R. D., Sargent, E. M., Kilwein, T. M., Stevenson, B. L., Kuvaas, N. J., & Williams, T. J. (2014). Alcohol use and alcohol-related consequences: associations with emotion regulation difficulties. American Journal Of Drug & Alcohol Abuse, 40(2), 125-130.

[107] Langer, E. (2004). Langer mindfulness scale user guide and technical manual. Worthington, OH: IDS Publishing Corporation.

[108] Demick, J. (2000). Toward a mindful psychological science: Theory and application. Journal of Social Issues, 56(1), 141.

[109] Brown, K. W., Ryan, R. M., & Creswell, J. D. (2007). Mindfulness: Theoretical Foundations and Evidence for its Salutary Effects. Psychological Inquiry, 18(4), 211–237.

[110] Leslie, M. (2005). How can we use moderate stresses to fortify humans and slow aging? Science of Aging Knowledge Environment : SAGE KE, 2005(26), nf49.

[111] Berry, R., 3rd, & López-Martínez, G. (2020). A dose of experimental hormesis: When mild stress protects and improves animal

performance. Comparative biochemistry and physiology. Part A, Molecular & integrative physiology, 242, 110658.

[112] Arumugam TV, Gleichmann M, Tang SC, Mattson MP. Hormesis/preconditioning mechanisms, the nervous system and aging. Ageing Res Rev 2006(5), 165-78.

[113] Kox, M., van Eijk, L. T., Zwaag, J., van den Wildenberg, J., Sweep, F. C., van der Hoeven, J. G., & Pickkers, P. (2014). Voluntary activation of the sympathetic nervous system and attenuation of the innate immune response in humans. *Proceedings of the National Academy of Sciences of the United States of America, 111*(20), 7379-7384.

[114] Mooventhan, A., & Nivethitha, L. (2014). Scientific evidence-based effects of hydrotherapy on various systems of the body. *North American journal of medical sciences, 6*(5), 199-209.

[115] Shevchuk, N. A., & Radoja, S. (2007). Possible stimulation of anti-tumor immunity using repeated cold stress: a hypothesis. *Infectious agents and cancer, 2*, 20.

[116] Ravussin, Y., Xiao, C., Gavrilova, O., & Reitman, M. L. (2014). Effect of intermittent cold exposure on brown fat activation, obesity, and energy homeostasis in mice. *PloS one, 9*(1), e85876.

[117] Sramek, P., Simeckova, M., Jansky, L., & Vybiral, S. (2000). Human physiological responses to immersion into water of different temperatures (Reponses physiologiques de l'homme a une immersion dans l'eau a differentes temperatures). European Journal of Applied Physiology, 81(5), 436-442.

[118] Shevchuk, N. A. (2008). Adapted cold shower as a potential treatment for depression. Medical Hypotheses, 70(5), 995-1001.

[119] Jungmann, M., Vencatachellum, S., Van Ryckeghem, D., & Vögele, C. (2018). Effects of Cold Stimulation on Cardiac-Vagal Activation in Healthy Participants: Randomized Controlled Trial. *JMIR formative research, 2*(2), e10257.

[120] De Ferrari, G. M., & Schwartz, P. J. (2011). Vagus nerve stimulation: from pre-clinical to clinical application: challenges and future directions. *Heart failure reviews*, *16*(2), 195–203.

[121] Hussain, J., & Cohen, M. (2018). Clinical Effects of Regular Dry Sauna Bathing: A Systematic Review. Evidence-based complementary and alternative medicine : eCAM, 2018, 1857413.

[122] Laukkanen, T., Kunutsor, S., Kauhanen, J., & Laukkanen, J. A. (2017). Sauna bathing is inversely associated with dementia and Alzheimer's disease in middle-aged Finnish men. Age and ageing, 46(2), 245–249.

[123] Laukkanen, J. A., Laukkanen, T., & Kunutsor, S. K. (2018). Cardiovascular and Other Health Benefits of Sauna Bathing: A Review of the Evidence. Mayo Clinic proceedings, 93(8), 1111–1121.

[124] Buijze, G. A., Sierevelt, I. N., van der Heijden, B. C., Dijkgraaf, M. G., & Frings-Dresen, M. H. (2016). The Effect of Cold Showering on Health and Work: A Randomized Controlled Trial. *PloS one*, *11*(9), e0161749.

[125] Dubois O, Salamon R, Germain C, Poirier MF, Vaugeois C, Banwarth B, Mouaffak F, Galinowski A, Olié JP. Balneotherapy versus paroxetine in the treatment of generalized anxiety disorder. Complement Ther Med. 2010;18(1):1-7.

[126] Daukantaitė, D., Tellhed, U., Maddux, R. E., Svensson, T., & Melander, O. (2018). Five-week yin yoga-based interventions decreased plasma adrenomedullin and increased psychological health in stressed adults: A randomized controlled trial. PloS One, 13(7), e0200518.

[127] Bordoni, B., & Zanier, E. (2014). Clinical and symptomatological reflections: the fascial system. *Journal of multidisciplinary healthcare*, *7*, 401–411.

[128] Stecco, A., Stern, R., Fantoni, I., De Caro, R., & Stecco, C. (2016). Fascial Disorders: Implications for Treatment. PM & R : the journal of injury, function, and rehabilitation, 8(2), 161–168.

[129] Bordoni, B., Marelli, F., Morabito, B., Castagna, R., Sacconi, B., & Mazzucco, P. (2018). New Proposal to Define the Fascial System. Complementary medicine research, 25(4), 257–262.

[130] Nair, S., Sagar, M., Sollers, J., 3rd, Consedine, N., & Broadbent, E. (2015). Do slumped and upright postures affect stress responses? A randomized trial. *Health psychology : official journal of the Division of Health Psychology, American Psychological Association, 34*(6), 632–641.

[131] Tozzi P. (2014). Does fascia hold memories?. Journal of bodywork and movement therapies, 18(2), 259–265.

[132] Frayn, M., Livshits, S., & Knäuper, B. (2018). Emotional eating and weight regulation: a qualitative study of compensatory behaviors and concerns. *Journal of eating disorders, 6*, 23.

[133] de Cabo, R., & Mattson, M. P. (2019). Effects of Intermittent Fasting on Health, Aging, and Disease. The New England Journal of Medicine, 381(26), 2541–2551.

[134] Faris, M. A., Kacimi, S., Al-Kurd, R. A., Fararjeh, M. A., Bustanji, Y. K., Mohammad, M. K., & Salem, M. L. (2012). Intermittent fasting during Ramadan attenuates proinflammatory cytokines and immune cells in healthy subjects. Nutrition research (New York, N.Y.), 32(12), 947–955.

[135] Halagappa, V. K., Guo, Z., Pearson, M., Matsuoka, Y., Cutler, R. G., Laferla, F. M., & Mattson, M. P. (2007). Intermittent fasting and caloric restriction ameliorate age-related behavioral deficits in the triple-transgenic mouse model of Alzheimer's disease. Neurobiology of disease, 26(1), 212–220.

[136] Grajower, M. M., & Horne, B. D. (2019). Clinical Management of Intermittent Fasting in Patients with Diabetes Mellitus. *Nutrients, 11*(4), 873.

[137] Duan, W., & Mattson, M. P. (1999). Dietary restriction and 2-deoxyglucose administration improve behavioral outcome and reduce degeneration of dopaminergic neurons in models of Parkinson's disease. Journal of neuroscience research, 57(2), 195–206.

[138] Brandhorst, S., & Longo, V. D. (2016). Fasting and Caloric Restriction in Cancer Prevention and Treatment. Recent results in cancer research.

Fortschritte der Krebsforschung. Progres dans les recherches sur le cancer, 207, 241–266.

[139] Froy, O., & Miskin, R. (2010). Effect of feeding regimens on circadian rhythms: implications for aging and longevity. *Aging, 2*(1), 7–27.

[140] Patterson, R. E., Laughlin, G. A., LaCroix, A. Z., Hartman, S. J., Natarajan, L., Senger, C. M., Martínez, M. E., Villaseñor, A., Sears, D. D., Marinac, C. R., & Gallo, L. C. (2015). Intermittent Fasting and Human Metabolic Health. Journal of the Academy of Nutrition and Dietetics, 115(8), 1203–1212.

[141] Baik, S. H., Rajeev, V., Fann, D. Y., Jo, D. G., & Arumugam, T. V. (2020). Intermittent fasting increases adult hippocampal neurogenesis. Brain and behavior, 10(1), e01444.

[142] Anton, S. D., Moehl, K., Donahoo, W. T., Marosi, K., Lee, S. A., Mainous, A. G., 3rd, Leeuwenburgh, C., & Mattson, M. P. (2018). Flipping the Metabolic Switch: Understanding and Applying the Health Benefits of Fasting. *Obesity (Silver Spring, Md.), 26*(2), 254–268.

[143] Dąbek, A., Wojtala, M., Pirola, L., & Balcerczyk, A. (2020). Modulation of Cellular Biochemistry, Epigenetics and Metabolomics by Ketone Bodies. Implications of the Ketogenic Diet in the Physiology of the Organism and Pathological States. Nutrients, 12(3), 788.

[144] Mattson, M. P., Moehl, K., Ghena, N., Schmaedick, M., & Cheng, A. (2018). Intermittent metabolic switching, neuroplasticity and brain health. Nature reviews. Neuroscience, 19(2), 63–80.

[145] Hartman, M. L., Veldhuis, J. D., Johnson, M. L., Lee, M. M., Alberti, K. G., Samojlik, E., & Thorner, M. O. (1992). Augmented growth hormone (GH) secretory burst frequency and amplitude mediate enhanced GH secretion during a two-day fast in normal men. The Journal of clinical endocrinology and metabolism, 74(4), 757–765.

[146] Aguiar-Oliveira, M. H., & Bartke, A. (2019). Growth Hormone Deficiency: Health and Longevity. Endocrine reviews, 40(2), 575–601.

[147] He, C., Sumpter, R., Jr, & Levine, B. (2012). Exercise induces autophagy in peripheral tissues and in the brain. *Autophagy, 8*(10), 1548–1551.

[148] Dorling, J., Broom, D. R., Burns, S. F., Clayton, D. J., Deighton, K., James, L. J., King, J. A., Miyashita, M., Thackray, A. E., Batterham, R. L., & Stensel, D. J. (2018). Acute and Chronic Effects of Exercise on Appetite, Energy Intake, and Appetite-Related Hormones: The Modulating Effect of Adiposity, Sex, and Habitual Physical Activity. *Nutrients, 10*(9), 1140.

[149] Klein, S., Sakurai, Y., Romijn, J. A., & Carroll, R. M. (1993). Progressive alterations in lipid and glucose metabolism during short-term fasting in young adult men. The American Journal of Physiology, 265(5 Pt 1), E801–E806.

[150] Tian, T., Li, X., & Zhang, J. (2019). mTOR Signaling in Cancer and mTOR Inhibitors in Solid Tumor Targeting Therapy. *International journal of molecular sciences, 20*(3), 755.

[151] Alirezaei, M., Kemball, C. C., Flynn, C. T., Wood, M. R., Whitton, J. L., & Kiosses, W. B. (2010). Short-term fasting induces profound neuronal autophagy. Autophagy, 6(6), 702–710.

[152] Wu, H. J., & Wu, E. (2012). The role of gut microbiota in immune homeostasis and autoimmunity. Gut microbes, 3(1), 4–14.

[153] Ekmekcioglu, C., & Touitou, Y. (2011). Chronobiological aspects of food intake and metabolism and their relevance on energy balance and weight regulation. Obesity reviews : an official journal of the International Association for the Study of Obesity, 12(1), 14–25.

[154] Tilg, H., & Kaser, A. (2011). Gut microbiome, obesity, and metabolic dysfunction. The Journal of clinical investigation, 121(6), 2126–2132.

[155] Mattson, M. P., Moehl, K., Ghena, N., Schmaedick, M., & Cheng, A. (2018). Intermittent metabolic switching, neuroplasticity and brain health. *Nature reviews. Neuroscience, 19*(2), 63–80.

[156] Cheng, C. W., Adams, G. B., Perin, L., Wei, M., Zhou, X., Lam, B. S., Da Sacco, S., Mirisola, M., Quinn, D. I., Dorff, T. B., Kopchick, J. J., & Longo, V. D. (2014). Prolonged fasting reduces IGF-1/PKA to promote hematopoietic-stem-cell-based regeneration and reverse immunosuppression. Cell stem cell, 14(6), 810–823.

[157] Sutton, E. F., Beyl, R., Early, K. S., Cefalu, W. T., Ravussin, E., & Peterson, C. M. (2018). Early Time-Restricted Feeding Improves Insulin Sensitivity, Blood Pressure, and Oxidative Stress Even without Weight Loss in Men with Prediabetes. Cell Metabolism, 27(6), 1212.

[158] Russo, M. A., Santarelli, D. M., & O'Rourke, D. (2017). The physiological effects of slow breathing in the healthy human. Breathe (Sheffield, England), 13(4), 298–309.

[159] Ma, X., Yue, Z. Q., Gong, Z. Q., Zhang, H., Duan, N. Y., Shi, Y. T., Wei, G. X., & Li, Y. F. (2017). The Effect of Diaphragmatic Breathing on Attention, Negative Affect and Stress in Healthy Adults. Frontiers in psychology, 8, 874.

[160] Zaccaro, A., Piarulli, A., Laurino, M., Garbella, E., Menicucci, D., Neri, B., & Gemignani, A. (2018). How Breath-Control Can Change Your Life: A Systematic Review on Psycho-Physiological Correlates of Slow Breathing. Frontiers in human neuroscience, 12, 353.

[161] Hermes-Lima, M., Moreira, D. C., Rivera-Ingraham, G. A., Giraud-Billoud, M., Genaro-Mattos, T. C., & Campos, É. G. (2015). Preparation for oxidative stress under hypoxia and metabolic depression: Revisiting the proposal two decades later. Free radical biology & medicine, 89, 1122–1143.

[162] Kox, M., van Eijk, L. T., Zwaag, J., van den Wildenberg, J., Sweep, F. C., van der Hoeven, J. G., & Pickkers, P. (2014). Voluntary activation of the sympathetic nervous system and attenuation of the innate immune response in humans. Proceedings of the National Academy of Sciences of the United States of America, 111(20), 7379–7384.

[163] Rhinewine, J. P., & Williams, O. J. (2007). Holotropic Breathwork: the potential role of a prolonged, voluntary hyperventilation procedure as an adjunct to psychotherapy. Journal of alternative and complementary medicine (New York, N.Y.), 13(7), 771–776.

[164] The Nobel Prize in Physiology or Medicine 2019. NobelPrize.org. Nobel Media AB 2020. Wed. 26 Aug 2020. <https://www.nobelprize.org/prizes/medicine/2019/summary/>

[165] Miller, T., & Nielsen, L. (2015). Measure of Significance of Holotropic Breathwork in the Development of Self-Awareness. Journal of alternative and complementary medicine (New York, N.Y.), 21(12), 796–803.

[166] Eyerman, J. (2013). A Clinical Report of Holotropic Breathwork in 11,000 Psychiatric Inpatients in a Community Hospital Setting. MAPS Bulletin Special Edition, 23(1), 24-27.

[167] Tupper, K., Wood, E., Yensen, R. & Johnson, M. (2015) Psychedelic medicine: A re-emerging therapeutic paradigm. CMAJ, 187(14), 1054-1059.

[168] Schenberg E. E. (2018). Psychedelic-Assisted Psychotherapy: A Paradigm Shift in Psychiatric Research and Development. *Frontiers in pharmacology, 9,* 733.

[169] Timmermann, C., Roseman, L., Williams, L., Erritzoe, D., Martial, C., Cassol, H., Laureys, S., Nutt, D., & Carhart-Harris, R. (2018). DMT Models the Near-Death Experience. Frontiers in psychology, 9, 1424.

[170] Zeifman, R. J., Palhano-Fontes, F., Hallak, J., Arcoverde, E., Maia-Oliveira, J. P., & Araujo, D. B. (2019). The Impact of Ayahuasca on Suicidality: Results From a Randomized Controlled Trial. *Frontiers in pharmacology, 10,* 1325.

[171] Ameisen, J. (2002). On the origin, evolution, and nature of programmed cell death: a timeline of four billion years. *Cell Death & Differentiation, 9,* 367-393.

[172] Lim, K., Kim, Th., Trzeciak, A. *et al.* (2020). In situ neutrophil efferocytosis shapes T cell immunity to influenza infection. *Nat Immunol,* 21, 1046–1057.

[173] University of Utah. (2008). When Cells Go Bad: Cells That Avoid Suicide May Become Cancerous. *ScienceDaily.* Retrieved July 30, 2022 from www.sciencedaily.com/releases/2008/10/081001093611.htm

[174] Wutzler, A., Mavrogiorgou, P., Winter, C., & Juckel, G. (2011). Elevation of brain serotonin during dying. Neuroscience letters, 498(1), 20–21.

[175] Balakrishnan, R., Nanjundaiah, R. M., & Manjunath, N. K. (2018). Voluntarily induced vomiting - A yoga technique to enhance pulmonary functions in healthy humans. Journal of Ayurveda and integrative medicine, 9(3), 213–216.

[176] Bouso, J., Fabregas, J., Antonijoan, R., Rodriguez-Fornells, A., & Riba, J. (2013) Acute effects of ayahuasca on neuropsychological performance: differences in executive function between experienced and occasional users. Psychopharmacology 230:415–424.

[177] Loizaga-Velder, A. & Verres, Rolf. (2014) Therapeutic effects of ritual ayahuasca use in the treatment of substance dependence — Qualitative results, Journal of Psychoactive Drugs, 46:1, 63-72.

[178] Leister, M. & Prickett, J. (2012) Hypotheses regarding the mechanisms of ayahuasca in the treatment of addictions. Journal of Psychoactive Drugs, 44:3, 200-208.

[179] Bouso, J., González, D., Fondevila, S., Cutchet, M., Fernández, X., & Ribeiro Barbosa, P. (2012) Personality, psychopathology, life attitudes and neuropsychological performance among ritual users of ayahuasca: A longitudinal study. PLoS ONE 7(8): e42421.

[180] Lindahl, J. R., Fisher, N. E., Cooper, D. J., Rosen, R. K., & Britton, W. B. (2017). The varieties of contemplative experience: A mixed-methods study of meditation-related challenges in Western Buddhists. PloS one, 12(5), e0176239.

[181] Kirschner, H., Kuyken, W., Wright, K., Roberts, H., Brejcha, C., & Karl, A. (2019). Soothing Your Heart and Feeling Connected: A New Experimental Paradigm to Study the Benefits of Self-Compassion. Clinical psychological science: a journal of the Association for Psychological Science, 7(3), 545–565.

[182] Opperman, M. C., and H. E. Roets. "The Creation And Manifestation Of Reality Through The Re-Enactment Of Subconscious Conclusions And Decisions." Journal Of Heart-Centered Therapies 12.1 (2009): 3-98.

[183] Massachusetts General Hospital. (2007, February 15). 'Wired To Connect': Physiologic Measurements Suggest Biologic Component To Empathic Connection Between Patients And Therapists. *ScienceDaily*.

[184] Chartrand, T. L., & Bargh, J. A. (1999). The chameleon effect: the perception-behavior link and social interaction. *Journal of personality and social psychology*, *76*(6), 893–910.

[185] Ardito, R. B., & Rabellino, D. (2011). Therapeutic alliance and outcome of psychotherapy: historical excursus, measurements, and prospects for research. *Frontiers in psychology*, *2*, 270.

[186] Alpert, P. T. (2011). The Health Benefits of Dance. *Home Health Care Management & Practice*, *23*(2), 155–157.

[187] Lindström, K., Lindblad, F., & Hjern, A. (2011). Preterm birth and attention-deficit/hyperactivity disorder in schoolchildren. *Pediatrics*, *127*(5), 858–865.

[188] Pyhälä, R., Wolford, E., Kautiainen, H., Andersson, S., Bartmann, P., Baumann, N., Brubakk, A. M., Evensen, K., Hovi, P., Kajantie, E., Lahti, M., Van Lieshout, R. J., Saigal, S., Schmidt, L. A., Indredavik, M. S., Wolke, D., & Räikkönen, K. (2017). Self-Reported Mental Health Problems Among Adults Born Preterm: A Meta-analysis. *Pediatrics*, *139*(4), e20162690.

[189] Due, C., Green, E., & Ziersch, A. (2020). Psychological trauma and access to primary care for people from refugee & asylum-seeker backgrounds: a mixed methods systematic review. *International journal of mental health systems*, *14*, 71.

[190] Reyes-Alvarado, S., Romero Sánchez, J., Rivas-Ruiz, F., Perea-Milla, E., Medina López, R., León Ruiz, A. M., & Alvarez Aldeán, J. (2008). Trastorno por estrés postraumático en nacidos prematuros [PTSD in premature newborns]. *Anales de pediatria (Barcelona, Spain : 2003)*, *69*(2), 134–140.

[191] Krol, K. M., & Grossmann, T. (2018). Psychological effects of breastfeeding on children and mothers. Psychologische Effekte des

Stillens auf Kinder und Mütter. *Bundesgesundheitsblatt, Gesundheitsforschung, Gesundheitsschutz, 61*(8), 977–985.

[192] Brattström, O., Eriksson, M., Larsson, E., & Oldner, A. (2015). Socio-economic status and co-morbidity as risk factors for trauma. *European journal of epidemiology, 30*(2), 151–157.

[193] Park S. & Schepp KG. A Systematic Review of Research on Children of Alcoholics: Their Inherent Resilience and Vulnerability. J Child Fam Stud (2015) 24: 1222.

[194] Idsoe, T., Vaillancourt, T., Dyregrov, A., Hagen, K. A., Ogden, T., & Nærde, A. (2021). Bullying Victimization and Trauma. *Frontiers in psychiatry, 11,* 480353.

[195] Yehuda, R., & Lehrner, A. (2018). Intergenerational transmission of trauma effects: putative role of epigenetic mechanisms. *World psychiatry : official journal of the World Psychiatric Association (WPA), 17*(3), 243–257.

[196] Andrade G. (2017). Is past life regression therapy ethical?. *Journal of medical ethics and history of medicine, 10,* 11.

[197] Otgaar, H., Muris, P., Howe, M. L., & Merckelbach, H. (2017). What Drives False Memories in Psychopathology? A Case for Associative Activation. *Clinical psychological science : a journal of the Association for Psychological Science, 5*(6), 1048–1069.

[198] Lieberman, A. F., Chu, A., Van Horn, P., & Harris, W. W. (2011). Trauma in early childhood: empirical evidence and clinical implications. *Development and psychopathology, 23*(2), 397–410.

[199] C.A. Courtois, C.A. (2017). Chapter 12 - Meaning Making and Trauma Recovery. *Reconstructing Meaning After Trauma, Academic Press,* 187-192. https://doi.org/10.1016/B978-0-12-803015-8.00012-7.

[200] Teh, A. L., Pan, H., Chen, L., Ong, M. L., Dogra, S., Wong, J., MacIsaac, J. L., Mah, S. M., McEwen, L. M., Saw, S. M., Godfrey, K. M., Chong, Y. S., Kwek, K., Kwoh, C. K., Soh, S. E., Chong, M. F., Barton, S., Karnani, N., Cheong, C. Y., Buschdorf, J. P., ... Holbrook, J. D. (2014). The effect of

genotype and in utero environment on interindividual variation in neonate DNA methylomes. *Genome research*, *24*(7), 1064–1074.

[201] Post, Stephen. "It's Good to Be Good: Science Says it's So." http://www.stonybrook.edu/bioethics/goodtobegood.pdf

[202] Hamilton, David. "Why Kindness is good for you." Hay House. 2010.

About the Author

Hi. My name is Luke. As a Wellbeing Coach and Somatic Therapist, I've been able to integrate my broad personal, academic, and professional experience into a unique approach for helping others. Today, I utilize compassionate inquiry, somatic practices, and healthy lifestyle strategies to help clients experience more vitality, authenticity, and inner peace in everyday life.

Something that my meditation practice – as well as guidance from my teachers Graham Mead, Gabor Maté, Rupert Spira, and Lenny Parracino – has taught me is that authentic change begins with silence, stillness, and the courage to look inward. We may not like what we find there, but getting into our body is where the real work of change is done. 'The Inner Work' transforms the way we relate to our mind, body & world. While this requires radical self-acceptance, ruthless honesty, and Yoda-like patience, present moment awareness is the greatest gift you bring into relationship.

The core of what I do is reconnecting clients with their body so that they learn how to listen to their body and wisdom it has to offer. I've worked with executives transitioning into a life of greater meaning, facilitated yoga and meditation for refugees in New Zealand, helped couples re-establish healthy and compassionate communication, worked with obese clients reclaiming their health, and led mindfulness sessions for professional fighters and recovering addicts.

My own personal journey through addiction and mental health challenges brought me back to the world of academia. After an eclectic journey through the academic world that included a Bachelor's in Accounting, a Master's in Sustainable Food Systems and a Postgraduate Diploma in Drug and Alcohol Studies, my doctoral psychology research examined meditation as an intervention for men with pornography addiction. Many men need support for their mental health. Men – and all human beings – turn to pornography or other behaviors as a way of coping with or avoiding uncomfortable emotional states. Currently, I am a practitioner, mentor, facilitator, and perpetual student of Compassionate Inquiry, a therapeutic approach developed by renowned Gabor Maté, aimed at helping people unearth the root causes of their suffering and self-destructive cycles.

***

Connect

You can learn more about Dr. Luke Sniewski, his practice, and his programs at www.LukeSniewski.com.

Take the next step in your healing journey with Dr. Luke Sniewski by scanning the QR code below, or visiting the link below:

www.LukeSniewski.com/Somawise-Online-Program

Printed in Great Britain
by Amazon

39352439R00165